Forest Management

Forest Management

Dr. Girish B. Shahapurmath
M.Sc. (Forestry) Ph.D.
Assistant Professor of Forest Management
Department of Natural Resource Management
College of Forestry, Sirsi (UK), Karnataka

Dr. Hanumantha, M.
M.Sc. (Forestry) Ph.D.
Assistant Professor of Forest Utilization
Department of Forest Products and Utilization
College of Forestry, Sirsi (UK), Karnataka

SSPH

SATISH SERIAL PUBLISHING HOUSE
403, Express Tower, Commercial Complex
Azadpur, Delhi-110033 (India)
Phone : 011-27672852, Fax : 91-11-27672046
e-mail : info@satishserial.com, hkjain1975@yahoo.com
Website : www.satishserial.com

Published by :

SATISH SERIAL PUBLISHING HOUSE
403, Express Tower, Commercial Complex, Azadpur, Delhi-110033 (INDIA)
Phone : 011-27672852 Fax : 91-11-27672046
E-mail : info@satishserial.com, hkjain1975@yahoo.com

ISBN 978-93-88020-63-3

Composed, Designed & Printed in India

About the Authors

Dr. GIRISH B. SHAHAPURMATH, M.Sc. (Forestry) Ph.D.
Assistant Professor of Forest Management
Department of Natural Resource Management
College of Forestry, Sirsi-581 401, Karnataka
University of Agricultural Sciences, Dharwad, India
E-mail: girishbshahapur@gmail.com /
shahapurmathgb@uasd.in

- Specialization in Silviculture and Agroforestry, Forest Management, Remote Sensing and GIS.
- Post Graduate Diploma in Agricultural Extension and Management (PGDAEM) by MANAGAE, Hyderabad during 2014-15.
- Post Graduate Diploma Computer Applications (PGDCA) by Infotech Computer Education and Manipal Institute of Computer Education (MICE) during 2008-09.
- Total 16 years of experience in the field of forestry (Teaching, Research and Extension).
- Presently working as Assistant Professor of Forest Management in Department of Natural Resource Management at College of Forestry, SIRSI (University of Agricultural Sciences, Dharwad, Karnataka (India).
- Recipient of "Outstanding Scientist Award" in Forestry by The Society of Tropical Agriculture, New Delhi, India in 7th International Conference on Agriculture, Horticulture and Plant Sciences held at Shimla (H. P.) during June 28-29, 2018.
- Recipient of "Best Teacher Award-2016" for outstanding contribution in the field of Forestry on the occasion of International Conference on "Rural Livelihood Improvement by Enhancing Farmers' Income through Sustainable Innovative Agri and Allied Enterprises (RLSIAAe)" organized by the Society for Upliftment of Rural Economy, Varanasi (India) during 30th October to 1st November, 2018 held at Birla Institute of Technology, Patna.
- Recognized as a Life Member for the "Society for Upliftment of Rural Economy, Varanasi (Membership No. LM/245/2018).
- First prize for Best Poster Presentation on Multistoreyed Cropping of Teak-perennial vegetables-legume based Agroforestry system

Presented in National Symposium (Silver Jubilee) on "Agroforestry Knowledge for Sustainability, Climate Moderation and Challenges Ahead" held at National Research Centre for Agroforestry, Jhansi (UP) from 15-17 December, 2008.

- First Prize for Best Poster presentation on "Forest Law and Models" presented in "National Kaanoonu Utsava" Exhibition held at Sirsi from 07.06.2014 to 06.07.2014 organized by Karnataka High Court, Bengaluru and District Law Service, Karwar and Bar Association, Sirsi.
- Worked as Principal Investigator and CO-Principal Investigator for 10 Research Projects.
- Field of interest - Silviculture and Agroforestry, Forest Management and Policy, Sustainable Forest Management, Remote Sensing and Geographical Information System in Forestry.
- Developed the course materials as reference books and for competitive exams, such as ASRB, IFS, ACF, RFO, KPSC, etc., in the field of forestry for students' purpose.
- Attended more than 15 Trainings/Summer/Winter schools, short courses, Seminars, Workshops, Conferences and undergone Agricultural Massive Open Online Courses (Ag MOOC).
- Published more than 100 publications including Research papers in NAAS rated journal/Research notes/Papers presented and published in symposium/seminar/conference/workshop/Training/ international conference/Popular articles published in journals/ newspapers/Books/chapters in books.

Dr. Hanumantha, M., M.Sc. (Forestry), Ph.D.
Assistant Professor of Forest Utilization
Department of Forest Products and Utilization
College of Forestry, SIRSI- 581 401, Karnataka
University of Agricultural Sciences, Dharwad, India

- Total 18 years of experience in the field of Forestry (Teaching, Research and Extension)
- Specialization in Wood Anatomy, Wood Science, Wood Products, Non-Timber Forest Products and Forest Mensuration
- Completed 18 months course of *"Instruction and Practical Training in Forestry and Allied subjects"* (RFO, Training) at State Forest Service College (SFSC), Coimbatore, Tamil Nadu from 01-04-2005 to 30-09-2006
- Post Graduate Diploma in Agricultural Extension and Management (PGDAEM) by MANAGE, Hyderabad during 2014-15
- Developed Course Materials as reference books and for competitive examinations (IFS, ACF, RFO) in the field of Forestry (Silviculture, Silviculture of Species, Forest Management, Forest Mensuration, Forest Policy and Legislation and ACF Solved Question papers in Forestry)
- Developed Lecture Notes on Wood Anatomy, Wood Science, Wood Products and Non-Timber Forest Products
- Participated in Two summer and winter school training
- Completed Eight Agriculture Massive Open Online Courses (AGMOOC)
- Recipient of "Young Scientist Award" for contribution in the field of Forestry by Society for Scientific Development in Agriculture and Technology (SSDAT). Received in International Conference on Global Research Initiatives for Sustainable Agriculture and Allied Sciences (GRISAAS-2018) during 28-30th October, 2018 held at Rajasthan Agricultural Research Institute, Durgapura, Jaipur, Rajasthan, India.
- Awarded National Young Leader Programme Award by Ministry of Youth Affairs and Sports, New Delhi and UAS, Dharwad for the year 2015-16 (awarded on 10-04-2017) for contribution towards NSS activities.
- Awarded First Prize for Best Poster / Chart presentation on "Forest Law and Models" in "National Kaanoonu Utsava" Exhibition held

at Sirsi from 07.06.2014 to 06.07.2014 organized by Karnataka High Court, Bengaluru and District Law Service, Karwar and Bar Association, Sirsi.

- Worked as Principal Investigator and CO-Principal Investigator for 13 Research Projects.
- Published more than 100 publications including Research papers in NAAS rated journal/Research notes/Papers presented and published in symposium/seminar/conference/workshop/Training/international conference/Popular articles published in journals/newspapers/Books/chapters in books.

UNIVERSITY OF AGRICULTURAL SCIENCES, DHARWAD
KRISHI NAGAR, DHARWAD-581 005
KARNATAKA STATE, INDIA

Hon'ble
Vice Chancellor

Foreword

The forest is a natural system that can supply different products and services. The working of natural system is influenced by the natural environment: climate, topography, soil, *etc.*, and also by biotic factors. The actions of humans in forests constitute forest management. In developed societies, this management tends to be elaborated and planned in order to achieve the objectives that are considered desirable.

Forest management is nothing but overall administrative, economic, legal, and social aspects, as well as scientific and technical aspects, such as silviculture, protection, and forest regulation. This includes management for aesthetics, fish, recreation, urban values, water, wilderness, wildlife, wood products, forest genetic resources, and other forest resource values. Management can be based on conservation, economics, or a mixture of the two. Techniques include timber extraction, planting and re-planting of various species, cutting roads and pathways through forests, and preventing fire. Some forests have been and are managed to obtain traditional forest products, such as firewood, fibre for paper, and timber, with little thinking for other products and services. Nevertheless, as a result of the progression of environmental awareness, management of forests for multiple use is becoming more common.

There has been increased public awareness of natural resource policy, including forest management. Public concern regarding forest management may have shifted from the extraction of timber for earning money for the economy, to the preservation of additional forest resources, including wildlife and old growth forest, protecting biodiversity, watershed management and recreation. Increased environmental awareness may contribute to an increased public mistrust of forest management professionals. But it can also lead to greater understanding about what professionals do for forests for nature conservation and ecological services.

Many tools like GIS and photogrammetry modelling have been developed to improve forest inventory and management planning. The abundance and diversity of birds, mammals, amphibians and other wildlife are affected by strategies and types of forest management. Forest management varies in intensity from a leave alone, natural situation to a highly intensive regime with silvicultural interventions. Forest Management is generally increased in intensity to achieve either economic criteria (increased timber yields, non-timber forest products, ecosystem services) or ecological criteria (species recovery, fostering of rare species, carbon sequestration).

The National Forest Policy, 1988, brought about a paradigm shift in the management of forests by acknowledging that the bonafide requirements of the villagers shall be the first charge on forest produce. In 1990, after the Government of India issued a circular on Joint Forest Management (JFM), enabling the states to initiate their own programmes. The forest departments then embarked on the partnership with the communities and two decades later the progress in the endeavour has been spectacular. JFM programmes are currently spanned in 29 states, represent 1,18,213 JFM committees protecting about 22.93 million hectare of forests. About one-third of the land with the forest department is being managed today in partnership with the people of the country.

The JFM programme has also contributed significantly towards the economic well-being of the people through increased availability of the forest resources, creation of employment opportunity and better flow of ecosystem services. Wherever a successful JFM programme has been implemented, it has led to improvement in forests which in turn imply better availability of water and more crop yields and thus, enhancing the livelihood and income of the people. The community assets created as part of the entry point activities has improved the infrastructure in the villages and supplemented the development efforts in the most remote and inaccessible habitations of India.

Textbooks on Management of Forests suitable for undergraduate and post graduate students are very few particularly in Forestry Colleges in India. This textbook on "Forest Management" by Dr. Girish B. Shahapurmath and Dr. Hanumantha, M., is a timely and welcome contribution in the forestry field. The authors have a considerable experience in teaching, research and extension in forestry/agroforestry and have presented the subject matter critically and systematically. This book will serve as a valuable source of information for the academicians in forestry institutes and also for the students for the preparation of competitive examinations in forestry discipline. I congratulate the authors for the hard work they put in, the systematic selection of topics and well documented and meticulous presentation.

I am hopeful that this text book will adequately meet the needs of students of forestry colleges and would be widely welcomed. I extend my best wishes to Dr. Girish B. Shahapurmath and Dr. Hanumantha, M. for the success of their book.

May, 2019
Dharwad, Karnataka

Dr. M.B. CHETTI
(Vice Chancellor)
University of Agricultural Sciences, Dharwad
and Former Assistant Director General (HRD),
ICAR, New Delhi

Preface

Forestry, as a subject, is being taught to students of the Forest Colleges in different Agricultural Universities in India. This subject had been introduced as a subject for degree courses in most of the Indian Agricultural Universities. Indian Council of Agricultural Research (ICAR) provided an opportunity to start state-run forestry colleges in various State Agricultural Universities (SAUs) in the country. Earlier as per the recommendation of the National Commission on Agriculture, ICAR had started a course in 'Farm Forestry' during 1976 in all SAUs. There was a growing concern among the academicians and politicians alike that the students of forestry should have a greater exposure and access to natural forests. There has been increased public awareness of natural resource policy, including forest management. Public concern regarding forest management may have shifted from the extraction of timber for earning money for the economy, to the preservation of additional forest resources, including wildlife and old growth forest, protecting biodiversity, watershed management and recreation. Increased environmental awareness may contribute to an increased public mistrust of forest management professionals. Therefore, this book has been written to meet the requirements of the students of the Forest Colleges as well as those of the students preparing for competitive examinations.

The book covers mostly the present syllabi of the Forest Colleges as well as those of the competitive examinations (Indian Forest Service and State Forest Services). I claim no originality in writing this book except for the arrangement and presentation of the subject matter. A large number of books, journals and proceedings of symposia and workshops have been consulted. A list of these references is given at the end of book as references / bibliography.

I, therefore, gratefully acknowledge the help taken from "Forest Management" by Ram Prakash., "A textbook on Forest Management" by M. R. K. Jerram., "Indian Forestry" by K. Manikandan and S. Prabhu and other publications mentioned in the references.

I am greatly indebted to Dean (Forestry) for constant guidance and help during the time of writing the book and improving it substantially. I am equally grateful to all the faculty members of College of Forestry, Sirsi (UAS, Dharwad, Karnataka) and officers of Karnataka Forest

Department for their valuable suggestions and help in writing the book as well as for reading through the chapters and making very valuable improvements.

Place: Sirsi, Karnataka
Date: 1st January, 2019

Dr. Girish B. Shahapurmath
Assistant Professor of Forest Management
Department of Natural Resource Managment
College of Forestry, Sirsi (UAS, Dharwad)
Karnataka, India

Contents

Chapter 1

Technical Terms used in Forest Management

- **Aerial photography :** Word 'photography' literally means 'writing with light'. Aerial photography means photographing or taking pictures of the earth from the air. Aerial photography is synonymously called as Aerial remote Sensing.
- **Afforestation :** The establishment of trees by sowing, planting or natural regeneration on areas from which trees have always or very long been absent.
- **Age class :** This is one of the intervals into which the range of age of the trees growing in a forest is divided for classification or use (e.g. trees falling into such an interval).
- **Age gradation :** An age class with one year as the interval.
- **Annual Plan of Operations (APO) :** APO is a tabular statement showing the order and extent of all works to be carried out during the year. Such a plan is based on the prescriptions of the working plan where it exists, otherwise on general silvicultural principles as modified by financial prescriptions/provisions.
- **Assessment :** The process by which information about forest management is collected with a view to establishing, within a defined framework of expectations, the current status and probable future direction of interactions between human beings and forests, using certain criteria and indicators.
- **Basal Area Factor (BAF) :** This is the multiplying factor, associated with any instrument used in horizontal point sampling.
- **Biological diversity :** The variability among living organisms from all sources including, inter alia, terrestrial, marine and other aquatic ecosystems and the ecological complexes of which they are part; this includes diversity within species, between species and of ecosystems.

- **Biomass :** The total above ground living organic matter in trees expressed as oven dry tons per unit area. It is referred to as biomass density when expressed as mass per unit area, e.g. tons per hectare. Excludes stumps and roots (belowground biomass), foliage, flowers and seeds. Different procedures in estimating biomass will be followed for the different vegetation types.
- **Block :** Block is main territorial division of forest, generally bounded by natural features and bearing a local proper name.
- **Circular plots :** Laying out of these plots is very easy on level ground, once its centre and radius is fixed. It has the minimum perimeter for a given area as compare to any other geometric shape and thus, has the minimum number of border line trees.
- **Cluster :** The term 'cluster' is used to define a Sampling unit, which is in fact a *group of smaller units*. The *cluster is the statistical unit,* whereas the *smaller ones are only record units.*
- **Community forestry :** Community forestry is an evolving branch of forestry whereby the local community plays a significant role in forest management and land use decision-making by themselves in the facilitating support of government as well as change agents.
- **Compartment :** A block is divided into several compartments, which are territorial units of a forest permanently defined for purposes of administration and record, designated by Arabic numbers 1, 2, 3, 4 etc.
- **Conservation forest :** Areas set aside by law or some other ruling for conservation purposes, for example: national parks, biological reserves, water reservoirs.
- **Control books :** It is usually maintained for each working circle for the years for which operations are prescribed in the working plan and shall be written up annually in Forms 3 & 4.
- **Control journal (Forest journal) :** This is a register in which all noteworthy occurrences, bearing on the management and improvement of forests, more particularly on the state of reproduction of more valuable species and on the suitability or system of management prescribed in the working plan.
- **Control maps :** Control map is the map showing the results of fire protection, prepared according to the directions from special Chief Conservator of Forests (CCF).

- **Conversion period :** Conversion period is defined as "The period during which a change from one Silvicultural system to another is effected."
- **Conversion :** Conversion is defined as "a change from one silvicultural system or one (set of) species to another".
- **Coupe :** A felling area usually one of an annual series unless otherwise stated, preferably numbered with roman numerals I, II, III, etc.
- **Criterion :** A category of conditions or process by which sustainable forest management can be assessed. A criterion is characterized by a set of related indicators, which are monitored periodically to assess change (Montreal Process, 1995).
- **Cutting Section (CS) :** A subdivision of FS formed with the object of regulating cuttings in some special manner.
- **De Liocourt's Law :** It is defined as "*in a fully stocked selection forest, the number of stems falls off from one diameter class to the next diameter class in geometrical progression*".Which means that the percentage reduction in the stem number from one diameter class to the next diameter class is constant. This is referred to as "De Liocourt's Law".
- **Deforestation :** A non-temporary change of land use from forest to other land use or depletion of forest crown cover to less than 10 per cent. Clear cuts (even with stump removal), if shortly followed by reforestation for forestry purposes are not considered deforestation.
- **Degradation :** Changes within the forest class (from closed to open forest), which negatively affect the stand or site and, in particular, that lower the biological productivity capacity and diversity.
- **Desertification :** Land degradation in arid, semi-arid and dry sub-humid areas resulting from various factors, including climate variations and human activities.
- **Diopter :** This is a measure of the value of an angle expressed as its Sine. One diopter is approximately equivalent to an angle of **0.57^0** or **34.36** minutes. Since Sin **0.57^0** = 1/100 = 1 diopter.
- **Ecosystem :** A community of plant and animal species and micro-organisms, considered together as a functional system which includes the complex, ever changing relations that exist among plants, animals and microbes, including man, and their environment. The term is used in identifying a certain forest site type (e.g. health forest). The

term 'habitat' is used in a general sense for the place where an organism is found (FAO, 1989).

- **Enumeration :** Enumeration is defined as "counting, singly or together, of individuals of one or more species, in a forest crop and their classification by species, size, condition, etc".
- **Exotic (introduced) species :** Any species growing or living outside its natural range of occurrence. Normally, this refers to species purposely or accidentally introduced into countries or regions they do not historically occur
- **Exploitable forest :** A forest on which there are no legal, economic or technical restrictions on wood and non-wood production. It includes areas where, although there are no such restrictions, harvesting is not currently taking place; for example, areas included in long-term utilization plans.
- **Felling cycle :** It is defined as "the time that elapses between successive main fellings on the same area".
- **Felling Series (FS) :** A forest area forming the whole or part of a working circle and delimited so as to distribute felling and regeneration to suit local conditions to maintain or create a normal distribution of age classes. The yield should be calculated for each FS which should have an independent representation of age classes.
- **Final yield :** (a) All the material that counts against the prescribed yield and which is derived from the main fellings in a regular forest. (b) As in the Yield Table, "it is the sum of the main crop and the subsidiary crop figures for the given crop age".
- **Forest degradation :** Impoverishment of standing woody material mainly caused by human activities, such as over-grazing, over-exploitation (for firewood in particular), repeated fires, or due attacks by insects, diseases, plant parasites or other natural causes, such as cyclones. Very often degradation does not show up so much in decrease of woody vegetation but rather as a gradual reduction in biomass, changes in species composition and soil degradation.
- **Forest ecosystem :** An ecological system composed of interacting biotic and abiotic components of the environment in which trees are a major constituent, such that their canopies cover 20 per cent or more of the area.
- **Forest goods and products :** Wood and non-wood forest products obtained from forests.

- **Forest inventory :** 'Forest inventory' is originally a commercial term means 'the record, showing the quantity and value of articles in a store'. It is also defined as "the tabulated, reliable and satisfactory tree information, related to the required unit, respectively units of assessment in hierarchy or sequence order". Forest inventory is synonymous with the term **"Cruise" in** North America and **"Enumeration"** in India.

- **Forest land :** Countries have defined forest land differently and, as such, a single definition is not possible here. When reporting, each country should provide its own definition for forest land.

- **Forest management unit :** A clearly demarcated area of land covered pre-dominantly by forests, managed to a set of explicit objectives and according to a long-term forest management plan. A forest management unit may cover several hundred hectares to fractions of. The entire area of the forest management unit will have to be clearly demarcated on the ground and usually also on a map. Under the broad objectives to which the entire management unit is subjected, sub-units may be managed under different and separate management regimes.

- **Forest management :** Forest management is defined as "the application of scientific, technical and economic principles of forestry". Forest management is the application of business methods and technical forestry principles to the operation of a forest property.

- **Forest services :** Environmental services (e.g. conservation of soil, water, biological diversity; micro and macro climatic effects; nutrient cycling) and socio-cultural services other than those provided by the production of wood and non-wood products (e.g. recreation and tourism, protection of cultural, aesthetic and scientific values) provided by forests.

- **Forest Type :** A category of forest defined generally with reference to its geographical location, climatic and edaphic features, composition and condition.

  OR

  Classification of forest land based on species forming a plurality of live-tree stocking. Type (e.g. low forest, multi-layered forest, even-aged forest, etc.) is determined on the basis of species plurality of all live trees that contribute to stocking (Pan-European Forest Process, 1994).

- **Forestry :** Activities related to the management of forests and other wooded land for the production and supply of wood and/or other goods and services.
- **Geographical Information System :** GIS is computer based integrated data base management system, in which large volumes of geo-referenced spatial data derived from variety of sources are, efficiently stored, organized, manipulated, retrieved, analyzed, displayed/presented according to the user defined specifications.
- **Global Positioning System (GPS) :** GPS is primarily satellite based radio navigation system for real time positioning. It provides three dimensional positions, navigation and time in information to suitability equipped users.
- **Growing stock :** Growing stock is defined as "the sum (by numbers or Volume) of all the trees growing in the forest, or a specified part of it". Growing Stock in a forest is the **Forest Capital.**
- **Increment Percent :** Increment Percent is an expression of the relation between the increment and volume. The average annual growth in volume (or basal area) over a specified period expressed as a percentage of the volume (or basal area) either at the beginning or more usually, half way through the period.
- **Increment :** Increment is defined as "the increase in girth, diameter, basal area, height, volume, quality, price or value of the trees or crops during a given period".
- **Intensive Forestry :** The basic principle of management is long-term sustainability of the ecosystem. In favourable localities, this science is applied to maximize financial return and is called **"Intensive Forestry"** which is defined as "the practice of forestry with the object of obtaining the maximum quantity of the desired quality of products per unit area through the application of suitable techniques of silviculture and management".
- **Intermediate yield :** "All the material from thinnings or operations proceeding the main felling in a regular forest, or its cash equivalent." (Syn - subsidiary crop).
- **Linear Tree Increment Plots (LTIP) :** LTIP is a linear plot with 20-40 m wide and of any desired length, often 1.0 km or more, lay across the fertility gradient. Very often it forms a line of trees of selected species maintained for the purpose of assessing diameter/age relation for species not characterized by annual rings.
- **Major Forest Products :** It comprises timber, small wood and fire-wood.

- **Microplan :** Microplan means the scheme of management of a village forest.

- **Minor Forest Products :** All forest produce, other than major forest produce, including grass, fruit, leaves, animal products, soil and minerals.

- **Multiple Use Forestry :** When forestry is practiced to achieve more than one purpose, it is called as **"Multiple Use Forestry",** which is defined as the practice of forestry for the simultaneous or sequential use of a forest area for two or more purposes. e.g. The production of wood with forest grazing and/or wildlife conservation, etc.

- **Natural forest :** A forest that has evolved and reproduced itself naturally from organisms previously established, and that has not been significantly altered by human activity.

- **Non-Wood Forest Products (NWFP) :** Goods of biological origin other than wood, derived from forests, other wooded land and trees outside forests.

- **Normal forest :** A forest which has a normal series of age gradations or age classes, a normal increment and a normal growing stock. A forest which, for given site and given objects of management, is ideally constituted as regards growing stock, age class distribution and increment, and from which the annual or periodic removal of produce equal to the increment can be continued indefinitely without endangering future yields. A forest by reason of its normalcy in these respects serves as a standard of comparison, for sustained yield management.

  OR

  Normal forest is defined as "a forest for a given site and given objects of management is ideally constituted as regards growing stock, age-class, distribution and increment and from which the annual or periodic removal of produce equal to the increment can be continued without endangering future yields".

- **Normal Growing Stock (NGS) :** It is defined as "the total volume of trees in a fully stocked forest with normal distribution of age-classes for a given rotation". NGS is the volume of stands in a forest with normal age classes and a normal increment.

- **Normal increment :** This is the best or maximum increment attainable by a given species and for a given rotation per unit area on a given site. Normal increment is the best or maximum increment attainable by a given species and for a given rotation per unit area on a given site.

- **Normal series of age gradations or age classes :** This is meant that the presence of trees of all ages from one year old to rotation age, when trees of each age occur on separate areas, they constitute a series of age gradations.
- **Normal yield :** "The yield from a normal forest".
- **Partial or Sample enumeration :** Enumeration is done only in a representative portion of the area.
- **Periodic Blocks (PB's) :** Periodic block is defined as "part or parts of forest set aside to be regenerated or otherwise treated during a special period".
- **Permanent sample plots :** These plots are laid out for measurements to be repeated at intervals over a period of time.
- **Plantation forests :** Forest stands established by planting or/and seeding in the process of afforestation or reforestation. They are either of introduced species (all planted stands), or intensively managed stands of indigenous species which meet all the following criteria: one or two species at plantation, even age class, regular spacing.
- **Plot Radius Factor :** This factor defines for each tree the radius of the circle within which the tree is tallied using an instrument with fixed critical angle. This factor is very useful in checking doubtful or borderline trees.
- **Price increment :** Price increment may be defined as "the increment in price, independently of quality increment, resulting from fluctuations in the market on account of changes in money value in general, and the demand and supply position in particular".
- **Production forest :** A forest managed to harvest forest products and to sustain the bioproductivity of the system.
- **Productive forest :** An area of forest capable of producing wood for more than a certain predicted amount, e.g. the increment volume is more than 1 m^3/ha/year in the foreseeable future.
- **Protected Area :** As defined by the International Union of Nature Conservation (IUCN), a protected area is an area of land and/or sea especially dedicated to the protection and maintenance of biological diversity, and of natural and associated cultural resources, managed through legal or other effective means.

- **Protection forest :** A forest that is generally situated on broken ground, or ground subjected to periodic or permanent floods, and therefore, rendered physically non-productive and difficult to manage, with the exception of the lands included in the category below.
- **Quality increment :** Quality increment is defined as "The increment in the value per unit volume of a tree or a crop, independent of any increase in the price of forest produce resulting from any change in money value in general, or the supply and demand position in particular."
- **Record of works :** It is the brief record to be written up annually in **FORM No.5** for each working circle of all works carried out in connection with the construction and repairs of communications, buildings, wells and tanks, etc. and in connection with demarcation, sowing, planting, thinning, cleanings, cultural operations, protection from fire, climber cutting, improvement felling and other tending operations, when they are different from the main exploitations prescribed in the working plan.
- **Reduced or modified area :** An area which would produce the same yield with uniform quality and/or density, as it produced by the existing areas with their various qualities and/or densities is called as ***Reduced or modified area.***
- *Reducing Factors :* The factors, by which each class must be multiplied to reduce it to the standard quality and/or density, are known as Reducing Factors.
- **Reforestation:** Artificial establishment of forests on land which carried forestry before and involving the replacement of the indigenous tree species by a new and essential different species or genetic variety.
- **Regeneration interval :** It is defined as the period between seeding felling and final felling on a particular area i.e., usually a compartment or a sub-compartment under one of the shelterwood systems.
- *Regeneration period:* This is the period required to regenerate the whole periodic block.
- **Regeneration :** Re-establishment of a forest stand by natural or artificial means following the removal of the previous stand by felling or as a result of natural causes, e.g. fire or storm.
- **Register of deviations from the Working Plan :** In this register all durations from the prescriptions of a WP in a serial order showing

the nature of the prescription, the nature of deviation and the authority sanctioning the deviation will be recorded.

- **Remote sensing :** This is the "science and art of obtaining information about an object, area, or phenomenon through the analysis of data acquired by a device that is not in contact with the object, area, or phenomenon under investigation".
- **Rotation/Production period :** The period which a forest crop takes between its formation and final felling.

  OR

  The planned number of years between the formation or regeneration of a crop (by seeding/ planting/ other means) and its final felling.
- **Sample :** Sample is defined as "a part of the population consists of one or more sampling units selected and examined as a representative part of the whole". Sampling fraction/Sampling intensity (SI) = Sample population/area x 100 Whole population/area.
- **Sampling intensity :** The ratio of sample to the whole population is called sampling fraction or sampling intensity, which is expressed as a percentage. e.g. 5%, 10%, 15%, etc.
- **Shrub and brush land :** Woody perennial plants, generally of more than 0.5 m and less than 5 m height, and often without a definite stem and crown. "Trees outside the forest" are excluded.
- **Square and Rectangular :** Such plots are most commonly used in India. Because of easy demarcation and lay out. Suited to plantations raised in rows. Usual size is ***0.1 ha and some times also follow 1.0 ha***
- **Stand table :** A table showing the distribution of stems by diameter classes for each of a series of crop diameters.
- **Stock Map :** Stock Map is "the map showing distribution of different forests or stand types which have a bearing on management, with information about their composition, age class, etc".
- **Strips :** Strips are laid across the forest from one end to other at a particular bearing at regular intervals and inventory of these strips made to serve as a sample.
- **Sub-compartment :** Sub-compartment is the sub-division of the compartment, generally temporary in nature, differentiated for special description and silvicultural treatment, designated by small letters a, b, c, etc.

- **Surround :** Surround is defined as "an area maintained round an experimental or sample plot ensure that the later is not being affected by the treatment applied to the area outside them both". It is also known as **isolation or buffer strip**, usually followed at least 15 m wide.
- **Sustainable development :** The management and conservation of the natural resources base, and the orientation of technological and institutional change in such a manner as to ensure the attainment and continued satisfaction of human needs for present and future generations. Such sustainable development (in agriculture, forestry and fisheries sectors) conserves land, water, plant and animal genetic resources, is environmentally viable and socially acceptable.
- **Sustainable Forest Management (SFM) :** It is the management of forests according to the principles of sustainable development. Sustainable forest management uses very broad social, economic and environmental goals. A range of forestry institutions now practice various forms of sustainable forest management and a broad range of methods and tools are available that have been tested over time.

  OR

  Sustainable Forest Management (SFM) : It is defined as "The stewardship and use of forests and forest lands in a way, and at a rate, that maintains their biodiversity, productivity, regeneration capacity, vitality and their potential to fulfill, now and in the future, relevant ecological, economic and social functions, at local, national, and global levels, and that does not cause damage to other ecosystems".
- **Sustained yield :** The material that a forest can yield annually (periodically) in perpetuity.

  OR

  The regular, continuous supply of the desired produce to the fullest capacity of the forest.
- **Temporary sample plots :** These plots are laid for measurements that are carried out once only. These are generally used in enumeration surveys.
- **The Joint Forest Management (JFM) :** This seeks to develop partnerships between local community institutions (as managers) and state forest departments (as owners) for sustainable management and joint benefit sharing public forest lands (usually degraded).

- **Topographical units (TU) :** TU is defined as "a sampling unit (SU) whose boundaries are pre-dominantly topographical or natural features such as nalas, streams, ridges, *etc*". These are shown on maps and fixed exactly on ground. Even artificial features, such as roads, inspection paths, block, compartment, sub-compartment boundaries also used as boundaries.
- **Total or Complete enumeration :** It is the enumeration, in which the desired species above the specific diameter is carried out over the entire area of the forest/given area.
- **Total yield :** "The standing volume of a crop including the total volume removed in thinnings since its establishment as a more or less even aged stand". Total yield is nothing but the sum of the final yield and intermediate yield.
- **Tree Factor :** It is the number of trees per hectare (or acre) represented by each tree tallied.
- **Tree:** A woody perennial with a single main stem, or in the case of coppice with several stems, having a more or less definite crown. Includes bamboo, palms and other woody plants meeting the above criterion. The definition excludes non-forest fruit tree species.
- **Trees outside forests:** Trees on land other than forest or other wooded land.
- **Unexploitable forest:** Forest and other wooded land on which there are legal, economic or technical restrictions on wood and non-wood production.
- **Unproductive forest :** A forest which is not regularly managed.
- **Vegetation type :** Mixture of vegetation covering a forest site. Used in identifying a certain forest site type, e.g. heath forest (Ministerial Conference on the Protection of European Forests and the Pan-European Forest Process; Geneva, 09/1994).
- **Village community :** Village community means such persons as are registered in the electoral rolls relating to village.
- **Village Forest Committee (VFC) :** Village Forest Committee means a committee constituted under sub-section (6) of Section 29 of the United Provinces Panchayat Raj Act, 1947 for the purposes of these rules.
- **Village Forest :** Village Forest means a village forest referred to in Section 28 of the Act.

- **Working Circle :** A forest area (forming a part or whole of a Working Plan area) organized with a particular object, and under one Silvicultural System and one set of Working Plan prescriptions. In certain circumstances, Working Circles may overlap.

- **Working plan :** Working plan is "a written scheme of management aiming at continuity of policy and action and controlling the treatment of a forest". It is synonymously called "Instrument of Forest Management/Management Plan".

- **Yield Capacity:** "The total quantity of material per anum, of given species, that an area is capable of producing under normal conditions, so long as the factors of locality remain unchanged".

- **Yield Determination:** The calculation of the amount of material which may be removed from a forest, annually or periodically over a stated period or of the annual or periodic area over which fellings may be made, consistent with the treatment prescribed.

- **Yield table :** A tabular statement which summarizes on a unit area (area/hectare) all the essential data relating to the development of a fully stocked and regularly thinned even aged crop at periodic intervals covering the greater part of its useful life.

❑❑❑

Chapter 2

History, Introduction, Definition, Object and Scope of Forest Management

History of Forest Management

History of Forest Management is divided into five distinct periods:

I. Pre-British period (1526-1700)

II. Early-British period (1750-1900)

III. Late-British period (1900-1947)

IV. Post-Independence period (1947-1975)

V. Post-Independence period (1985-till date)

I. Pre-British period (including epic period - 1526-1700)

- Dhandakaranya and Nandana Vanas (Epic period)
- Dravidians (Rishimunis)
- Buddhism and Jainism (Both appreciated nature)
- Kautilya formed Arthashastra that envisages functions and importance of forests (400 BC)
- Ashoka emphasized on symbiotic relationship between man, trees and animals (300 BC)
- Mughal invasion (1526-1700) - Avenue planting and canal plantations.

II. Early-British period (1750-1900)

- Concepts of sustainable yield, Rotation, Normal forests and Control of forests (1800).

- British introduced agriculture into forestry and establishment of Nilambur teak plantation (1842)
- Commercial interference i.e. committee constituted on harvestable material mainly evergreen forests (1850)
- Beginning of forest administration in India (1864)
- Brandis–First Inspector General of Forests (IGF) introduced scientific forest management and forest administration (1855)
- Scientific forest management started with introducing sustainable yield and normal forests (1864)
- First ever Indian Forest Act was passed (1865)

III. Late British Period (1947-1975)

- Importance was given for Industrial plantations
- Second World was (1939-1945) – Loss of large area forests
- Howard retired as IGF under British rule
- Indian Forest Act, 1927 was enacted

IV. Post-Independence Period (1900-1947)

- National Forest Policy revised (1952)
- Emphasis on agriculture
- Functional classification of forests, such as :

  Protection forests

  National forests

  Village forests and

  Tree lands

V. Post-Independence Period (1985-till date)

- Wildlife (Protection) Act, 1972
- Forest Conservation Act, 1980
- National Forest Policy, 1988
- Biodiversity Act, 2002 – Biological Diversity Act was signed by India (UN convention on biodiversity)
- Recognition of Forest Rights, 2006
- National Forestry Policy, 2018

Forest:

Forest is derived from the Latin word "*Foris*" means outside the village boundary/away from the inhabited land.

Legally : Forest is an area of land proclaimed to be a forest under a forest law.

Ecologically : Forest is a living system dominated by tree species.

SAF definition : "Forest is a biological community dominated by trees and other woody species" (SAF – Society of American Foresters).

BCFT definition : Forest is a plant community pre-dominantly of trees and other woody vegetation usually with closed canopy (British Commonwealth Forestry Terminology-BCFT).

FAO definition : All lands bearing vegetative associations dominated by trees, capable of producing wood or exerting an influence on local climate or on the water regime or providing shelter for wildlife.

Forest : Forest is defined as an area set aside for the production of timber and other forest produce or maintained under woody vegetation for certain indirect benefits, which it provides. e.g. Climatic or productive.

Forestry : Forestry is defined as the theory and practice of all that constitutes the creation, conservation and scientific management of forests and utilization of their resources.

Silvicutlure : Silviculture is that branch of forestry which deals with the establishment, development, care and reproduction of stands of timber (Toumey and Korstian). Silviculture is nothing but the art and science of cultivating forest crops (FRI, Dehradun).

Silvics : The study of life history and general characteristics of forest trees and crops with particular reference to environmental factors as the basis for thc practice of silviculture. The practice of silviculture is applied Silvics.

Management : It is a mechanism by which a defined human group peruses a determined set of objectives through systematic group efforts for their implementation most effectively and economically. This can be viewed as a group effort towards a common goal in which team behaviour plays an important role.

Definitions of Forest Management

1. **Forest Management** is defined as the practical application of the scientific, technical and economic principles of forestry (British Commonwealth Forestry Terminology-BCFT).
2. **Forest Management** is that branch of forestry whose function is the organization of a forest property for management and maintenance, by ordering in time and place the various operations necessary for the conservation, protection and improvement of the forest on the one hand, and the controlled harvesting of the forest on the other.
3. **Forest Management** is the application of business methods and technical forestry principles to the operation of a forest property.

The above definitions depict that the forest management is the practical application of science, technology and economics to a forest estate for the achievement of certain objectives mainly production of wood, timber, raw materials for industries and other forest products (NTFPs), such as resin, gum, tan bark, etc. it is based on the knowledge of a number of basic subjects/sciences, such as silviculture, Ecology, Geology, Pedology, Botany, Mensuration, Pathology, Economics, Finance, etc.

Management of forests broadly involves three main tasks, *viz.*,

I. Control of composition and structure of the growing stock

II. Harvesting and marketing of forest produce

III. Administration of forest property and personnel.

The most of the forests in India are State owned forests (95.8%) which are maintained for a multiplicity of purpose i.e. productive, protective, climatic, wildlife, recreational and bio-aesthetic, with one use dominant i.e. production of wood.

Intensive Forestry : The basic principle of management is long-term sustainability of the ecosystem. In favourable localities, this science is applied to maximize financial return and is called **"Intensive Forestry"** which is defined as "the practice of forestry with the object of obtaining the maximum quantity of the desired quality of products per unit area through the application of suitable techniques of silviculture and management".

Multiple Use Forestry : When forestry is practiced to achieve more than one purpose, it is called as **"Multiple Use Forestry"**, which is defined as the practice of forestry for the simultaneous or sequential use of a forest area for two or more purposes. e.g. The production of wood with forest grazing and / or wildlife conservation, etc.

Scope of Forest Management

Management of forests involves a process of making and implementing policy decisions to achieve the objectives of the owner. These decisions involve a plan of action. Planning is the responsibility of the states and the Centre in case of State-owned forests with broad principles in the National and the State Forest Policies. Detailed plans are prepared by Forest managers at the Professional level and executed by the technician level staff. Forest Manager has to constantly manage the growing stock to achieve given objects of management by deciding 'how much, when, where and how to cut'.

Scope of Forest Management is very extensive; it encompasses, broadly, the following main activities:

I. Control of Growing Stock, its Structure and Composition

i) Site adaptation
ii) Choice of species
iii) Manipulation of stands
iv) Harvesting of produce
v) Regeneration
vi) Protection

II. Distribution and Marketing of Produce

i) Transportation and Communication
ii) Logging plan
iii) Marketing data
iv) Sale of produce
v) Revenue

III. Administration of Forest Property

i) Forest organization
ii) Management of personnel
iii) Monitoring and control of works
iv) Labour management and welfare
v) Financial control and economic efficiency
vi) Fulfillment of social obligations
vii) Record for present and future references

Objectives of Forest Management

Objects of management broadly express the basic purpose of the forestry enterprise rather than the production of a specific product. The object of management may be:

a) **Economic :** Production of the maximum yield of forest product.

b) **Protective :** Preservation of the physical features, conservation of soil and moisture.

c) **Bio-aesthetic :** Enhancing the scenic beauty and preservation of flora and fauna.

d) or a judicious combination of all these.

General objectives of Forest Management

The general objects of management provide the framework for the entire forest estate under a management plan. Primary object of good management is provision of the maximum benefit to the greatest number of people for all time (Brasnett). The object of management under any circumstances is the most advantageous utilization possible of the soil allotted to forestry (Knuchel, 1953).

In the State owned forests, the management plans (Forest Working Plans) invariably stipulate the following general objects of management as applicable to the entire forest estate under the specific plan providing the broad framework for management :

i) Maintaining and raising the productive capacity of the soil and of the forest stands consistent with the maximum site potential.

ii) Promoting the protective effect of the forest, against soil erosion, avalanches, floods and protection of the physical factors, such as natural scenery, local flora and fauna.

iii) Execution of silvicultural operations and regulation of fellings in such a way so as to bring the forest to a condition of as near normality as possible i.e. attainment of a *normal forest* is one of the principal objects.

iv) Satisfaction of rights of the right holders in respect of timber, firewood, grazing, etc., in particular and to meet the bonafide requirements of the local population in general.

v) Subject to the above Silvicultural, Conservational and Social considerations, providing the maximum possible volume of valuable of timber for constructional and industrial purposes and other forest produce for meeting the market demands and securing the highest possible financial results.

Special objectives of Forest Management

Special objects are laid down for different regions/locations, with different site factors and forest types, more suited for specific purposes. Accordingly, Working Plans invariably specify general objects for the entire Working Plan area and in addition special objects of management of each Working Circle, which is characterized by a distinct vegetation type, more suited for certain purposes as compared to others. i.e. Priorities of objects are rearranged. Some examples are given below :

i) Badly eroded areas and steep hill slopes may be constituted into a Protection Working Circle, where the special objects will be protection, afforestation, soil and water conservation; satisfaction of only the minimum social needs of the local population, ignoring considerations for market supplies and financial returns.

ii) In the watershed of municipal water supplies, irrigation and hydroelectric generation dams, the special objective will be the maintenance of an undisturbed protective vegetative cover including all other forms of use.

iii) In forest areas of natural scenic beauty, wood lands near urban habitation, recreation will be the dominant objects where timber felling, grazing and even hunting will have to be entirely stopped.

Such forest serve as "magnificent playgrounds for tired mankind seeking peace and spiritual strength" (V.S.Rao).

iv) Mixed miscellaneous open forests, heavily grazed and felled in the past, with low proportion of valuable timber and industrially important species are clearfelled and converted into plantation of desired species (pure or simple compatible mixtures). Such areas have extensively been constituted into Plantation Working Circles and /or Industrial Timber Working Circles in plains and terai areas of UP and West Bengal, Bihar, Odisha, with a view to meeting increasing demand for industrial raw material for pulp, match and plywood industries.

v) In Chir pine forests, one of the special objects is invariably the production of resin for resin and turpentine industries.

vi) In dry and moist mixed deciduous forests, containing quantities of *Khair* and *Semal,* one of the special objects will be to ensure their reproduction and increase their proportion to feed Cutch / Katha and Match industries.

Special features of Forestry

Following are the constraints of managing Indian Forests :

1. Forestry is a long term investment and there is a long interval between the formation and harvesting of forest crops.
2. Income/Annual increment of the forest is not distinct from the capital/growing stock.
3. Identity of the product and the manufacturing plant - Trees themselves are the machinery which manufacture the raw material (wood).
4. Multiple and varied uses of forests.
5. Incomputable benefits, such as soil conservation, carbon sequestration, etc.
6. Inaccessibility - Generally occupy more remote, less accessible and less fertile lands as compared to agricultural land.

Chapter 3

Forest Organization

Forest Organization

Forests are classified into various (six) categories for purposes of description, administration, management and record.

1. Ecological (Geographical and climatic) : Done by Champion and Seth

1. Tropical forests

- Tropical wet evergreen forests
- Tropical semi-evergreen forests
- Tropical moist deciduous forests
- Tropical dry deciduous forests
- Littoral and swamp forests
- Tropical thorn forests
- Tropical dry evergreen forests

2. Montane sub-tropical forests

- Broad leaved hill forests
- Pine forests
- Dry evergreen forests

3. Montane temperate forests

- Himalayan temperate forests
- Wet temperate forests
- Dry temperate forests

4. Sub-alpine forests

5. Alpine scrub

- Moist alpine scrub
- Dry alpine scrub

2. Functional classification : According to National Forest Policy, 1952

i) Protection forests
ii) National forests
iii) Village forests
iv) Tree-lands

3. Legal classification : (IFA, 1927)

i) Reserved forests/State Forests – (Section 4-initial notification Section-17 –final notification)
ii) District forests – (Section -33)
iii) Minor forests – (Section -35)
iv) Section – 4, notified forests
v) Village forests – (Section - 29)
vi) Private forests – (Section – 37)
vii) Un-classed forests – are forest lands owned by government. These are generally heavily burdened with rights and are excessively grazed and felled and even burnt. These includes C&D class lands under the control of forest department.

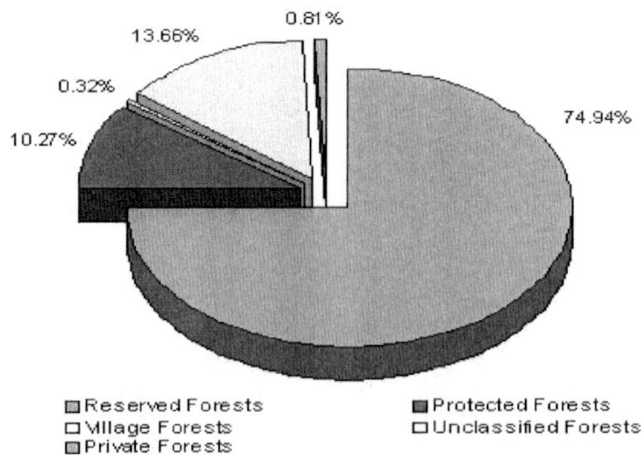

Classification of Karnataka state forests on legal basis

Source: Annual Report, 2002-03, Karnataka Forest Department

4. Territorial classification

Forests are divided into Block, Compartment and Sub-compartment for **executive** and **protective** works :

i) **Block :** It is main territorial division of forest, generally bounded by natural features and bearing a local proper name.

ii) **Compartment :** A block is divided into several compartments, which are territorial units of a forest permanently defined for purposes of administration and record, designated by Arabic numbers 1, 2, 3, 4, *etc.* This is the **smallest permanent working plan unit** of management.

iii) **Sub-compartment :** It is the sub-division of the compartment, generally temporary in nature, differentiated for special description and silvicultural treatment, designated by small letters a, b, c, *etc.*

5. Management (Silvicultural) classification

1. **Working circle :** A forest area (forming whole or part of working plan area) organized with a particular object, subject to one and the same silvicultural system and same set of working plan prescriptions (Fig. 1).

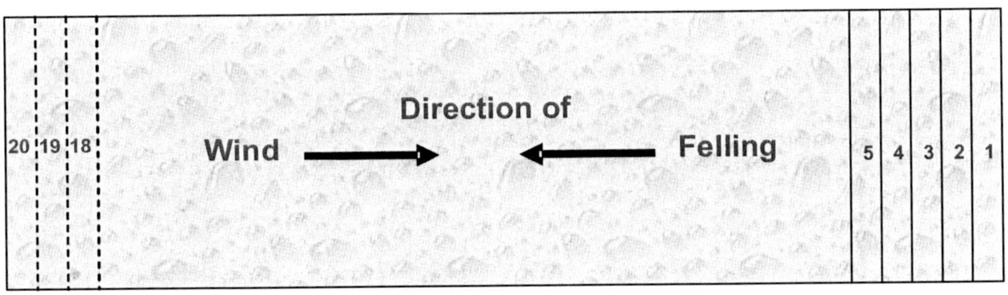

Fig. 1: Plan of an undivided Working Circle with 20 Coupes

2. **Felling series :** A forest area forming the whole or part of a working circle and delimited so as, a) to distribute felling and regeneration to suit local conditions. b) to maintain or create a normal distribution of age classes. The yield should be calculated for each FS which should have an independent representation of age classes (Fig. 2).

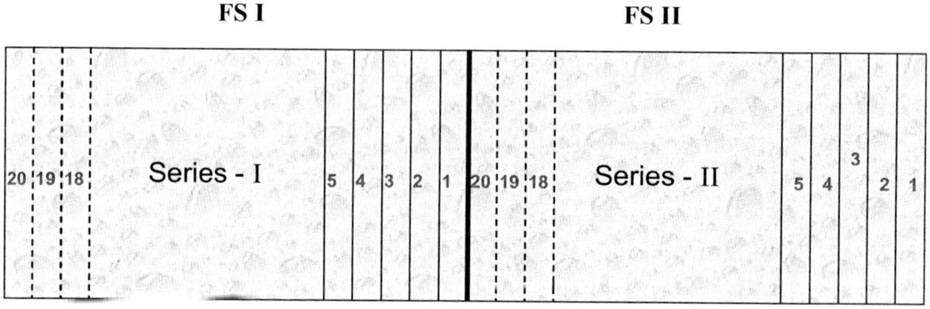

Fig. 2: Plan of the same Working Circle divided into two equal felling series, with twenty coupes in each

3. **Cutting section :** A sub-division of FS formed with the object of regulating cuttings in some special manner, a planned separation of fellings in successive years (Fig. 3).

4. **Coupe :** A felling area usually one of the annual series unless otherwise stated, preferably numbered with roman numerals I, II, III, *etc.* (Fig. 4)

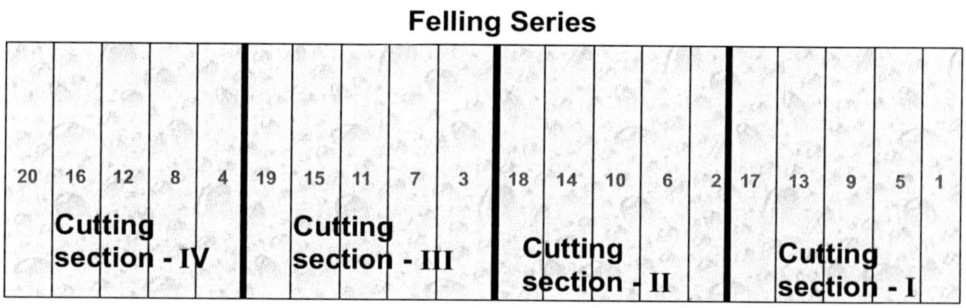

Fig. 3: Felling series divided into 4 Cutting sections with 5 annual coupes each

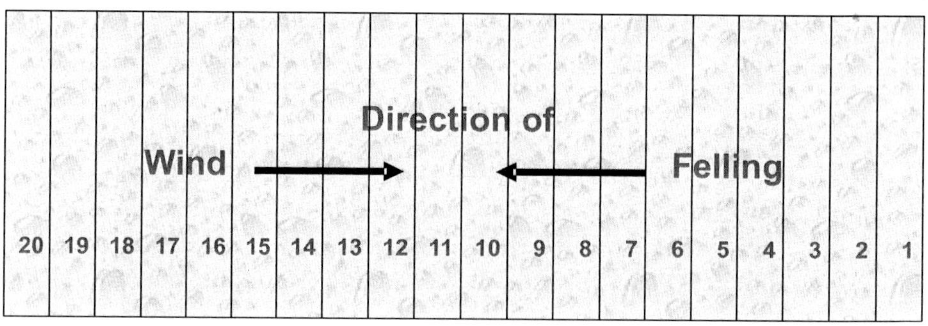

Fig. 4: Plan of an undivided Working Circle with 20 Coupes

Periodic Blocks

Periodic blocks: It is defined as *"part or parts of forest set aside to be regenerated or otherwise treated during a special period"*.

a) **Floating or Single Periodic Block :** The regeneration block is called as **"Floating or Single"**, when it is the only periodic block allotted at each working plan revision.

b) **Fixed or Permanent Periodic Block :** When all the periodic blocks are allotted and retain their territorial identity at working plan revision, they are termed as "**Fixed or Permanent periodic blocks**".

Under the Regular Shelterwood (or Uniform) System of natural regeneration, **age classes** take the place of **age-gradations** and **periodic blocks** take the place of **annual coupes**, each containing one age class instead one age-gradation.

- **Regeneration period :** The period required to regenerate the whole of a periodic block (PB).
- **Age gradation :** An age class with one year as the interval.
- **Age class :** One of the intervals into which the range of age of trees growing in a forest is divided for classification or use (trees falling in an interval).
- **Working Plan : Working plan** is *"a written scheme of management aiming at continuity of policy and action and controlling the treatment of a forest"*. It is synonymously called as "**Instrument of Forest Management**" or "**Management Plan**".
- **Felling Cycle :** The time that elapses between successive main fellings on the same area.

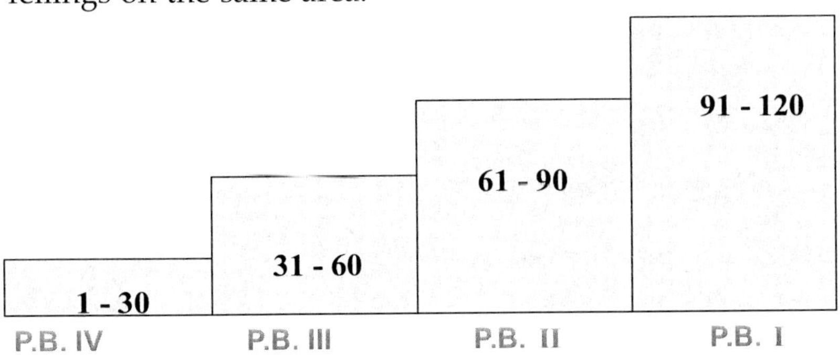

Fig. 5: Arrangement of age- classes / P.Bs. in a F.S. worked under uniform system

Sub Chapter : Organization of Management Areas

Working circle (WC) : WC is a forest area (forming whole or part of working plan area) organized with a particular object, subject to one and the same silvicultural system and same set of working plan prescriptions.

Since the entire working plan area is usually large and heterogeneous in site and crop composition, different silvicultural treatments have to be given in different parts and different working rules called prescriptions drawn up for different parts. Such parts called Working circles.

Felling series (FS) : FS is a forest area forming the whole or part of a working circle and delimited so as :

a) To distribute felling and regeneration to suit local conditions

b) To maintain or create a normal distribution of age classes. The yield should be calculated for each FS, which should have an independent representation of age classes.

To distribute works of all kinds over one or more ranges working circle may be divided into felling series.

Division of WC into several FS enables effective control and distribution of work in different ranges. When a WC is not divided, it is of course one FS.

Periodic blocks (PB) : It is defined as *"part or parts of forest set aside to be regenerated or otherwise treated during a special period".*

Under regular shelter wood or uniform system of natural regeneration, **age classes** takes place the age gradations and **periodic blocks** takes place the annual coupe, each containing the one age class instead of one age gradation.

1. **Floating or single PB** : Only one periodic block is allotted at each working plan revision.
2. **Fixed or permanent PB :** When all PB's are allotted and retain their territorial identity at working plan revision.

e.g., In Chir pine forests

Rotation period is 120 years and Regeneration period is 30 years

$$\text{No. of PB's} = \frac{\text{Rotation period}}{\text{Regeneration period}}$$

$$= \frac{120}{30} = 4PB$$

Each PB is regarded as approximately even aged. The fewer the no. of age gradations included in the age class in a PB (shorter the regeneration period and larger the no. of PBs, the more nearly it is even aged).

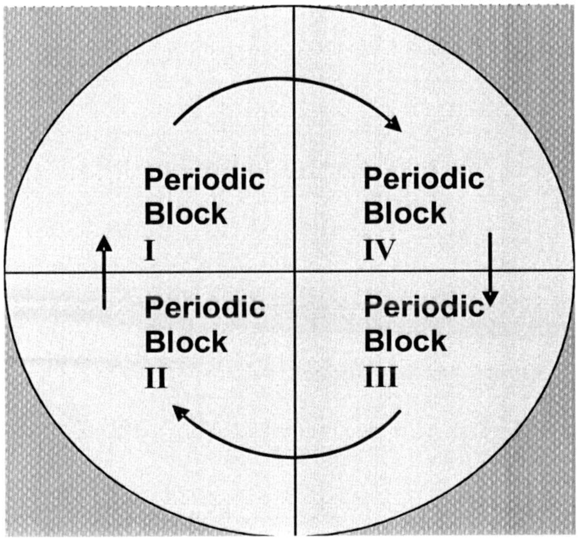

Fig. 9: Sequence of movement of forest in various Periodic Blocks

Felling cycle (FC)

Felling cycle is ***"the time that elapses between successive main fellings on the same area".***

It may vary from 10-30 years (some cases 5-40 years) depending on the intensity of working. Working of the entire WC is neither practicable nor desirable. The usual practice is to divide the area into number of coupes and each of which is worked at an interval of planned number of years known as Felling cycle.

The numbers of coupes will absolutely is equal to the number of years in the felling cycle and they may be made up of one or more compartments. If 100 years is the rotation and 10 years the FC, there will be 10 felling coupes, each being one-tenth of the FS and worked at intervals of 10 years.

6. Administrative (organizational) classification

Principal Chief Conservator of Forests (PCCF) - HOFF

↓

Principal Chief Conservator of Forests (PCCF) - Wildlife

↓

Additional Principal Chief Conservator of Forests (APCCF)

↓

Chief Conservator of Forests (CCF)

↓

Conservator of Forests (CF) – Head of Circle

↓

Deputy Conservator of Forests (DCF) – Head of Division

↓

Assistant Conservator of Forests (ACF) – Head of Sub-division

↓

Range Forest Officer (RFO) – Head of Range

↓

Forester – Head of Section

↓

Forest Guard – Head of Beat

↓

Watcher

** HOFF – Head of Forest Force

Table: Classification of recorded forest area in Karnataka on the basis on forest types

S.No.	Forest type	Area (Sq. Km)	%
1.	Evergreen forests	4,350	11.36
2.	Semi-evergreen forests	1,450	3.79
3.	Moist deciduous forests	5,780	15.10
4.	Dry deciduous forests	7,270	18.99
5.	Thorn forests (Scrub)	8,340	21.78
6.	Un-wooded	11,094	28.98
	Total	38,284	100.00

Source: Annual Report, 2002-03, Karnataka Forest Department

Table: Karnataka forest types as per Champion and Seth classification

S.No.	Forest type	Symbol
1.	Southern hilltop tropical evergreen forests	1 AC 3
2.	West coast tropical evergreen forests	1 AC 4
3.	Cane breaks	1 E 1
4.	Wet bamboo breaks	1 E 2
5.	Pioneer Euphorbiaceous scrub	1 2S 1
6.	West coast semi-evergreen forest	2 AC 2
7.	West coast secondary evergreen dipterocarp forest	2 A 2 S 1
8.	Moist bamboo brakes	2 E 3
9.	Lateritic semi-evergreen forest	2 E 4
10.	Secondary moist bamboo brakes	22 S 1
11.	Slightly moist and moist teak forest	3 BC 1 a,b
12.	Southern moist mixed deciduous forest	3 BC 2
13.	Southern Sec. moist mixed deciduous forest	3.B 2S 1
14.	Sub montane hill valley swamp forests	4 C FS 1
15.	Riparian fringing forests	4 E RS 1
16.	Dry teak forest	5 AC 1b
17.	Southern dry mixed deciduous forest	5 AC 3
18.	Dry deciduous scrub	5 DS 1
19.	Dry savannah forest	5 DS 2
20.	Euphorbia scrub	5 DS 3
21.	Dry grass-land	5 DS 4
22.	Hardwickia forest	5 E 4
23.	Laterite thorn forest	5 E 7

24.	Dry bamboo brake	5 E 9
25.	Southern dry tropical reverian forest	5 1 S 1
26.	Sec. dry deciduous forest	5 2 S S 1
27.	Southern thorn forest	6 AC 1
28.	Southern thorn scrub	6 ADS 1
29.	Southern euphorbia scrub	6 ADS 2
30.	Western sub-tropical hill forest	8 AC 2

Classification of Forest Cover into density classes

- Very Dense (Canopy Density > 70%)
- Moderate Dense (Canopy Density 40% to 70%)
- Open Forest (Canopy Density 10% to 40%)
- Scrub: Degraded forest lands (Canopy density <10%)
- Non-forest: Lands not included in above classes

Canopy-Wise Forest Cover

Class	Area (sq. km)	Percent of Geographic Area
Very Dense Forest	98,158	2.99
Moderately Dense Forest	3,08318	9.38
Open Forest	3,01,797	9.18
Total Forest Cover*	7,08,273	21.54
Scrub	45,979	1.40
Non-Forest	25,33,217	77.06
Total Geographical Area	32,87,469	100.00

* Includes 4,921 sq.km under Mangrove Cover (Percentage rounded off)

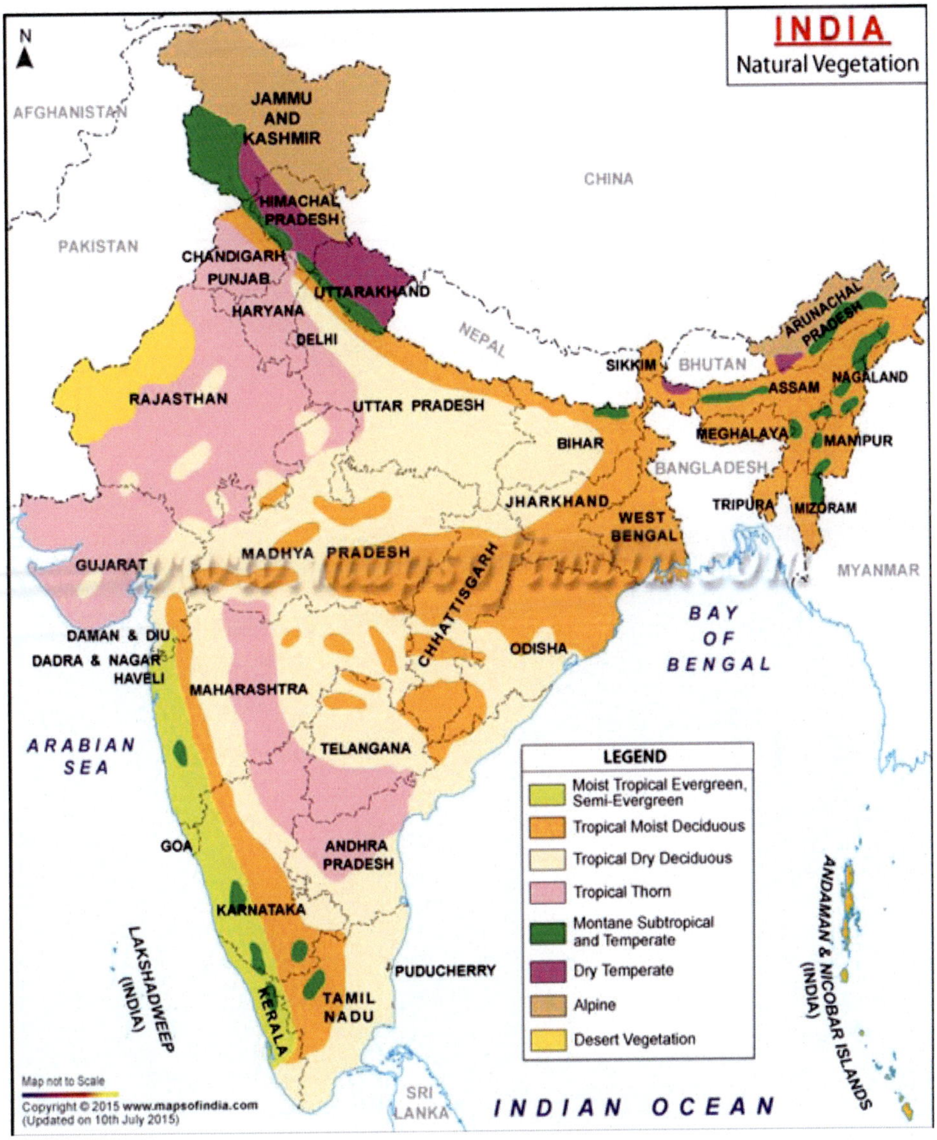

Fig. Distribution of forests in India

Chapter 4

Sustained Yield Concept

Sustained Yield

DEFINITION : Sustained yield is defined as ***"the material that a forest can yield annually (periodically) in perpetuity".*** OR

The regular, continuous supply of the desired produce to the fullest capacity of the forest.

***Sustained Yield* is defined and/or expressed variously as:**

i) a) " The material that a forest can yield annually (or periodically) in perpetuity.

b) As applied to policy, method or plan of management (*Sustained Yield Management),* it implies continuous production with the aim of achieving at the earliest practical time at the highest practical level an approximate balance between net growth and harvest by annual or somewhat longer periods." (BCFT).

ii) "The regular, continuous supply of the desired produce to the full capacity of the forest." (Osmaston)

iii) "The yield of timber or other forest produces from a forest which is managed in such a way as to permit the removal of approximately equal volume or quantity of timber or other forest produce annually or periodically in perpetuity.

Sustained Yield may be annual or periodic, depending on whether a complete series of age-gradations (or ages mixed together) is maintained or only an incomplete series.

Periodic Yield is also considered as sustained, provided the period is short.

Intermittent Yield is defined as the material or cash return obtained from time to time from a forest not organized for continuous production.

Principle of Sustained Yield

The principle of maximum sustained yield has been the ***back bone of forest management*** and considers sustained yield synonymous with good forest management. It ensures stability and continuous supply of raw material to the industries and to meet the social and domestic needs of the people.

The principle of sustained yield envisages that ***"the annual or periodic fellings do not exceed the annual or periodic growth"***. Concept of sustained yield has been evolved from the basic considerations that the later generations may derive from the forest at least as much of the benefits as the present generation.

Pre-requisites for Sustained Yield management

1. Normal age class gradations
2. Normal Increment
3. Normal Growing Stock (NGS)

How to achieve the objective of Sustained Yield concept?

The simplest method of achieving the objective of sustained yield is to maintain a complete succession of equal areas of crops of all ages from one year old upto the age of maturity (say 10 years) and remove the 10 years old wood annually and plant up the area again.

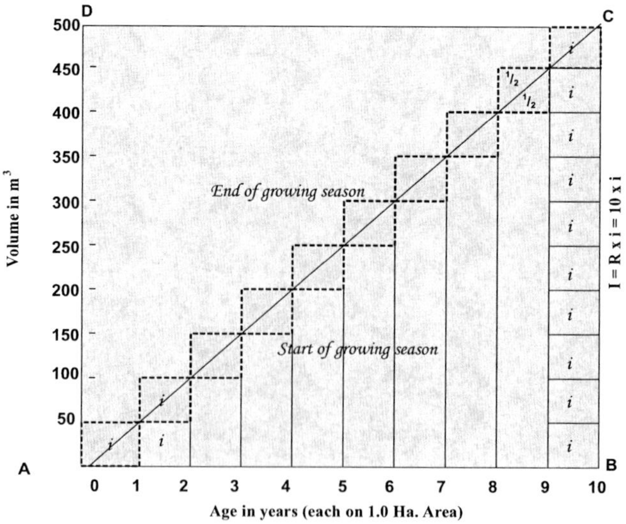

Fig. 6: Theoretical Normal Growing Stock in a series of R (10) equal Age-gradations (one hectare each)

This matured wood represent the increment of the whole forest and difficulty of removing the annual increment from each unit area, say one hectare, is overcome by removing accumulated production of 10 hectare on $1/10^{th}$ part of the total area, as illustrated in the figure.

Such series of trees or crops of all ages, from seedling to maturity, so as to enable the removal of the oldest is known as a ***"Complete series of age gradations"***.

As the forest in the above example has equal area of every age in it, an equal area will be available for felling at maturity. The establishment of such a series of age-gradations is one form of the crop necessary for ***"Sustained Yield Management"*** and for maintaining it in perpetuity. Such a forest provides a conceptual picture of *"Normal Forest"*.

The ideal of a Normal forest is a logical corollary (consequence result) to the principle of *Sustained Yield* in perpetuity.

Advantages / Merits of Sustained Yield

1. It facilitates budgeting and regulation of taxation; ensures steady income to the state.
2. Constant employment to the local labour and their skill improvement.
3. Staff employed is fully and permanently engaged.
4. Contractors employed on felling, conversion and transport have an assured and steady permanent employment.
5. Wood using industries have an assured continuous supply of raw materials.
6. Local people will get sustained supplies of wood for their domestic and agricultural needs.
7. Markets can be developed and their confidence can be gained with the sustained supplies.

Disadvantages / Demerits

Some of the arguments against the principle of sustained yield may be summarized as follows:

1. Sustained yield management treats timber production as only a biological function rather than a response to economic demand.
2. It ignores the cost involved in producing a fixed quantity i.e. production is carried on irrespective of price fluctuations resulting in inefficient resource management.
3. Fixed supply is economically inefficient.
4. It ignores inter-relationship between forestry and other sections of national economy.
5. Such a rigid (inflexible) policy is not suitable for a dynamic or growing economy.
6. In practice sustained yield has merely been ideal; wide fluctuations in yield are quite common.

Concept of Progressive Yield (PY)

The concept of progressive yield is advocated by a German Forester ***Hartig.***

This concept takes into account of both the gradual evolution of the economy as well as the progress in the silvicultural techniques, as a result of experience and research, which is considered as an important ingredient of scientific management.

The concept of progressive yield envisages that ***"raising the productivity of soil, and of the crop, by silvicultural treatments, judicious tending, and enrichment of the forest by changing the crop composition and by replacement of the original inferior forest by valuable species".***

The principle of production of maximum quantity of the kind of produce in market demand that can be produced by the soil, in the shortest possible time, would cover the principle of **"Progressive Yield".**

It also stipulates avoidance of loss of increment by effective protection and tending and adoption of quick and efficient regeneration techniques.

Comparisons between Sustained Yield (SY) and Progressive Yield (PY)

S.No.	Contents	Sustained Yield (SY)	Progressive Yield (PY)
1.	*Principle*	*Static* (same yield in perpetuity)	*Dynamic* (acts according to the changed conditions and requirements)
2.	*Economy*	Practiced in ***stagnant economy***	Practiced in ***developing economy***
3.	*Products*	Continuous supply with ***same products***	Continuous supply with ***needed products***
4.	*Suitability*	Economically ***less suitable***	Economically ***more suitable***

❑❑❑

Chapter 5

Rotation and Types of Rotation

Rotation / Production Period

It is defined as ***"the planned number of years between the formation or regeneration of a crop (by seeding/planting/other means) and its final felling". OR*** The period which a forest crop takes between its formation and final felling.

The period which a forest crop takes between its formation and final felling is known as ***Rotation or Production Period.*** This term is also defined in various other ways by different authors; some of these definitions are given below:

i) "The planned number of year between the formation or regeneration of a crop and its final felling. In the case of a selection forest, the average age at which a tree is considered mature for felling" (Glossary).

ii) "The number of years fixed by the *Working Plan* between the formation or regeneration and the final felling of a crop (Brasnett).

iii) "Rotation age is the age of trees or crops at which when they are felled, objects of management for the time being are best served" (Knuchel).

iv) "Rotation or Production Period is the interval of time between the formation of a young crop by seeding, planting or other means and its final harvesting" (Osmaston).

v) "Rotation is the period which elapses between the formation of a wood and the time when it is finally cut over" (Jerram).

Concept of Rotation in Regualr and Irregular Crops

The term *Rotation*, strictly / correctly applicable to regular crops only. *In Clear-felling System and plantations, rotation is a definite period of interval between the year of formation and final felling*. In these, and regular forests in general, entire crops of trees of a sizeable area are felled at a time or during a comparatively short period (regeneration period in Regular Shelterwood System) when ready for felling. There is, more or less, a clear production period which can be planned in advance to give timber which satisfies the object of management.

In the latter case, rotation is fixed for the whole working circle a unit, as the average length of time between the establishment of crops and their harvesting. Though this system facilitates better planning and organization of work, it does not take into consideration that:

i) Rate of growth will vary with site variation, even for the same species.

ii) It involves sacrifice of immature trees / crops, as some will not have reached exploitable size.

iii) Accidents, such as fire, disease, and wind-throw may happen, necessitation felling earlier than planned.

iv) If profit is the main object of management, some difficulties may arise, as the degree of profit is affected by rotation, rate of growth, size/price gradients of timber and the cost of growing it. To obtain desired profits, stands will have to be finally at various times depending on their rate of growth.

In uneven aged (irregular) selection forests, trees are selected individually on their merit for felling, depending on:

i) Qualities of size, vigour and suitability for markets.

ii) Adjustment of proportion of different sizes.

iii) Silvicultural principles; e.g., removal of inferior stems in favour of better ones.

Types of Rotation

Rotation is an important factor in the regulation of yield and proper management of the forest as a whole which depends on mainly the objects of management.

Various types of rotation recognized in forestry are :

1. Physical Rotation

"It is the rotation which coincides with the natural lease of life of a species on a given site". **The natural life-span (longevity) of trees** varies greatly with species and the site factors. This rotation is applicable only in case of protection and amenity forests, park lands, and in some case roadside avenues.

Another interpretation of Physical Rotation is the age upto which the **trees remain sound**, or produce viable seed in high forests and also reliable coppice shoots in coppice crops. It is very variable, fairly long and also indefinite. This rotation is **not of any relevance / importance** to economic forestry.

Applicability - Protection and amenity forests, park lands and trees in National parks and Wildlife sanctuaries.

2. Silvicultural Rotation

"It is the rotation through which a species retains satisfactory growth and reproduction on a given site". It can neither be lower than the age at which trees start producing fertile seed in sufficient quantity nor beyond the age when stop doing so. It very long and may be used in combination with other rotations such as technical rotation.

Silvicultural Rotation may be useful in forests managed primarily for **aesthetic and recreational purposes**, where large old trees with accompanying regeneration provide scenic beauty. *Some foresters do not distinguish between physical and silvicultural rotations.*

Applicability - Aesthetic, Recreational forests and Avenue trees.

3. Technical Rotation

"It is the rotation under which a species yields the maximum material of specified size or suitability for economic conversion or for special use". It aims at producing the **maximum material of specific dimension or size,** such as railway sleepers, saw logs, mine props, transmission poles, match wood, paper wood, *etc.*

Technical rotation is adopted, particularly, by industrial firms which own forests/plantations for the purpose of supplying raw material for their plants (e.g., NEPA and West-Coast Paper Mills, WIMCO match factory).

Applicability - Wood based industries that have their own forests and plantations. West coast paper mills, NEPA, WIMCO match industry.

4. Rotation of Maximum Volume Production

"It is the rotation that yields the maximum annual quantity of material i.e., the age at which the MAI culminates and intersect with CAI".

This rotation yields largest volume per unit area per annum and is an important rotation and used frequently with combination of other rotation.

In this rotation, M.A.I refers to the stand and the quantity refers to the material from all thinning and the final volume felled at the end of *rotation.* The length of this rotation will coincide with the year when the average rate of growth, or volume increment per unit area, reaches the maximum, i.e., the age indicated by the **point of intersection** of C.A.I. (Current Annual Increment) and the M.A.I. (Mean Annual Increment).

This rotation is particularly suitable for adoption where the total quantity of woody material is important and not the size and specification, e.g. firewood, raw material for paper pulp fibreboard and industries based on disintegration processes of wood. Common practice in forestry is to adopt a combination of *Rotation of Maximum Volume Production and Financial Rotation.*

Applicability - suitable for adoption where the total quantity of material is important and not the size or specification. *e.g.,* fire wood, fiber board, particle industries.

5. Rotation of Highest Income/Revenue

"It is the rotation which yields the highest average annual gross or net revenue irrespective of the capital value of the forest".

It is calculated without interest or irrespective of the times, when the items of income or expenditure occur. This rotation is important from the overall national point of view.

The private owner of a forest estate is interested in maximum net revenue (gross income minus expenditure, both discounted to date) by keeping the rotation period as short as possible.

6. Financial or Economic Rotation

"It is the rotation which yields the highest net return on the invested capital. This rotation is most profitable rotation".

It differs from the rotation of highest income in that all items of revenue and expenditure are calculated with compound interest at an assumed rate, usually the rate at which the government is able to barrow money. This rotation is also defined as:

i) "the rotation which gives the highest discounted profit, usually at its commencement."

ii) "the rotation which is most profitable."

iii) "the rotation which gives the highest net return on capital value, i.e., under which the ***Soil Expectation Value*** **(Se)** calculated with a given rate of interest is the maximum.

It is determined by :

a) Based on soil expectation value (Faustmann's formula)

b) Based on financial yield

a) **Based on the *Soil Expectation Value* (Se) of the land**, i.e., value based on the net income which it is expected to yield, and calculated at selected rate of interest, at different rotations ***Faustmann's Formula***.

Soil (land)Expectation Value: The discounted present value of all future returns from a property minus the discounted present value of all future expenses necessary to earn these returns, the discounting done at a given rate of interest at compound interest.

b) **Based on the financial yield,** i.e., the rate of interest or *Mean Annual Forest Percent (M.A.F. %),* which the forest enterprise yields on investment. M.A.F. % is merely a financial equivalent of M.A.I. and used the same way as M.A.I. is used to determine rotation of maximum volume production.

The last two types of *rotations* are concerned with money return from the forest and but it is difficult to depict which one is the correct rotation to adopt for Indian State forests.

i) However, in cases when money has to be borrowed at compound interest for making new plantations the **Rotation of Highest Income/Revenue** would be better, as it gives the maximum interest on the capital.

ii) For ordinary Indian forests, the most paying rotation would probably be the rotation of ***highest sustained net income***.

Main groups based on objectives

Choice of type / kind of rotation is as follows:

i) Rotations controlling the supply of certain services are:

Type of rotations: Physical and Silvicultural rotation

ii) Rotations controlling the output of material, forest products in form, size and quantity are:

Type of rotations - Technical rotation and Rotation of maximum volume production

iii) Rotations controlling the financial returns are:

Type of rotations - Rotation of maximum income and financial rotation

Choice of suitable rotation

Mainly depends on the following factors :

i) Objects of management

ii) Silvicultural requirements of the species

iii) Productivity of the site

iv) Market demands and national requirements

v) Financial and economic aspects

vi) Socio-economic policy of the state (labour condition and employment).

Length of Rotation

The choice of the type of rotation depends on the object of management, but the length of rotation depends on the **interaction of several physical and economic factors** given below :

a) Rate of growth
b) Silvicultural character of the species
c) Response of the soil
d) Economic considerations such as cost and prices
e) Social conditions
f) Climatic and topographic factors

a) **Rate of Growth :** This will vary with species, site fertility (soil, climate, topography, etc.) and intensity of thinnings, etc.

b) **Silvicultural Characteristics of the Species :** For example, natural span of life, age of fertile seed production, age at which rate of growth culminates, age at which the quality of its timber is most desirable or begins to fall, etc.

c) **Response of the Soil :** That is, deterioration or exhaustion of soil due to exposure (short coppice rotation) biotic influence, etc.

d) **Economic Considerations :** Depending on a combination of factors of cost, prices of different sizes, time required to reach those sizes, etc. a factor tending to lengthen the rotation is the increase in value of large-size timber – though not economically sound to grow large-size timber over a long rotation.

e) **Social Conditions :** Socio-economic and employment policy of the State.

f) **Climatic and topographical factors :** Climate and topography may necessitate long, protective rotation or the adoption of uneven aged forestry, whatever the economics may be. Some of the above factors may affect the management policy. The inevitable combination of factors may require different rotations in different parts of a forest and thereby complicate management.

Table: Rotation or Conversion period of important Indian tree species

S.No.	Tree species	Locality / Division / State	Rotation / Conversion period (yrs)	Remarks
1	Teak (*Tectona grandis)*	Gorakhpur (U.P)	60	Teak Taungya W.C.
		Haldwani (U.P)	50	Under-planting; Teak introduction Working circle.
		Darjeeling (W.B.)	80	Teak Conversion W.C.
		North Betul (M.P.	100	Conversion to Uniform System: Teak Conversion W.C.
		Hoshangabad (M.P) (Bori)	120	Bori Species Teak W.C. Conversion to Uniform and Selection – cum improvement.
		Hoshangabad (M.P) (Bori)	80	General Teak W.C. Conversion to uniform.
		Allapalli (maharastra)	120 100	Modified Uniform System with P.Bs. (Elchil F.S.) (Plains F.S.) Teakconversion W.C.; Teak conversion W.C.; Modified Uniform System with P.Bs.
		Nilambur (Kerala)	60	(Teak F.S.) Clear felling and planting
2	(Sal) *Shorea robusta*	South Raipur (M.P)	180	Sal High Forest W.C. Conversion to Uniform.
		South Raipur (M.P.)	40	C.W.R; Coppice rotation.
		Gorakhpur (U.P.)	75 & 90	Sal Taungya W.C.
		East Dehra (U.P.)	120	Uniform
		Haldwani (U.P.)	150	Irregular Shelterwood W.C. ; Floating P.B.
3	Blue Gum *Eucalyptus Globulus* Nilgiris	South (T.N.)	10	Simple Coppice.
4	*Eucalyptus Hybrid (E . Tereticornis)*	U.P., Punjab, Haryana	8 to 12	Simple coppice.
5	Wattle *(Acacia Mearnsii* Syn. *A.mollissima)*	Nilgiris South (T.N.)	10	Clear felling with natural regeneration, supplemented by artificial regeneration.
6	Deodar (*Cedrus deodar)*	Kulu (H.P.)	150	Punjab (Modified) Shelterwood System.
		Chakrata (U.P.)	160	Uniform system.
7	Chir *(Pinus roxburghii)*	Kangra (H.P.)	120	Punjab (Modified) Shelterwood system.
		Chakrata (U.P.)	100	Uniform with Floation P.B.
8	Fir (*Abies pindrow, Abies spectabilis)*	Kulu (H.P.)	90	Modified clear felling (over 40 cm dia.) and planting; selection on slopes.

Rotation and Conversion Period

The term **conversion** is defined as : **"a change from on e silvicultural system or one (set of) species to another"**.

Conversion period is defined as : "The period during which a change from one Silvicultural system to another is effected."

Rotation and conversion period as defined above are basically the two entirely different terms. *Conversion Period* is indicated where a change in silvicultural system is contemplated, or where a forest is brought under scientific management for the first time, and no rotation can be calculated or applied straight away for various reasons. While it is necessary to fix a Rotation in case of regular forests, it is not so with *conversion period;* the latter is fixed where it is considered necessary to minimize sacrifice. For the purpose of management and yield control it takes the place of rotation, usually in the first rotation. *Conversion period* is usually less than *Rotation;* may be sometimes even more than rotation, but when equal, it is not distinguished.

***Conversion Period* is usually kept less than *Rotation* when it is desirable to remove the mature crop earlier that the rotation period due to:**

a) Crop not likely to survive the full rotation period.

b) Crop has suffered from some injury.

c) Crop is very openly or irregularly stocked.

d) Crop is putting on small increment.

e) Advance growth is already present on the ground and, therefore, time required for replacement of mature crop by new one can be shortened.

The shortening of the conversion period, or the extent to which it can be shortened would be limited by:-

i) Size of the material produced and its marketability, as compared to the size produced in the contemplated rotation.

ii) The extent of sacrifice involved. The greater the difference between the conversion period and *rotation* greater is the sacrifice and more difficult it is to bring the forest on to the contemplated *Rotation* at the end of *Conversion Period.*

For example : Suppose take a teak plantation with a spacing 2 m x 2 m (2500 trees) and its conversion depends on the object of felling.

- 2m x 4m (1250 trees) - 1250 trees are removed for purpose of **small poles**
- 4m x 4m (625 trees) – 625 trees are removed for purpose of **small timber**
- 625 trees retained are maintained for the purpose of **merchantable timber**.

❑❑❑

Chapter 6

Normal Forest and its Concept

Normal forest

In order to achieve the object of sustained yield, foresters evolved a concept of *"Normal Forest"*. **Normal forest** is, thus, a conception of forest management based on the principle of *Sustained Yield.* It was evolved in early **19th century by German Foresters**. The term *"Normal Forest"* is variously described or defined as:-

i) ***"A forest which, for a given site and given objects of management, is ideally constituted as regards growing stock, age class distribution and increment, and from which the annual or periodic removal of produce equal to the increment can be continued indefinitely without endangering future yields.*** A forest which by reason of its normalcy in these respects serves as a standard of comparison for sustained yield management." (Glossary).

A forest which has a normal series of age gradations or age classes, a normal increment and a normal growing stock.

ii) "A forest which, corresponds in every way to the objects of management is called a *Normal Forest.* It serves as an ideal to be aimed at, though it may never be altogether reached or, if established, not permanently maintained. Normal state of a forest, under given set of conditions, depends chiefly on the presence in it of:-

a) A normal increment.

b) A normal distribution of age-classes, and

c) A normal growing stock." (Schlich)

iii) "That forest which has reached and maintains a practically attainable degree of perfection in all its parts for the full satisfaction of the purpose of management" (Osmaston).

iv) "A forest which has (a) a normal series of age-gradations or age-classes, (b) a normal increment, and consequently, (c) a normal growing stock, it termed a *normal forest.* It follows that there is nothing absolute in the term. A forest normal under one method of treatment or rotation, would be abnormal under any other treatment or rotation" (Darcy).

v) "A forest which contains a regular and complete succession of age-gradations or classes (several age-gradations thrown together) in correct proportion so that an annual or periodic felling of the ripe woods results in an equalization of the annual or periodic yields" (Jerram).

vi) "Normality is that practically attainable degree of perfection in a forest which we strive to secure in all parts of the forest and to maintain it in perpetuity" (Knuchel).

Basic factors (Attributes/characteristics) of the Normality

(Trinity of the norms of the normal forest by Osmaston)

- Normal series of age gradations or age classes.
- Normal increment and.
- Normal growing stock.

1. **Normal series of age gradations or age classes;** is meant that the presence of trees of all ages from one year old to rotation age, **when trees of each age occur on separate areas, they constitute a *series of age gradations*.**
2. **Normal increment:** is the best or maximum increment attainable by a given species and for a given rotation per unit area on a given site.
3. **Normal growing stock:** is the volume of stands in a forest with normal age classes and a normal increment.

Distribution of age classes

1. Normality/distribution of age classes in regular forests:

In Clear felling system

1. In **clear felling system**, all age gradations from ***one year*** to ***rotation age*** are present, each occupying equi-extensive/equi-

productive areas, in which rotation age coupe is felled and regenerated every year, offers the simplest example of a conventional normal forest, capable of giving annual sustained yield.

2. In **short rotation species** such as coppice system of some fast growing species it seldom practical to distinguish between age differences of only one year. In such cases 5-10 or even more age gradations may be grouped together to form one age class. e.g., If rotation period is 100 years, 10 age classes are made of 10 years age, such as 1-10, 10-20, 20-30, 30-40, ...90-100 and occupies 1/10th of the equi-productive area of the felling series. The oldest class (90-100) will be felled and regenerated in 10 years.

In shelter wood system (Uniform system), this concept may be extended to the division forest area into Periodic Blocks (PB's). See the examples below with diagrammatic representation :

1. Rotation is 100 years, and then the entire forest area worked to be divided into 5 PB's of 20 years each. Each PB is felled and regenerated, in turn during 20 years regeneration period in a regular manner (See Fig a).
2. In Chir pine, rotation is 120 years, No. of PB's = 4, the oldest PB (91-120 years) is felled and regenerated in 30 years (See Fig b). This kind of organization is not only simple, but provides some flexibility, which are both useful to meet the market fluctuations and essential to vary fellings designed for natural regeneration.

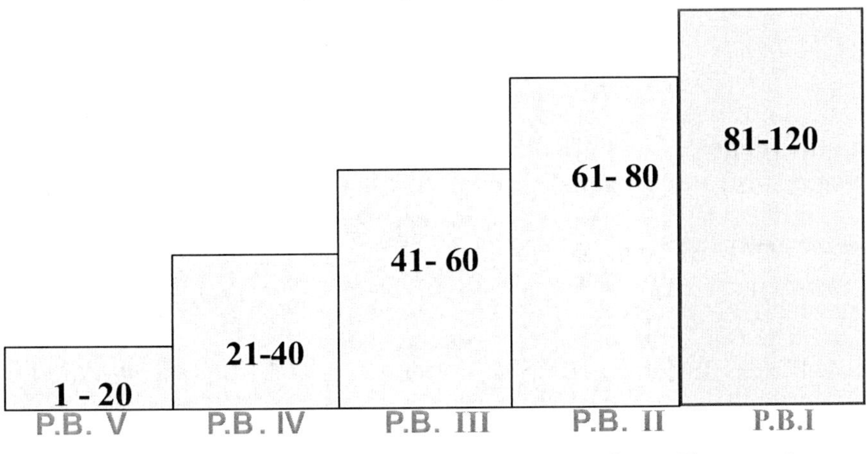

Fig. a) Arrangement of P.Bs in a F.S. worked under uniform system

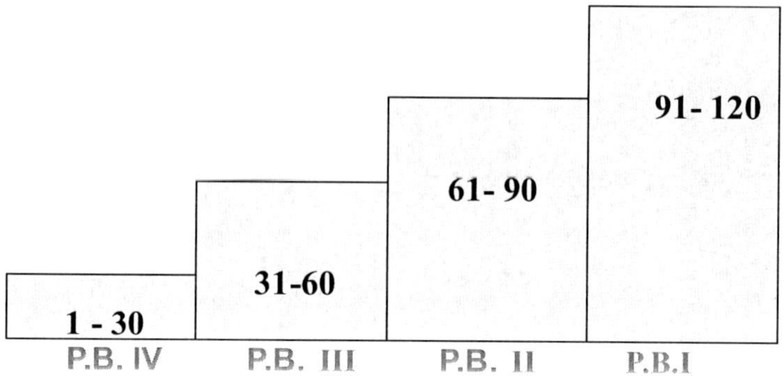

Fig. b) Arrangement of P.Bs in a F.S. worked under uniform system

It will be readily appreciated that: ***Shorter the regeneration period - Narrow age classes - then it is more even aged stand***

Longer the regeneration period - Wider age classes - then less even aged

Thus, shorter rotation plantations of *Eucalyptus sp.* worked under annual coupes with one year age classes are absolutely even aged, but in chir pine converted crops worked under uniform system on 120 years rotation with 30 years regeneration and 30 year age classes are only more or less even aged.

Strictly speaking occupation of equal areas by each class is not essential, but the proportion of different ages should be correct. In other words, in theory each of the age gradations must occupy in series of areas of equal productiveness. Such a proportion between various age gradations is known as ***Normal proportion.***

2. Normality/distribution of age classes in irregular/uneven aged forests

In an entire uneven aged forest worked under selection system, trees of all ages (sizes) are found mixed together on every unit of area. Younger and smaller trees occur in groups under older and larger trees and partly in gaps or openings of upper canopy. The oldest/ largest trees are scattered everywhere singly or in pairs. In such circumstances neither the ***ages of trees*** can be known nor the ***area*** occupied by the each class.

Fellings, therefore, cannot be distinguished either by ***area*** or ***age,*** nor ***thinning*** can be separated from final fellings and yield. Consequently definite areas cannot be set aside every year either for final felling of intermediate yields.

Large mature trees are felled when they reach ***exploitable size*** or their increment falls below acceptable level. Other trees are removed on principles of thinnings to give proper growing space to the better stems.

Hence, age and rotation are meaningless concepts in selection forests. Hence, the only scheme in the ***arrangement of growing stock is the proper intermingling of different sized trees in their ideal proportion,*** so that a regular sequence of maturing trees is obtained, in general assumption that, on an average, size indicates the age.

Therefore, normality of an uneven aged selection forest can be ascertained by the number of trees in each size class, it must have ***Normal series of size gradations*** instead of age gradations of the normal even aged forest. In addition, it must have the normal volume and normal increment, as well as the amount of irregularity per unit area that is deemed to be most satisfactory.

Although it is obvious that normal uneven aged forest contains large number of small trees than the bigger ones/hectare, hence it is not possible to devise a simple model, such as the triangle of the normality for even aged forests to represent the numbers or volumes of trees in the various size classes. ***We do not have yield tables for irregular forests,*** to show that what the normal number of trees should be in each size class.

To bring the irregular forests to normally productive state, the fellings, thinnings and regeneration operations have to be so regulated that all undesirable irregularity is smoothened out and the forest is brought to correspond to a properly balanced irregular forest.

De Liocourt's Law

It is defined as "***in a fully stocked selection forest, the number of stems falls off from one diameter class to the next diameter class in geometrical progression***".

Which means that the percentage reduction in the stem number from one diameter class to the next diameter class is constant. This is referred to as **"De Liocourt's Law"**.

If the quotient of the series is known and the number of stems in any class is given, the whole series can be worked out and this should give the proportionate distribution in an ideal selection forest or its balanced composition.

This series is represented by the geometrical progression

$a, a\,q^{-1}, a\,q^{-2}, a\,q^{-3}, \ldots\ldots\ldots\ldots\ldots\ldots a\,q^{-(n-1)}$

a = number of stems in lowest diameter class

q = co-efficient of reduction in number of stems: the quotient

Meyer (1933), simplified De Licourt's Law in the form of an exponential function :

$Y = Ke^{-ax}$

Y = Number of stems in the diameter interval

x= Diameter at breast height

a = Percentage reduction in number of stems for each diameter class

K = Relative stand density, which is dependent on site conditions

e= 2.71828, the base of Napierian logarithms

Kinds of Abnormality: Forests may be abnormal usually in the following ways :

1. Overstocked

A forest past the age of maturity, or having excessive distribution of older age classes, will have more volume per unit area than the normal forest. This condition will also bring about by a reduction in the rotation. Reduction in rotation, thus, results in surplus growing stock to dispose off (as shown in the fig.).

2. Under-stocked

This condition may be caused due to pre-ponderance (excess) of younger age classes, poor density or extension in rotation.

In such cases conservative treatment, i.e., felling less than the permissible amount in order to build up a proper reserve of growing stock is indicated. The accumulation of growing stock to remedy a deficit is often secured by adopting a rotation longer than that necessary, or by cutting less then the possibility.

3. Normal growing stock but abnormal distribution of age classes or age gradations

In this case they may be disproportionate; some of them may be even missing. This is worst form of abnormality because the entire forest may be practically of one age class (allowing a variation of about 20 years).

The conversion of such a forest to normality is a very difficult problem, involves either an interruption in sustained yield or sacrifice of material by decay or unsoundness.

4. Increment may be sub-normal

This condition may be caused by defective density, fire, disease, etc; or it may be due to pre-ponderance of over-mature trees.

5. Normal increment volume in an abnormal forest

Annual increment of a forest may be correct volume for normal increment, but unless it is laid on to trees of the right size class in the right proportion, it is not a normal increment.

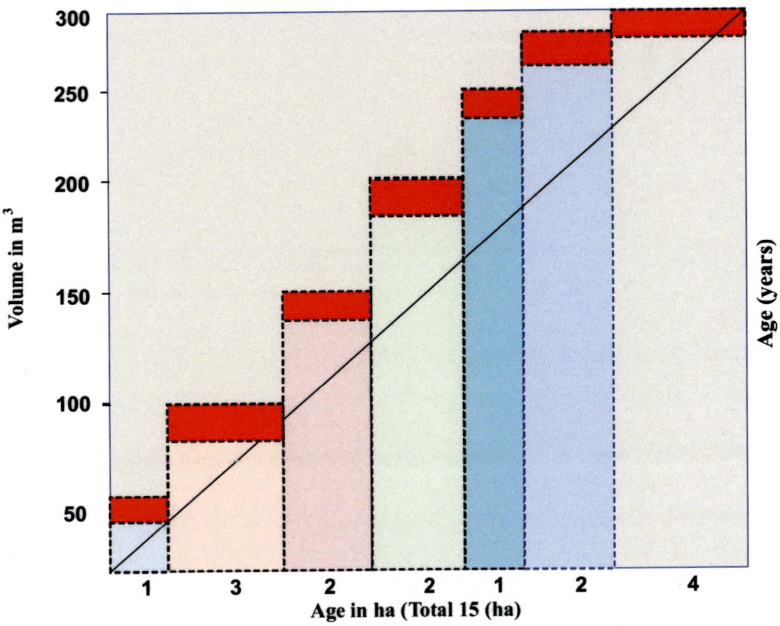

Fig. Abnormal growing stock of 15 years on 15 ha area (Red shaded portion represents CAI of various age gradations)

□□□

Chapter 7

Increment and Types of Increment

Increment

Increment is the increase in growth of a tree or a crop with age. It may be in terms of physical increase of wood content, or may refer to any of the factors which increase with age–diameter, height, basal area, volume, quality, price or value. It may be determined for any given period, by measuring/evaluating these parameters at the beginning and at the end of the period. Methods of measurement of diameter, height, basal area and volume are covered in the subject of forest mensuration. *In forest management, the term increment refers usually to only volume increment, and that too of crops rather than of individual trees.* Increment of both individual trees and crops is influenced by species, site quality, silvicultural treatment (tending operation) and also the nature of the crop - whether even aged or uneven-aged.

Increment is defined as ***"the increase in girth, diameter, basal area, height, volume, quality, price or value of the trees or crops during a given period".***

Classification of increment : Different types of increment are as following:

1. **Current Annual Increment (CAI)**: CAI is the increment which a tree or crop puts on a single year. The increase in growth that takes place in a particular year is called the current annual increment (C.A.I.) for that year. It may be expressed, figuratively, as $CAI = V_{n+1} - V_n$

   V_{n+1} is volume produced in n+1 years V_n is volume in 'n' years

2. **Periodic Annual Increment (PAI):** PAI is the average annual increment for any short period. It is also known as *Periodic Mean Annual Increment.*

3. **Mean Annual Increment (MAI):** MAI is the mean or average volume of a tree or crop at the desired age. The mean or average of all CAIs, i.e. the total increment upto a given age.

$MAI = V_n / n$

Where, V_n is volume upto 'n' years

'n' is age or rotation period

If MAI is calculated for a portion of the total age, it is called as **Periodic mean annual increment**, if it is calculated to the rotation age, it is called as **Final mean annual increment.**

Total Increment: It is the increment that a tree or a crop puts on from its origin upto the age at which the tree or crop is cut. It is the sum of the CAI and therefore, represents the volume of the tree or crop.

Relationship between CAI and MAI (Graphical representation)

1. CAI is the expression of actual response of any one year (Individual) MAI is the expression of average yearly response (Average).
2. CAI and MAI do not go inside with each other through out the life of the tree or stand

   Except One at the end of the first year and

   Second at the year of culmination of MAI
3. CAI is not uniform through out the life of a tree or stand; it rises to a maximum and gradually falls off. The MAI also increases to a maximum but at much lower rate.
4. The MAI continues to rise towards a maximum, even after the CAI has started falling.
5. When MAI reaches maximum and starts falling off at that junction it meets CAI, this point of intersection is called **Rotation of Maximum Volume production**.
6. CAI will be zero when there is no growth and negative, when the tree or stand is cut off or decay or rot occurrence.
7. MAI will never be zero and in no circumstances it is negative, until the tree stand is cut or destroyed, the MAI is always positive.

The relationship between CAI and MAI is explained with graphical illustration as follows:

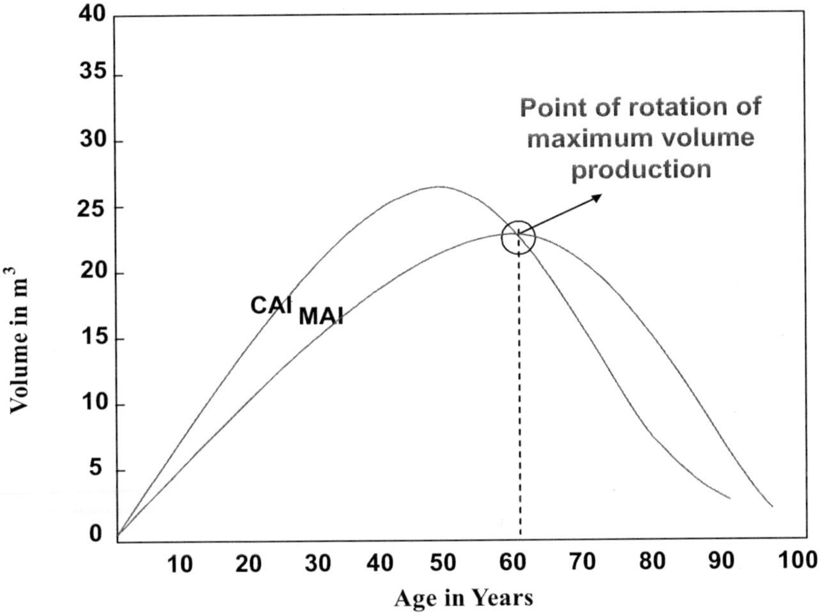

Fig. 7: Relationship between CAI & MAI

Increment Per Cent

The term ***Increment Per cent*** is an expression of the relation between the ***increment*** and ***volume***. The average annual growth in volume (or basal area) over a specified period expressed as a percentage of the volume (or basal area) either at the beginning or more usually, half way through the period.

$$\textbf{Increment Per cent (IP)} = \frac{Increment}{Volume} \times 100$$

Types of Increment Per cent

1. **Current increment per cent:** It is the relation of the increment during a given year to the volume at the beginning of the year.
2. **Periodic increment per cent**: It is the relation of the increment during a given period to a basic volume which may be taken as the mean or average volume for the period, or the volume at the beginning of the period.

3. **Mean annual increment per cent**: It is the per cent ratio which the MAI for a given age bears to the total volume at that age.

The main purpose for which the increment per cent is utilized is to **test the maturity** or **ripeness of individual trees or crops**, which is very useful information for **fixing the rotation or the yield**. Those trees or crops, which show the lowest increment per cent on their present volume compared with other trees or crops, should be **selected for felling**. The object of such selection is to remove from the forest the greatest possible **volume of wood capital**, while at the same time reducing the increment of the crop by the smallest possible amount. If this is done, the effect is to transform the forest capital from a condition in which the ratio of increment to volume is low, to one in which the ratio is materially increased for the forest as a whole. On individual trees the increment can be found by **stem-analysis**, by means of **Pressler's increment borer**, by repeated **direct measurements** or is taken from the **yield tables**.

Rate of growth : According to present concept, a fast grown species is one which yields a minimum of **10m³/ha/annum**. In case of younger plantations, the height increment must **not be less than 60 cm per annum**.

Pressler's Formula for Increment Per cent

Let us consider **"V"** is the volume of the crop at present

V - Present volume of the crop

v - The volume "n" years ago

If "n" is fairly short (not more than 10 years)

$$\text{Then } CAI = \frac{V\text{-}v}{n} \rightarrow (i)$$

The average volume of the crop producing this increment =

$$\textbf{MAI} = \frac{V\ \text{-}v}{2} \rightarrow \ (ii)$$

Therefore, from equations (i) and (ii), increment per cent (P) will be

$$\textbf{Increment Per cent (P)} = \frac{\text{Increment}}{\text{Volume}} \times 100 = \frac{(V\text{-}v)/n}{(V+v)/2} \times 100$$

$$= \frac{(V\text{-}v)}{n} \times \frac{2}{(V+v)} \times 100$$

Increment Per cent (P) $= \frac{(V\text{-}v)}{(V+v)} \times \frac{200}{n} \rightarrow$ This is known as *Pressler's formula*

Note:

1. This formula is used based on the assumption that the increment is laid on in equal annual installments.
2. If any felling has been made in the intervening period, its volume must be added to "V" to obtain correct result.

These two points are to be taken into consideration while calculating increment per cent (P).

Solve the following problems

1. If the volume at the age of 50 years is equal to 2500 cft and at the age of 60 years the volume will be 3500 cft. In the intervening period, thinning done at the age 55 years yield 300cft. Calculate the increment per cent (P) by Pressler's formula.

Solution : In the above problem V = Present volume = Volume at 60 years = 3500 cft

v = Volume at 50 years (10 years ago) = 2500 cft

Felling at 55 years = V+ 300 cft n = 10 years

Therefore, Pressler's formula for increment per cent (P) can be calculated as follows:

$$\text{Increment Per cent (P)} = \frac{Increment}{Volume} \times 100$$

$$= \frac{(V\text{-}v)}{(V+v)} \times \frac{200}{n}$$

$$= \frac{(3500+300) - 2500}{(3500+300) + 2500} \times \frac{200}{10}$$

$$= \frac{1300}{6300} \times \frac{200}{10}$$

Increment Per cent (P) = 4.126 %

2. Calculate the increment percent (P) by Pressler's formula when the volume at the age of 70 years be 100 m^3 and the volume ten years ago be 70 m^3. But a thinning was carried out at 5 years ago and yielded 10 m^3.

Solution : In the above problem

V = Present volume = Volume at 70

years = 100 m^3 v = Volume at 60

years (10 years ago) = 70 m^3 Felling at 65

years = V + 10 m^3 n = 10 years

Therefore, Pressler's formula for increment per cent (P) can be calculated as follows :

$$\text{Increment Per cent (P)} = \frac{Increment}{Volume} \times 100$$

$$= \frac{(V\text{-}v)}{(V+v)} \text{ x } \frac{200}{n}$$

$$= \frac{(100+10) - 70}{(100+10) + 70} \text{ x } \frac{200}{10}$$

$$= \frac{40}{180} \text{ x } \frac{200}{10}$$

Increment Per cent (P) = 4.44 %

Relationship between CAI and MAI

Increment per cent is very large in the early life of the crop but decreases very rapidly thereafter as shown in graph (fig.)

This is like imagining the per cent growth rate of **young seedlings, saplings and poles and then of older trees** when they reach maturity.

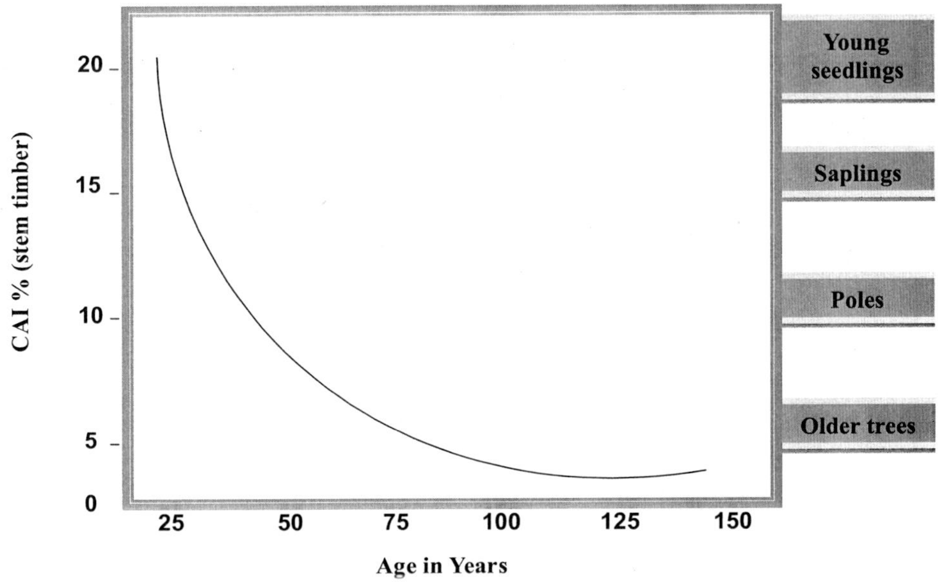

Fig. CAI per cent in *Shorea robusta* (Sal) on site quality II

Relationship between CAI and MAI

Law of great importance in Forest Management

Pressler has also discovered a "**law of great importance in Forest Management"** stating that the increment per cent for the year "r", in which the MAI culminates.

This can be expressed by the formula: **p = 100/r**

We know that, Pressler's formula

$$\text{Increment Per cent P} = \frac{(V\text{-}v)}{(V+v)} \times \frac{200}{n}$$

$$\text{i.e. } \mathbf{P} = \; = \frac{(V - v)}{n} \times \frac{2}{(V + v)}$$

In the year "r", when MAI culminates, CAI = MAI

$$\text{CAI}=\frac{(V\text{-}v)}{n} \text{ and } \text{MAI}=\frac{[(V\text{-}v)/2]}{r}=\frac{(V+v)}{2r}$$

When CAI= MAI

$$\frac{\text{(V-v)}}{\text{n}} = \frac{(V+v)}{2r}$$

$$\frac{\text{(V-v)}}{\text{n}} = \frac{(V+v)}{2} \times \frac{1}{r} \rightarrow (i)$$

Substitute equation (i) in Pressler's formula $\mathbf{P} = \frac{\text{(V-v)}}{\text{n}} \times \frac{200}{(V+v)}$

Therefore, $\text{P} = \frac{\text{(V+v)}}{\text{n}} \times \frac{1}{r} \times \frac{200}{(V+v)}$

$P = \frac{100}{r} \rightarrow$ **This is a law of great Importance in Forest Management**

This is an increment per cent for the year "r", when CAI = MAI

Schneider's formula for Increment Percent

The most convenient formula for finding the increment per cent (p) of standing trees is that developed by **Professor Schneider in 1853.** This formula is based on the determination of the diameter at breast height and the number of rings in the last centimentre (or inch) of the radius as found by the "**Pressler's Borer**".

Volume Increment Per cent $\mathbf{P} = \frac{400}{nD}$

Where D - dbh at present

n - No. of rings in the last centimetre or inch

Quality and Price Increment

Quality increment

Quality increment is defined as "**The increment in the value per unit volume of a tree or a crop, independent of any increase in the price of forest produce resulting from any change in money value in general, or the supply and demand position in particular.**"

As a tree or crop grows with age, there is increase in the value per unit volume, as larger sizes always fetch higher prices (size /

price gradient) due to higher utilization per cent and, secondly, there is a reduction in the cost of production of unit volume of timber (proportion of stem wood to branch wood increases). The increase in the value per unit volume in case of firewood is limited upto medium sizes (the case of firewood may be left out of consideration). **Quality increment per cent** can be determined and expressed in the same way as volume increment per cent. By using Pressler's method the expression will be:

Quality increment per cent = p = $\dfrac{K_2 - k_1}{K_2 + k_1} \times \dfrac{200}{n}$

Where p - Increment per cent,

k_1 - The value of unit volume rising to value K_2 during the course of *n* years.

Price increment

Price increment may be defined as "**the increment in price, independently of quality increment, resulting from fluctuations in the market on account of changes in money value in general, and the demand and supply position in particular**".

In countries like India with developing economics, there is always a rise in prices as the *per capita* consumption of wood has also been increasing. Increment per cent for price may also be determined in the same way as the increment per cent for volume or quality. Supposing P_1 was the price of a unit volume of wood *n* years ago, and the present price is P_2;

Then the increment per cent *p* by Pressler's method is expressed as:

Price increment per cent = p = $\dfrac{P_2 - p_1}{P_2 + p_1} \times \dfrac{200}{n}$

Effect of thinning on volume increment

1. The mathematical relationship between the CAI and the MAI depends on the rise and fall of the CAI, which is a regular one. This is correct provided the growing conditions remain constant and the measurements are taken on the same trees. Seasonal

variations of rainfall, temperature, etc., do not upset the regularity because the interval between the measurements is quite long (say 5 to 10 years).

2. Thinnings are carried out do introduce a complication, and if these are heavy or irregular, curves may rise or fall with every thinning.
3. Regular thinnings of a fixed grade carried out in sample plots (on the basis of preparation of yield tables) do not disturb the smooth rise and fall of the curves.
4. In practice, some of the trees from the lower class (unmeasured) come into the measurement class. It must be ensured (within the practical limit)that the calculations are based on the total yield i.e. volume of the existing crop plus the volume removed in thinnings. If this is not done, neither the rise and fall will be regular, nor will it be correct to establish any relationship between the CAI and MAI
5. If the data information of yield from thinnings of a crop is not available, measurements should be taken before thinning, or both after thinning, for purpose of comparison of the MAI with the CAI.
6. Natural or artificial thinning of a crop does not create a complication, when the increment of a tree is considered.
7. Studies on the effect of the kind of thinning on the increment reveal that the increment of individual trees is markedly stimulated by repeated liberation of the crown, but it is doubtful, when the whole crop is opened out.
8. Studies on various grades of thinnings depicted that:
   a) The amount of increment of the even-aged stands cannot be greatly affected by the nature of periodic thinning and
   b) The total volume yield is practically unaffected by thinning treatment (e.g. multiple yield tables for deodar).
   c) The value production is substantially increased by the fact that the possible increment of a stand is concentrated on the best trees.

The value of a tree increases with its size because:

a) It has a larger volume and
b) The value per m3 is higher

The total increase in value is expressed by 1.0 t = 1.0 v x 1.0 p

When, t = annual increment per cent in value of the tree

v = annual increment per cent in volume of the tree

p = annual increment per cent in price per m^3

Determination of the Increment

It is relatively easy to determine the CAI on individual trees by stem analysis on felled trees, by **Pressler's increment borer** on standing trees, by **repeated direct measurements** or from the **yield tables**.

The most accurate method consists in **calculating the periodic mean increment** from the difference between two measurements. This is suitable for calculating the increment not only on the whole stand but also by size classes.

Increment estimation by yield tables

Yield tables (for fully stocked, pure, even-aged crops of important species) provide information about the behaviour of the volume increment as a function of age of the crop, as well as about the increment of other parameters of growth viz., diameter, basal area and height.

a) Increment from MAI

Increment of the felling series, or the yield, can be determined from the final MAI.

In a normal forest, the annual yield, or increment of the series will be as follows:

The annual yield or increment of the series = MAI at rotation age x Area of the FS

If the forest is under-stocked or over-stocked, the yield must be reduced or increased accordingly, by an amount equal to the difference between the actual and the normal growing stock; divided by the equalization period (Heyer's formula).

b) Increment from CAI

The increment can also be estimated from the CAI figures in the yield tables by:

i) Area method

ii) Per tree method

iii) By increment percent method

i) **Area method** : From the data of area under each age class, its average site quality and density, and increment per unit area, increment of each age (or diameter) class, and the total increment of the series can be determined.

Sl.No.	Dia. class	No. of trees	Vol / tree	CAI / tree	Total increment
1	d_1	n_1	v_1	c_1	$n_1v_1c_1$
2	d_2	n_2	v_2	c_2	$n_2v_2c_2$
3	d_3	n_3	v_3	c_3	$n_3v_3c_3$
4	d_4	n_4	v_4	c_4,	$n_4v_4c_4$
Then, the total increment = $n_1v_1c_1 + n_2v_2c_2 + n_3v_3c_3 + n_4v_4c_4$					

ii) **Per tree method** : Suppose from the enumeration of the growing stock,

d_1, d_2, d_3, d_4, etc. are the diameter classes

n_1, n_2, n_3, n_4, etc., are the number of trees in the diameter classes

v_1, v_2, v_3, v_4, etc., are the volume per tree in the diameter classes and

c_1, c_2, c_3, c_4, etc., are the CAI per tree in the diameter classes.

Note

a) The **volume per tree** is obtained from the yield table by dividing the standing volume corresponding to the crop diameter by the number of trees per hectare.

b) The **CAI in each diameter class** is obtained from graph; the CAI per tree being equal to CAI per hectare divided by the number of trees.

iii) **By increment per cent method**: The increment per cent may be obtained from the yield table by **Pressler's formula**. It can also be calculated with a fair degree of accuracy on standing trees by **Pressler's increment borer**, with the help of **Schneider's formula.**

The increment per cent method can be used both for regular and irregular crops by determining the growth per cent in selected sample trees representing all the diameter classes and site qualities. This method is very useful in the absence of precise growth data, such as the preparation of first working plan, and for extensive areas.

For practical application of this growth per cent method : total standing volume in each diameter class is known (from enumeration data), with the calculation of increment per cent of each diameter class (from above method) we can calculate increment in each diameter class (or the yield) on its present volume, and sum of increments (yields) of all the diameter classes gives the total increment of the forest area (FS) on the yield.

From this, the average increment per cent of the entire FS can also be worked out as:

Average increment per cent of the entire FS

$$= \frac{\text{Total increment of all diameter classes}}{\text{Total standing volume of all dia. classes}} \times 100$$

The CAI and increment per cent are affected by the degree of stocking. The increment determined by the above method is **lower side for under-stocked forests and higher for over-stocked crops**.

Increment determination in irregular crops: When enumeration of growing stock is done above a certain diameter, usually over 20 cm in Indian Forest Management, MAI can be calculated by the following method:

Let n_1, n_2, n_3, etc. be the number of trees in different dia. classes
p, q, r, etc., be the true ages of the dia classes; and
x, the age corresponding to dia over which enumeration are done (say 20 cm)

Then **mean age (A) of the crop by Andre's formula** is:

$$A = \frac{n_1 (p - x) + n_2 (q - x) + n_3 (r - x)}{n_1 + n_2 + n_3}$$

The MAI would be Ga/A, where Ga is the actual volume of the growing stock.

Increment determination by successive enumerations

This was given by **Biolley's methods du controle**, which is based on successive inventories for determination of increment / yield.

If v_1 = Initial volume of growing stock

V_2 = Final volume of growing stock

N = Material removed during the period (thinnings, etc.)

P = Recruitment, i.e., the growing stock, which has passed the minimum enumeration limit (usually 20 cm dia)

n = Period between successive enumerations (short; usually 5 to 10 years)

Then, the MAI during the period is $= \dfrac{(V2 - v1) + N - P}{n}$

❑❑❑

Chapter 8

Growing Stock

Definition

Growing Stock (GS): Growing stock is defined as **"the sum (by numbers or volume) of all the trees growing in the forest, or a specified part of it"**. Growing stock in a forest is the **"Forest Capital"**.

Normal Growing Stock (NGS): is defined as **"the total volume of trees in a fully stocked forest with normal distribution of age-classes for a given rotation"**.

General concept

- Growing stock (GS) in a forest is the **forest capital** and the other basic factor of this capital is the forest soil. So, ultimately the G.S. which gives the return (yield) is the aim of every enterprise. It represents the investment of the owner from which he receives the income.
- Any increase or decrease in the capital (GS), is immediately reflected in the income (increment/yield).
- In forestry enterprise, the G.S. (capital) may be **over-stocked, normally-stocked** or **under-stocked** (just as in case of a business enterprise, the investment may be overcapitalized, normally-capitalized or under-capitalized).
- An over-mature and/or very **densely stocked** crop may have an excess GS to the extent that it is **overcrowded,** and not only the increment is retarded but even the excess GS may also gradually be lost by decay.
- Besides the **volume** of the GS, **composition** and **age-classes** are important to continue to provide mature trees for regular sustained fellings (annual yields). Therefore, regularization of the GS and also its composition are very important factors in the

practice of forestry. Both these variables (**GS and also its composition**) can be accurately determined by regular and frequent inventories or enumerations by age-gradations / classes. These inventories indicate the trend of the progress of the G.S. (forest capital) and increment (interest) thereon.

- **Growing stock** (GS) is defined as *"The sum (by numbers or volume) of all the trees growing in the forest, or a specified part of it"* (glossary).
- **Normal Growing Stock (NGS)** is defined as *"The total volume of trees in a fully stocked forest with normal distribution of age-classes for a given rotation"* (glossary).

Determination of Actual Growing Stock

Actual growing stock can be determined by any of the following methods with the help of ***Volume tables :***

a) By Total or Complete enumeration

- Not widely practiced
- Practiced only in very valuable forests in limited extent

b) By Partial or Sample enumeration

- Statistically accepted methods are adopted for this purpose
- Gives reasonably accurate results for the purpose

c) By Sample plot measurement

- Followed in selected representative areas of the crop

In determination of Actual Growing Stock, *"Aerial Photography"* is being used for the preparation of inventories of large forest areas and these methods have been extensively adopted by the Directorate of Forest Resources of India for estimation of GS in various regions of the country.

Determination of Normal Growing Stock (NGS)

Definition: Normal growing stock (NGS) is defined as *"The total volume of trees in a fully stocked forest with normal distribution of age-classes for a given rotation"*.

Normal Growing Stock of forests worked under various representative silvicultural systems can be determined by the following methods :

I) N.G.S. In Clear Felling System

Normal Growing Stock of forests worked under **clear felling system** can be determined by one of the following methods :

a) Based on MAI (Mean Annual Increment)

b) By using Yield Tables

a) Determination of Normal Growing Stock by MAI (Mean Annual Increment)

N.G.S. in Clear felling system (from sustained yield concept)

From the figure,

Area = 10 ha

Age gradations/Equi-productive areas = 10

Rotation 10 years

10 year old crop is felled and regenerated

In figure, age gradations shown along the base line AB, with the theoretical volumes standing on each, which are represented by a number of equal rectangles. Each equivalent to one year growth. Assuming the each hectare of plantation puts on equal volume of wood every year of its life.

Thus, each year growth I each plantation = i

Thus, the volume of each age gradation from one year old to 10 years old will be i, 2i, 3i, 4i, 5i, 6i, 7i, 8i, 9i and 10 i

If the volume of the 10 years old plantation/gradation on one hectare is 500 m^3

Then, final MAI at this rotation age (10 year) $\frac{500}{10} = 50m^3$

r x i = sum of the MAI's of all the 'r' age gradations = I

Therefore, in figure, volume of the oldest or rotation age is equal to

i) r x i = I, or

ii) Final MAI of any age gradation 'i' multiplied by 'r' rotation or

iii) The sum of CAI's (i) of all 'r' age gradations

iv) The total MAI of all the series

The yield of the normal forest is the volume of the oldest or rotation 'r' age gradation; it is equal to the increment is equal to the increment of the forest and may be based on any of the above four items.

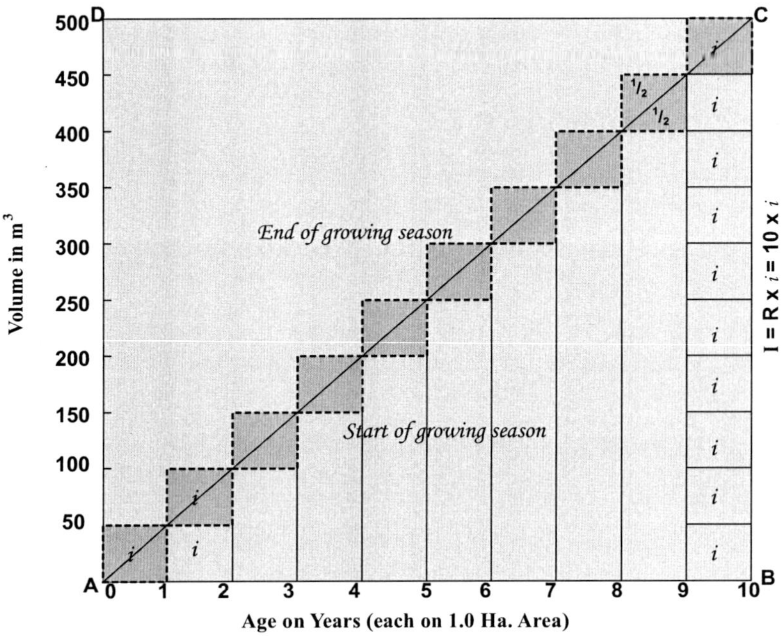

Fig. 8: Theoretical Normal Growing Stock (NGS) in a series of 'R' (10) equal age gradations (one ha each)

Total GS on 'r' age gradations, one to 'r' year old is the sum of the series i, 2i, 3i,................ (r-1)i, ri, in **Arithmetical Progression (AP),** at the end of the growing season and before the oldest 'r' year old, plantation is felled.

We know that, according to AP, sum of natural numbers $= \frac{n(n+1)}{2}$

Therefore, NGS = i+2i+3i+............... +(r-1)i+ri

= i [1+2+3+.................+(r-1)+r]

$$= i\frac{[r(r+1)]}{2}$$

$$=\frac{r.ri}{2}+\frac{ri}{2}$$

Substitute I for ri, so **NGS =** $\left(r\times\frac{I}{2}\right)+\frac{I}{2}$ **This is at the *end of the growing season(i)***

Similarly, with the removal of oldest plantation (volume = r x i = I)

The Increment I of the whole series is removed and the volume at the *beginning of the next growing season* will be,

NGS = $\left(I\times\frac{r}{2}\right)-\frac{I}{2}$ **This is at the *beginning of the next growing season (ii)***

Therefore, the volume of NGS in the *middle of the growing season* is the average of the above two values (i) and (ii).

Therefore, **NGS** = $I\times\frac{r}{2}$ **This is at the middle *of the growing season (iii)***

Assume that half the increment is laid by the middle of the growing season, the total volume of the G.S. will be represented by the area of the triangle $ABC=I\times\frac{r}{2}$

Whereas, at the ***end of the growing season,*** it will be

= Δ^{le} ABC + 'r' small Δ^{les} above the Δ^{le} ABC (each = i/2)

$$=I\times\frac{r}{2}+i\frac{r}{2}$$

$$=I\times\frac{r}{2}+\frac{I}{2}$$

Similarly, at the ***beginning of the growing season,*** after the old plantation (I) is felled, but no further growth has taken place, the volume of the G.S will be,

$$=I\times\frac{r}{2}-\frac{I}{2}$$

For all practical purposes, the mid-season formula is used.

Examples

1. Find out the NGS for Eucalyptus plantation worked on 10 years rotation, on 10 ha, one ha under each gradation, when the volume of 10 years gradation being 500 m^3 and calculate the average NGS per ha also.

Calculate NGS for eucalypts plantation using the formulae for the following example :

e.g., Eucalyptus plantation was worked on 10 years rotation, on 10 ha, one ha under each gradation, the volume of 10 years gradation being 500 m^3, then the NGS will be:

a) $I \times \frac{r}{2}$ = 500 x 10/2 = **2500** m^3 at the middle of growing season

b) $I \times \frac{r}{2} + \frac{I}{2}$ = 2500 + 500/2 = **2750** m^3 at the end of the growing season

c) $I \times \frac{r}{2} - \frac{I}{2}$ = 2500 – 500/2 = **2250** m^3 at the beginning of the growing season

This NGS at the mid season, i.e. 2500 m^3, is standing on 'r' ha area

So, the Average NGS per ha in this case is = 2500/10 = 250 m^3

Solve the following problems

1. Calculate the NGS for *Eucalyptus globules* (blue gum) plantation worked on 10 years rotation, on 10 ha area, one ha under each gradation, when the volume of 10 years gradation being 800 m^3 and also find out the average NGS per ha.
2. Calculate the NGS for *Eucalyptus tereticornis* (*Eucalyptus* hybrid) plantation worked on 8 years rotation, on 8 ha area, one ha under each gradation, when the volume of 8 years gradation being 600 m^3. Find out the average NGS per ha.

b) Determination of NGS from Yield Tables

The yield table gives the volume of each age-gradation at an interval of one year and the G.S volume can be readily calculated by adding up the volumes of successive years. But the volume of N.G.S. can be accurately determined by plotting the yield table data on a graph paper, drawing a smooth curve and computing the area below the curve either by a *plani-meter,* area-square or by counting the squares in case of yield tables of five or ten years. But this is a cumbersome procedure.

The GS can also be calculated mathematically by regarding the two successive entries in the yield table as the first and the last terms of an arithmetic progression.

From the yield table the N.G.S for middle of growing season will be calculated from the following formula :

Let "n" be the Yield Table interval

A, B, C, and D be the volumes given in the yield table at ages n, 2n, 3n and 4n, respectively. Then, sum of volumes of age gradations from 0 to n, n to 2n, 2n to 3n and 3n to 4n years are respectively as follows :

$(0+A)\ (n+1)/2,\ (A+B)\ (n+1)/2,\ (B+C)\ (n+1)/2$ and $(C+D)\ (n+1)/2$

Therefore, the sum of volume of NGS will be,

$NGS=[(0+A)\ (n+1)/2]+[(A+B)\ (n+1)/2]+[(B+C)\ (n+1)/2]+[(C+D)\ (n+1)/2]$

$= (n+1)/2\ (0+A+A+B+B+C+C+D)$

$= (n+1)/2\ (2A+2B+2C+D)$

Here, the volumes A,B & C of n,2n & 3n age gradations must be deducted as these volumes except last one (D) are included twice.

NGS $= [(n+1)/2\ (2A+2B+2C+D)]\ [(A+B+C)]$

$= [(n+1)\ (A+B+C+D/2)] - (A+B+C)$

$= n\ (A+B+C+ D/2) + (A+B+C+ D/2) - (A+B+C)$

N.G.S. = n (A + B + C + D/2) + D/2 ------- (i) At the end of growing season

This is NGS at the **end of growing season**, before the felling of the oldest age gradation

Where, A, B, C, D is the yield in particular years

n = the difference between the two periods at which the yield is taken

N.G.S. = n (A + B + C + D/2) - D/2 ––––––-(ii) At the beginning of growing season

This is NGS at **the beginning of growing season** (If the oldest age gradation is felled after growing season GS must be reduced by D).

N.G.S. = n (A + B + C + D/2 ––––––––––––-(iii) At the middle of growing season

This is NGS at the **middle of growing season** (average of the above two values).

In practice, the mid-season formula (equation iii) is generally used.

Note: *This result applies to an area of as many units of area (acres / hectares, on which yield tables are based) as the age of the oldest (rotation year old) age gradation (4n in above case).*

Graphical Illustration of the Above Formula (Mid-Season Formula)

Let us assume a yield table showing only four entries at intervals of *n* years (as in the above case). The volumes A, B, C and D are shown in figure by rectangles in the years n, 2n, 3n and 4n respectively. The volumes are plotted against age and a smooth curve ELMNP drawn through the plotted points. Total volume of mid-season or summer NGS for the rotation r = 4n or "r" hectares, is represented by the area below the curve (fig).

i.e., Area EKPNMLE = Triangle ELF + Trapeziums (FGML + GHNM + HKPN).

(Here, segments EL, LM, MN and NP of the curve may assumed to be straight lines).

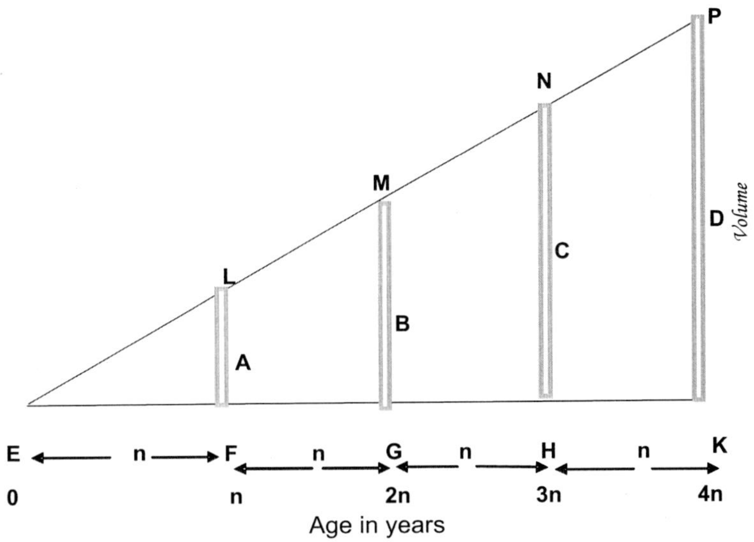

Fig. Graphical illustration of the mid-season formula for Normal Growing Stock

$$\text{Therefore, NGS } = \frac{1}{2}nA + n\frac{(A+B)}{2} + n\frac{(B+C}{2} + n\frac{(C+D)}{2}$$

$$= \frac{n}{2}(\text{A+A+B+B+C+C+D})$$

$$= \frac{n}{2}(\text{2A+2B+2C+D})$$

N.G.S. $= n(A + B + C + \frac{D}{2})$ This is NGS at the **middle of growing season**.

For the sake of convenience only four values have been taken in the above example.

If the rotation is *r* years, n the yield table interval, and Vn, V2n, V3n, ... Vr-n and Vr the volumes at ages n, 2n, 3n, ... r – n and r years,

Then the general formula can be written as:

NGS = n(Vn + V2n + V3n +........ Vr-n + Vr)

Numerical examples on calculation of GS

Solve the following problems on Normal Growing Stock (NGS)

Problem 1. Calculate the average N.G.S. per ha in a teak plantation of Site Quality II, worked on a rotation of 40 years to which the following yield tables apply. Write the inference.

Sl. No.	Age (Years)	Final Yield (Stem Timber m3)
1	05	---
2	10	00.70
3	15	08.40
4	20	27.99
5	25	51.43
6	30	73.82
7	35	94.81
8	40	114.75

Solution

i) By **MAI formula,** N.G.S. on 40 ha $= I \times r/2$

$= 114.75 \times 40/2$

$= 2295\ m^3$

Average N.G.S. per ha $= 114.75 \times 40/2 \times 1/40$

$= 57.38\ m^3/ha$

ii) **From Yield Table,** N.G.S. on 40 ha $= n(A + B + C + \frac{D}{2})$

$$= 5\ (0 + 0.70 + 8.40 + 27.99 + 51.43 + 73.82 + 94.81 + \frac{114.75}{2})$$

$= 5 \times 314.53\ m^3$ or

$$\text{Average N.G.S. per ha} = \frac{5 \times 314.53}{40} = 39.31\ m3\ /\ ha$$

Inference: NGS calculated by MAI method is greater than that of yield table method for 40 year rotation.

Problem 2. Calculate the total and average NGS per ha in a deodar plantation of site quality II worked on a rotation of 100 years to which the following yield table apply. Write the inference.

Sl. No.	CropAge in years	Final Yield (Stem Timber and small wood m^3)
1	10	-
2	20	9.80
3	30	74.17
4	40	210.62
5	50	347.06
6	60	490.50
7	70	574.47
8	80	656.34
9	90	734.01
10	100	806.77

Problem 3. Teak plantation of site quality II was worked on a rotation of 50 years bearing the final yield (Stem Timber m^3) as given in the following yield table. Calculate the total and average NGS per ha with the following yield table. Write the inference.

Sl. No.	CropAge in years	Final Yield (Stem Timber and small wood m^3)
1	05	-
2	10	01.10
3	15	10.30
4	20	31.35
5	25	53.34
6	30	75.25
7	35	101.15
8	40	124.54
9	45	136.90
10	50	157.85

Comparison of Real and Theoretical NGS – Flury's Constant

Flury (Swiss Forest Service) suggested that in the mid-season formula, **GS = I x r x ½**, a variable constant "C" (different from each rotation) should be substituted for "½", to obtain more correct results and the formula would read as **GS = I x r x C**, wherein "C" is known as **Flury's Constant.** Flury actually calculated values of "C" at various ages to substitute for "½" in the formula, for various species, various rotations and varying sets of growing conditions. ***"The value of "C" will be less than "½" for short rotations, and more than "½" for long rotations".***

Determination of Flury's Constant "C"

We have already discussed with two numerical examples for calculation of NGS in which NGS real and theoretical were determined by Yield Table and MAI methods. Now, we shall equate MAI formula results with variable "C", to the Yield Table method results and find the value of variable "C".

Example 1

According to the numerical example for calculation of NGS,

The real or correct NGS by Yield Table Method = **GS = 350.04 m^3/ha**. Then, the real or correct NGS by MAI formula = **GS = I x r x C** over "r" ha,

where I = 806.77 m^3

$$\therefore "C" = \frac{350.04}{806.77} = 0.43$$ which is a **Flury's constant**

Example 2

According to the numerical example for calculation of NGS,

$$\frac{I \times r \times C}{r} = 39.31 \text{ m3/ha}$$

114.75 x C = 39.31

$$\therefore "C" = \frac{39.31}{114.75} = 0.34$$ which is a **Flury's constant**

II) N.G.S. in Uniform Regular Shelter Wood System

It is necessary that the whole periodic block should be regenerated within the regeneration period (whatever the regeneration interval for a coupe or a compartment)

Regeneration interval : It is defined as the period between seeding felling and final felling on a particular area i.e., usually a compartment or a sub compartment under one of the shelterwood systems.

Regeneration period : It is the period required to regenerate the whole periodic block.

In shelter wood systems, felling and regeneration is done according to the regeneration fellings. **Fischer**, evolved a formula for a condition, when part of the G. S. has been removed under regeneration fellings.

The N. G. S under such working would be = $(V + V_1)$ x P/2 x D

Where **V** = Initial Growing Stock

V_1= Growing Stock at the end of regeneration period

P = Regeneration period

D = Crown density

Example : Calculate the NGS of a chir pine forest containing 600 m^3 per hectare at the age of 100 years. In the regeneration fellings over 20 years period, 75% of the volume was removed, the rest was left as part of the future crop. The density was reduced to 0.25.

Solution: According to Fischer N. G. S = $(V + V_1)$ x P/2 x D

V =600 m^3/ha, V_1 = 150 m^3/ha (25% of V), P = 20 yrs, D = 0.25

Substituting above values in Fischer's formula,

G.S. = (600 + 150) x 20/2 x 0.25

= 1875 m^3 for 20/2 (or 10) years

NGS = 187. 5 m^3/ha/year.

III) N.G.S. in Selection System

N.G.S. in selection system is determined by the old methods. Due to the assumed similarity between the G.S. in a normal even aged forest and a selection forest, the N.G.S. is often been determined by the use of the M.A.I. This is also easier to apply.

A formula evolved by **Munger (U.S.A.)** is based on CAI. He considers that the N.G.S. in a selection forest can be better found on the basis of CAI, rather than the MAI.

His Normal G.S. (Gn)

G.S. (Gn) = $\frac{\text{i x f.c.}}{2}$ **+ reserved timber per felling area x the number of areas**

Where, i = the CAI over the whole reserved timber

f.c = Felling cycle

Example : Calculate GS using Munger formula in 100 ha area having 500 m^3 increment (CAI) over the whole reserved timber producing 25000 m^3 reserved timber over the whole area with a felling cycle of 10 years.

Solution: According to Munger formula,

G.S. (Gn) = $\frac{i \times f.c.}{2}$ + reserved timber per felling area x the number of areas

Suppose the total area = 100 ha,

i = 500 m^3,

f.c = 10 years,

Reserved timber = 25000 m^3 over the whole area (250 m^3 /ha).

$$\text{Then G.S.} = \frac{\{500 \times 10 + 25000\}}{2} \; m^3 \text{ for 100 ha}$$

G.S = 27500 m^3

G.S / ha = 275 m^3/ha

Here, Reserved Timber/Residual G.S. is the G.S. below the exploitation diameter left standing after the fellings are over, usually under a felling cycle.

Relationship between Growing Stock (GS) and Yield (as shown in figure)

A complete picture of NGS at the end of the forest rotation is given in the figure.

The 10 years old crop will be felled at the beginning of the next rotation and will be immediately regenerated by planting or coppice. Similarly, every plantation will reach maturity and in turn, felled to give a annual yield.

Then, the Growing Stock removed during a rotation of 'r' years will be:

= I (Annual coupe/yield) x r (Rotation)

GS = I x r

As represented by Rectangle ABCD

Which is **twice the triangle ABC = the NGS triangle**

Thus, during a rotation, **the yield is twice the existing GS**, the other half coming from the increment put on by the GS during the interval (Rotation) i.e. **Y = 2GS**

In other words, during a rotation, **half the yield is produced by the existing GS and the other half by the increment.**

Only half the increment occurring during the rotation is used in this way, the other half goes to form the GS of the next rotation. In this way although volume equal to the increment only is felled during the rotation (i x r) and this is what it should be, it is composed of the GS received from the previous rotation and this loan is repaid to the next rotation.

From the figure,

Annual yield is 10 i

GS = Δ^{le} ABC

GS = ½ I x R = ½ Ri x R = ½ x 10i x 10 = 50 i (Y = 2GS = 100i)

Y = 100 i

$$\text{Annual Yield} = \frac{2\ GS}{R} = \frac{2 \times 50}{10} = 10$$

Annual Yield = 10 i

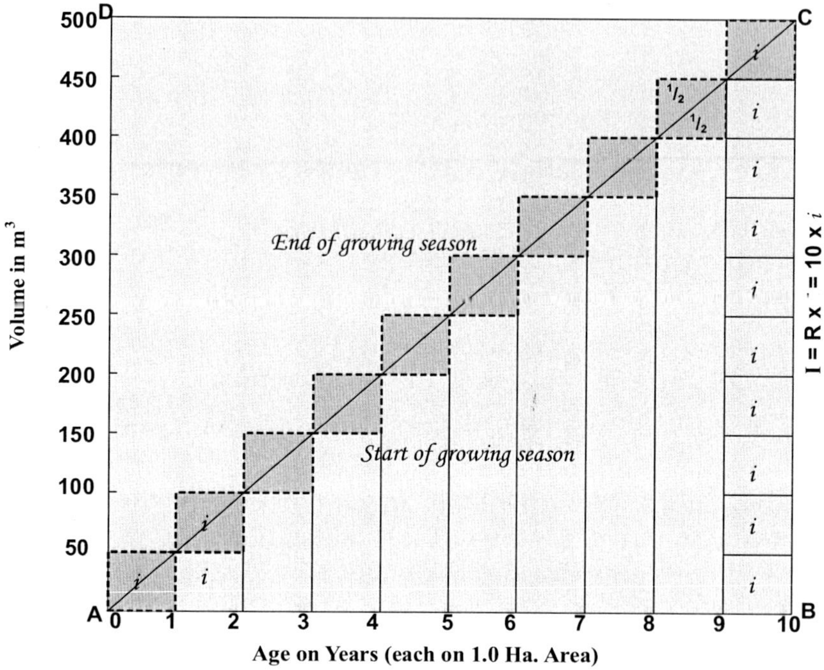

Fig. Theoretical NGS in a series of 'R' (10) equal age gradations (one ha each)

Utilization Percent : It is the per cent ratio of Normal Yield to the NGS

It is expressed as $\frac{\text{Yn}}{\text{NGS}} \times 100$

Where Yn = Normal Yield

The term is also applied to the percentage ratio between volumes as estimated from the standing tree or the log and the actual merchantable outturn.

$$\frac{\text{Volumes as estimated from the standing tree or the log}}{\text{The actual merchantable out turn}} \text{ x } 100$$

Comparison of Real and Theoretical NGS – Flury's Constant

Since the yield tables are not always available, it has led many foresters to find some modification to the more convenient MAI formula, which would allow for varying conditions under different systems of management. Amongst them, **Flurry (Swiss Forest Service)** is the more prominent.

He suggested that in the mid-season formula, **GS = I x r x 1/2,** a variable constant C (different for each rotation) should be substituted for ½, to obtain more correct results and the formula would read as,

GS = I x r x C, wherein C is known as Flury's constant.

Flury actually calculated values of G at various ages to substitute for ½ in the formula, for various species, various rotations and varying sets of growing conditions.

Reducing (or Reduction) Factors – Reduced (or Modified) Areas

Reduced or modified area: An area which would produce the same yield with uniform quality and/or density, as it is produced by the existing areas with their various qualities and/or densities is called as ***Reduced or modified area.***

The factors, by which each class must be multiplied to reduce it to the standard quality and/or density, are known as ***Reducing Factors.***

While preparing yield table (sample plots) from data collected on normally stocked forests (**fully stocked is expressed as unity i.e. 1.00**), two most important factors in which conditions are likely to differ are **density and quality.**

Both density of stocking and quality of the locality have to be brought on to a common basis, before allotment to the annual coupes or periods is made because the potential volume production of different site qualities varies considerably (it is essential for sustained yield management).

a) Reduction (or modification) for density

Density of a stand which is not normally/fully stocked is expressed by decimal (e.g. 0.6, etc). It is usually assessed by **comparison of actual basal area with that of yield table basal area, per hectare**. The area occupied by the crop is multiplied by its density of stocking to get equivalent area in terms of crop with normal density (1.0)

Example: The density of 40-year old teak plantation is 0.8, where the final yield (stem timber)is 114.75 m^3 on site quality II worked on a rotation of 40 years.

Therefore, the volume per hectare would be 114.75 x 0.8 = 91.80 m³. Thus, 0.8 is a reducing (or modifying) factor for density.

Example with illustration of Reduction (or modification) for density

Illustration: Let the area of Felling Series (FS) in clear felling or coppice system be 1000 ha, of this 300 have normal density, 200 ha 0.75, 400 ha 0.50 and the remaining 100 ha have 0.25 density. If the total area is to be divided into 25 equi-productive coupes, area of each will be worked out as follows:

Reduced (modified) area of the FS in terms of unit (normal) density is equal to = (300x1.0) + (200x0.75) + (400x0.50) + (100x0.25) = **675 ha (fully stocked)**

Reduced / modified area of each annual coupe of normal density (1.0) = 675 / 25 = **27 ha**

In distributing crops to 25 equi-productive coupes, area of each coupe in various density crops will be as follows:

27 ha in density 1.0 crop

27 / 0.75 = 36 ha in density 0.75 crop

27 / 0.50 = 54 ha in density 0.50 crop

27 / 0.25 = 108 ha in density 0.25 crop

e.g. If a crop has density of 0.7 in course of time and then become 0.9 or normally stocked (1.0) as a result of **regeneration operations.** Thus, the stocking factor is not a permanent one. It varies from age to age and rotation to rotation.

b) Reduction (or modification) for quality

Variation in GS due to yield capacities of different site qualities is, more or less, a permanent factor of the locality and has to be taken into account. Indication of different qualities is given by the MAI.

For e.g., in case of plantation teak, the yield capacity (MAI) for total wood for a rotation of 60 years is (from yield tables):

Quality I - 9.30 m3/ha

Quality II - 6.79 m3/ha

Quality III - 4.20 m3/ha

In order to determine the areas under different qualities which will produce the same yield, a reduction or modification of the area will have to be made on the basis of their production capacity, i.e. MAI.

Reduction may be made in either of the three ways :

i) Reduction to the most prevalent quality

ii) Reduction to the mean quality of the whole area

iii) Reduction to any suitable quality – whether present in the area or not.

In Chakrata Forest Division, U.P., the most prevalent quality of forest included in Deodar Working Circle is II. Taking this as the standard quality, reduction factors of other site qualities based on their MAI at rotation, are worked out as 1.37, 1.20, 1.00 (standard), 0.83 and 0.63 for qualities I, I/II, II, II/III and III respectively.

The quality most represented is called the standard quality, in which the reduction of other qualities is usually made. This is done by applying the inverse proportion of their MAI.

Reduced area: actual area = MAI of the quality: MAI of the standard quality.

$$\frac{\text{Reduced area}}{\text{Actual area}} = \frac{\text{MAI of the quality}}{\text{MAI of the standard quality}}$$

The factor

$$\frac{\text{MAI of the quality to be reduced}}{\text{MAI of the standard quality}}$$

This is known as the *reducing factor for quality*

Example with illustration

e.g. In a plantation, teak felling series of 1000 ha worked on 60 years rotation, the reduced area in terms of the standard II quality will be worked out as follows:

Quality class	Actual area (ha)	MAI (m^3/ha)	Reducing factor	Reduced / modified area (ha)
I	300	9.38	9.38 / 6.79 = 1.38	300x1.38 = 414
II	**500**	**6.79**	**6.79 / 6.79 = 1.00**	**500x1.00 = 500 (Standard quality)**
III	200	4.20	4.20 / 6.79 = 0.62	200x0.62 = 124
IV	1000			

From the above table,

$$\text{MAI of the mean quality} \quad \frac{(300x9.38) + (500x6.79) + (200x4.20)}{1000}$$

$$= \frac{2814 + 3395 + 840}{1000} = \frac{7049}{1000} = 7.05 \text{ m3/ha}$$

The modified / reduced area of each of the various qualities will be: $= \dfrac{\text{Actual area x its MAI}}{\text{MAI of mean quality}}$ as

i) Reduced area of 300 ha, Quality I = $\dfrac{300x9.38}{7.05} = 399.15$ ha

ii) Reduced area of 500 ha, Quality I = $\dfrac{500x6.79}{7.05} = 481.56$ ha

iii) Reduced area of 200 ha, Quality I = $\dfrac{200x4.20}{7.05} = 119.15$ ha

999.86 ha = 1000 ha

Note : Total reduced area should be equal to the actual area, i.e. 1000 ha as all areas have been reduced to the mean quality. The difference of 0.14 ha is due to rounding off decimal fractions.

❑❑❑

Chapter 9

Enumeration of Growing Stock

Plots and types of plots

Experimental plots : Experimental plots are the plots which are mainly designed for the purpose of laying experiments, such as for comparing the yield, growth, fruit productions, *etc.* with given treatments. These are usually laid out according to the statistical designs, such as CRD (Completely Randomized Design), CRBD (Completely Randomized Block design), Factorial design, split plot design, *etc.*

Sample plots : It is a plot chosen as a representative of a larger area.

In forestry sample, plots are used mainly to study the growth of stands and to study effects of certain treatments. These are applicable to pure, even aged and uniformly stocked crops.

Types- based on objectives

1. **Temporary sample plots** – laid for measurements that are carried out once only. These are generally used in enumeration surveys.
2. **Permanent sample plots** – laid out for measurements to be repeated at intervals over a period of time.

Permanent sample plots are designed for :

- Preparation of yield tables
- Determination of crop volume and crop increment at all stages of development of even aged crops
- Comparison of growth in different qualities of locality
- Measuring the effects of certain treatments, such as grades and intensity of thinning, application of fertilizers, *etc.*

Selection of plots : Plots are generally laid out in fully stocked and even aged/pure crops and are well distributed over the whole range of quality, type and geographical distribution of the species.

In absence of fully stocked crops, plots are laid in crop with uniform stocking without large gaps and patchy growth. Trees at the edge of the crop or the crowns spreading in a gap are avoided.

Number of plots : Depends upon the species, number of age classes, quality classes and variations in treatment. For each decade of age, each quality class, each variation of thinning regime, there should be a minimum of two plots. About ***600 plots*** for each thinning regime for one species are considered enough for preparation of yield tables.

Shape of plots : The shape of the plots may be circular, rectangular or square. In India rectangular or square plots are most commonly used.

Size of sample plots : The plot size should be such that it should not be so small as to be affected by treatments outside the plot; at the same time it should not be so large that the crop is not uniform all over.

A plot size of ***0.1 to 0.2 ha*** is considered sufficient

Layout of plots: It includes layout of surround, demarcation of plot boundary, marking cross marks and numbering of trees in the plots and preparing a plot chart showing layout of plot and trees in it.

Surround: It is defined as an area maintained round an experimental or sample plot ensure that the later is not being affected by the treatment applied to the area outside them both. It is also known as isolation or buffer strip, usually followed at least 15m wide.

Permanent preservation plots (Permanent sample plots)

Laid out for measurements to be repeated at intervals over a period of time. These are designed for :

- Preparation of yield tables
- Determination of crop volume and crop increment at all stages of development of even aged crops
- Comparison of growth in different qualities of locality

- Measuring the effects of certain treatments, such as grades and intensity of thinning, application of fertilizers, *etc.*

Linear Tree Increment (LTI) plots : The only way to determine increment in tree without annual rings is to make periodic measurements in Linear Increment Plots (LIP) or sample plots.

LIP is a linear plot with ***20-40 m*** wide and of any desired length, often 1.0 km or more, lay across the fertility gradient. Very often it forms a line of trees of selected species maintained for the purpose of assessing diameter/age relation for species not characterized by annual rings.

Applicability : LTI plots is applicable to :

- Uneven aged crops
- Irregular stocked forests
- Mixed forests
- Isolated forests

Routine markings and fellings prescribed by the working plan are carried out in LIP along with the rest of the compartments. LIP is selected so as to be representative of the whole range of quality, type and geographical distribution of the species to be selected.

All the trees in plots are not necessarily kept under detailed observation, only some trees suitable for the purpose are selected to cover all diameter classes, crown classes, age classes. These trees are given cross marks and serially numbered. The central line of the plot is cleared, if necessary and durable pegs or posts are driven in at every 20 m. Measurements of the selected trees are taken periodically and compiled to draw curves, which indicate the increment in those trees.

Purposes of LTI plots

1. Determination of average time required to pass through the each diameter class of typical trees.
2. Determination of rotation and yield
3. Comparison of increment of trees of different age, diameter and crown classes as guide for suitable treatment.
4. Comparison of effect of adverse or favorable influences on diameter or increment of trees.

5. Collection of data for determination of crop increment in irregular forests.

Destructive Sample plots : These are the sample plots laid out in the forest area/plantations, which are going to be felled in the near future. In these plots the trees are felled before final harvesting and used for stem analysis purpose, estimation of form factor, analysis of different wood parameters, *etc.*

Enumeration of Growing Stock

Forest Inventory : It is originally a commercial term means 'the record, showing the quantity and value of articles in a store'.

It is also defined as 'the tabulated, reliable and satisfactory tree information, related to the required unit, respectively units of assessment in hierarchy or sequence order'.

Forest inventory is synonymous with the term **'Cruise"** in North America and **'Enumeration'** in India. The forest inventory therefore has to necessarily provide information about the size and shape of the area and the qualitative and/or quantitative information of the growing stock.

Enumeration is defined as the 'counting, singly or together, of individuals of one or more species, in a forest crop and their classification by species, size, condition, *etc.*

Objectives of Forest inventory

1. To determine the volume of timber of the forest in order to estimate the yield.
2. To assess the value of timber growing in a forest.
3. To determine the increment (CAI, PAI, MAI).
4. To prepare the map of the area showing the high or low volume production areas.
5. Helps to set up the industries and pre-investment decision on forest industry establishment or expansion.
6. To supply the information for forest management and planning.

Types of Inventory

Based on the objective and the extent of the area covered, inventories may be :

1. Regional or national inventories
2. Management based inventories
3. Compartment or stand inventories
4. Cruises

Sampling intensity : The ratio of sample to the whole population is called sampling fraction or sampling intensity, which is expressed as a percentage. e.g 5%, 10%, 15%, etc.

Sampling fraction/sampling intensity (SI)

$$\frac{\text{Sample population/area}}{\text{Whole population/area}} \times 100$$

Sample : It is defined as a part of the population consists of one or more sampling units, selected and examined as a representative part of the whole.

Suppose total area is **100 ha**, sample area is **10 ha**, and then the SI is $\frac{10}{100} \times 100$ Then, the SI is **10%**

Table. Sampling intensities used for different forest types and different plots

Type of forest	SI (%)
Tropical wet evergreen forest	10
Tropical moist deciduous forest	2.5
Sub tropical pine forest	5

Terrain	Method	SI (%)
Plains	Strip sampling	5-10
	Line plot survey	2-5
Hills	Topographical units	20-25 (if area is > 2000 ha)

Forest Inventory Design

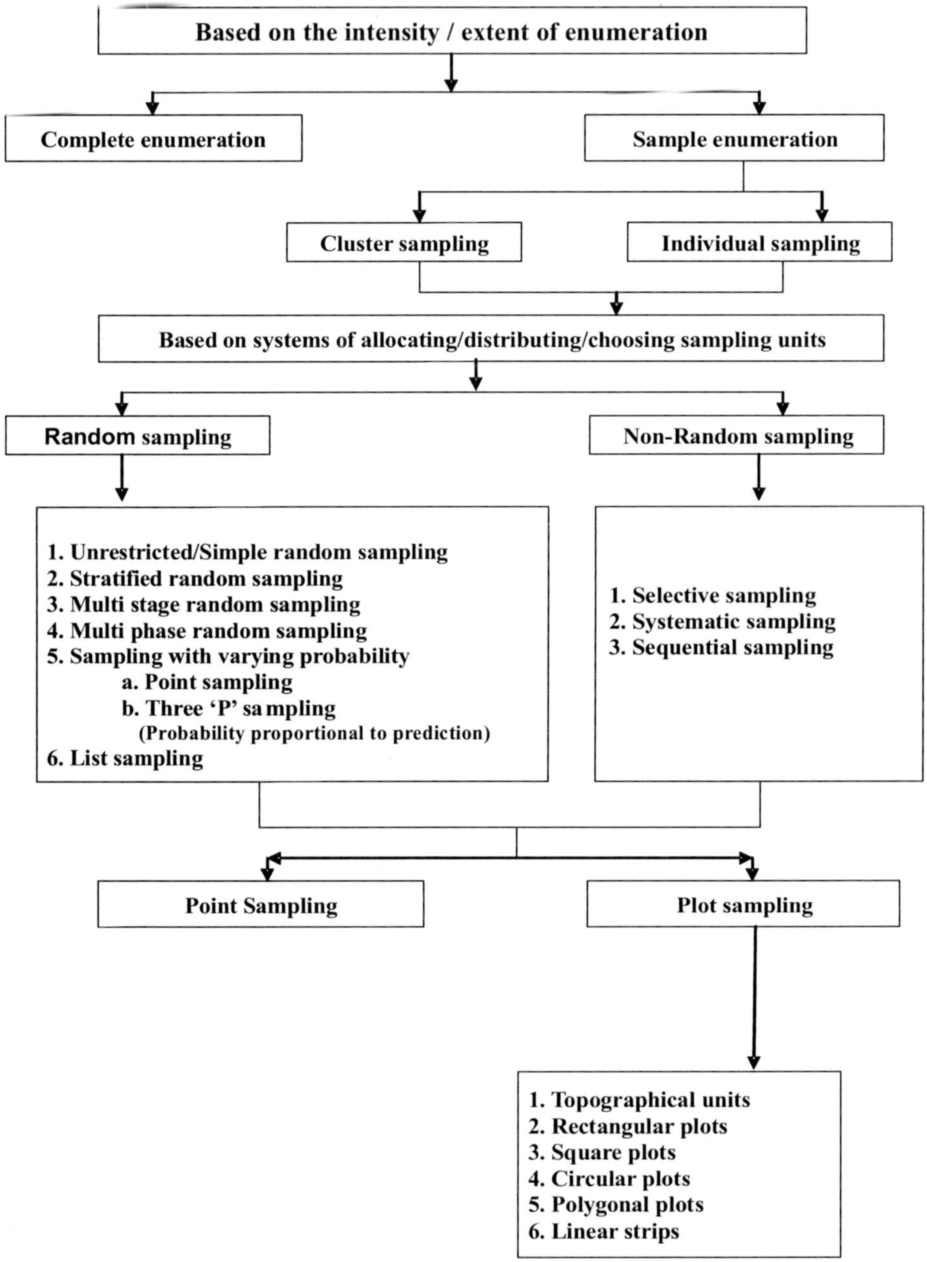

Sample size = Total number of sampling units (plot size)

Sample unit size = Size or area of each sampling unit/plot

e.g. Total area is **1000 ha**

Sampling intensity is **10%**

Then, area to be enumerated is $\frac{1000}{10} = 100$ ha

$$\mathbf{100 \times 10{,}000 = 10{,}00{,}000\ m^2}$$

Sample size is 100 ha

Plot size 50 x 50 =2500 m^2 = 400 plots (400 x 2500)

100 x 100 = 10,000 m^2 = 100 plots (10,000 x 100)

Sample size = 400 or 100 plots (100 ha)

Sample unit size = 50 x 50m Or 100 x 100 m (100 ha)

Kinds of enumeration

1. Total or complete enumeration
2. Partial or sample enumeration

1. Total or complete enumeration

In this method, enumeration of the desired species above the specific diameter is carried out over the entire area of the forest/given area.

Disadvantages

- It is expensive and time-consuming
- More labour and money needed

Applicability

- Done in smaller areas of valuable or intensively managed forests
- Done in miscellaneous forests, where the No. of species is very large
- Carried out for statistical studies as check on results of partial enumeration

2. Partial or sample enumeration

In this method, enumeration is done only in a representative portion of the area.

Advantages of partial enumeration

1. Reduced cost and time-saving
2. Relative accuracy
3. Knowledge of error
4. Greater scope

Methods of Sampling

I. Random sampling methods

1. Unrestricted/Simple Random Sampling

Samples are selected by random process from the whole population or the area. In this method sampling units are selected by some strictly random process from the whole population or area without dividing it into homogeneous blocks.

Examples:

1. If you want to report on general height of the 500, 5 years old *Samanea saman* avenue trees. We have to sample 50 trees (10%). Prepare 500 chits and pick the 50 chits and for those numbered trees, measure the height and calculate the average height from the sampled 50 trees.
2. If sampling unit is 1.0 ha, and the population area is 100 ha, the population area is divided into 100 sampling units and each of them given a number 0 to 100. Now for a 10% unrestricted random sampling, 10 different numbered chits are selected among the 100 chits randomly. Then, enumeration is done in selected 10 plots (10 ha), results extrapolated to whole area (100 ha).

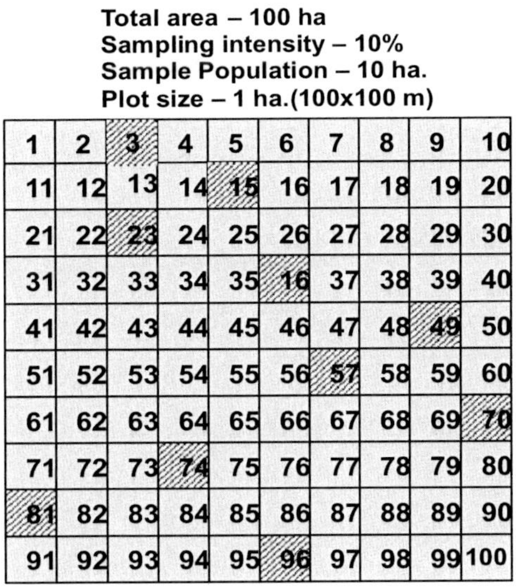

Fig. 10: Simple Random sampling

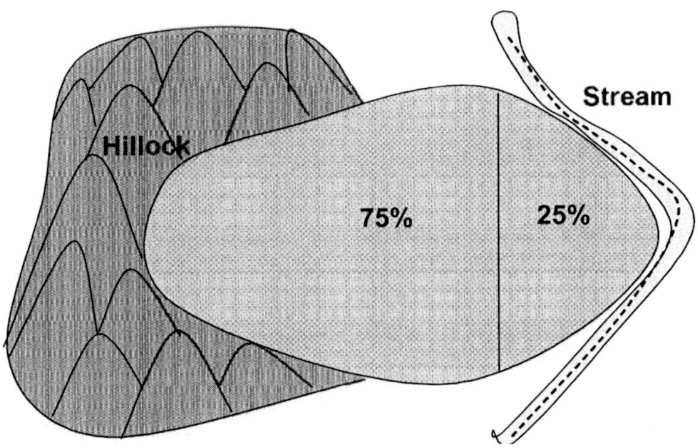

Fig. 11: Stratified random sampling

2. Stratified Random Sampling

It is the method of sampling, in which the population is divided into sub populations of different strata and then sampling units are selected from each of them in proportion to their size. Simple random sampling method gives good results only if the forest crop is uniform, but generally forest populations are characterized by considerable heterogeneity. In such situations, the area is divided into homogeneous blocks; this method of division into homogeneous groups/blocks is called stratification.

This method of division is done by forming strata by ***species, site qualities, crop density, etc.***

Applied when there is more heterogeneity in the species composition, site factors within the enumeration area.

3. Multistage Random Sampling

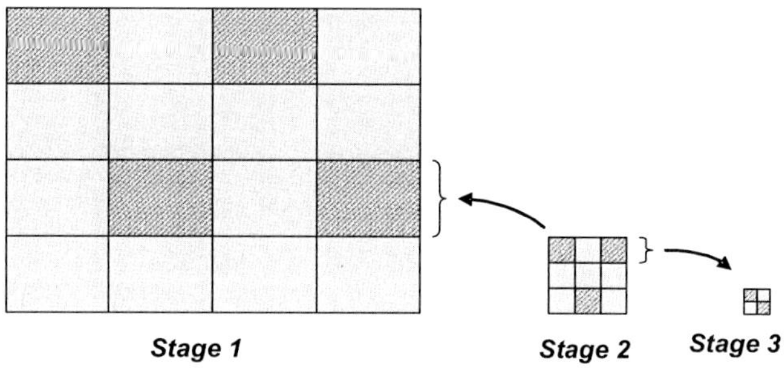

Fig. 12: Multistage sampling

In the earlier methods sampling units are drawn from a population at one time or at one stage, therefore it is called ***Single - stage sampling***. But sometimes, it is cheaper to take some samples at the stage and then divide them to take some more sample units at the next stage and so on. As the sampling units are taken out in two or three stages, the method of sampling is called ***multi-stage sampling.***

e.g., A forest to be inventoried might consist of numerous **compartments** that could be considered **primary units** in design. Some compartments may be selected in the primary stage. They may be broken into **plots** of which some would be selected at the secondary stage. **Trees** selected in these plots for volume measurement could be the third stage.

4. Multiphase Random Sampling

In this method, some of the sampling units are used at the different phases of sampling to collect different information by different methods. Two-phased sampling is in forest inventories and because of the two phases, it is often referred to as **Double sampling or two phased sampling.**

e.g., if the number of clumps and culms in the 50 ha bamboo forest is to be calculated, (Sample area= 5.0 ha) then,

- In first phase, choose sample unit size of 0.1 ha (then Sample size is 50 plots) and count No. of clumps in 50 plots.
- In second phase, No. of culms/clump is to be determined in 20 plots (0.1 ha size).

Estimate these information to the entire 50 ha forest

Phase 1. Average No. of clumps in 0.1 ha =10 the in 1.0 ha =100

In 50 ha = 50 x 100 = 5000 clumps

Phase 2. Average no. of culms/clump = 40

Total No. of culms/50 ha = 5000 x 40 = 200000 culms

5. Sampling with varying probability

In the random sampling methods described above, the chances of selection of all sampling units are the same at all times. But in certain populations, the chances may vary as the sampling proceeds and therefore, sampling with varying probability is used.

This method of sampling has become increasingly important in forest inventories in recent years.

a) **Point sampling (PPS):** It involves sampling from point. It is also called as :

- Angle count cruising
- Pointless cruising
- Variable plot clustering
- Poly aerial plot sampling
- Probability proportional to the size (PPS)

Methods

1. Horizontal point sampling (HPS)(measures basal area/ha)

It is developed by Bitterlich.

2. Vertical point sampling (measures mean stand height)

It is developed by Japanese forester Hirata

Instruments used in HPS

1. Wedge prism
2. Simple angle gauge
3. Spigeal relaskop
4. Wide scale relaskop
5. Tele relaskop
6. Ravi-altimeter

b) Three 'P' sampling or Probability Proportional to Prediction

6. List sampling

It is another form of sampling with varying probability. The method consists of making a list of sampling units along with their measure of size in any order.

II. Non-random sampling methods

Non-random sampling is that method of sampling in which samples are selected according to the subjective judgement of the observer on the basis of certain rules or guidelines indicating what sample should be chosen. As the selection is based on judgement of the observer, it is likely to be biased. The following are the different methods of non random sampling methods used in forest inventories:

1. Selective sampling

It consists of choosing samples according to the subjective judgement of the observer. It may give good approximations of population parameters, if it is properly used by a person with intensive knowledge of the population. 4PEA (Picking plots by personal prejudice and/or each of access) is one of the form of it. It is described by Gydeland and La Bou for quick and rough estimates.

2. Systematic sampling

In this sampling units are selected according to the pre-determined pattern with out recourse to the random sampling. Most commonly, the pattern envisages regular spacing of units.

e.g., Sampling units may be located 80 m apart in rows which may be 200 m apart. The selection of the first unit may be either random or according to a fixed arbitrary rule and this will result in distinguishing two varieties of systematic sampling.

When the first unit is selected at random and other according to a fixed pattern, the sampling is referred to as systematic sampling with a random start.

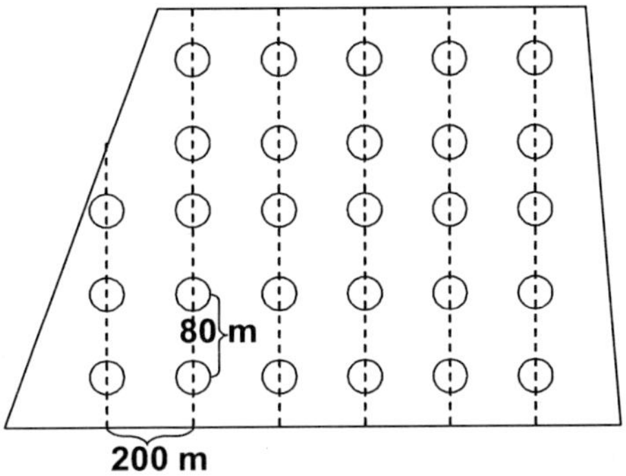

Fig. 13a: Systematic sampling

1	2	3	4	5	6	7	8	9	10
11	12	13	14	15	16	17	18	19	20
21	22	23	24	25	26	27	28	29	30
31	32	33	34	35	16	37	38	39	40
41	42	43	44	45	46	47	48	49	50
51	52	53	54	55	56	57	58	59	60
61	62	63	64	65	66	67	68	69	70
71	72	73	74	75	76	77	78	79	80
81	82	83	84	85	86	87	88	89	90
91	92	93	94	95	96	97	98	99	100

Fig. 13b: Systematic sampling

Advantages:

1. Simplicity
2. Easy in location of sample units
3. Reduction in cost
4. Uniform distribution of samples

3. Sequential sampling

In this method sampling is continued till a desired precision is reached. It is a method of sampling, whose characteristic feature is that, the number of observations in the sample is not determined in advance, but sampling units are taken successfully from a population. Each sample includes all the sample units of the former sample. The confidence interval at each stage will go on decreasing. Sampling is stopped, when the desired precision is reached.

This type of sampling is usually adapted to test a hypothesis. The hypothesis is tested each time, a new observation is made to determine whether the hypothesis should be rejected or accepted.

Sampling design : In order that sampling may give the most accurate estimate of the population, it is necessary that the sampling design should be statistically sound. Choice of the design depends upon certain factors; some of the important ones are :

1. The objective of the inventory
2. The desired precision
3. Time and money available for the work
4. Topography and accessibility to and within the forest.
5. Availability of personnel and equipment
6. Availability of satellite imageries, aerial photographs and maps
7. Availability of automatic data processing equipment
8. Results of the previous surveys carried out in the area.

- **Kinds of sampling units (SU) :** Mainly of two kinds:

  1. Sampling units having a fixed area
  2. Sampling units having a shape

1. **Sampling units having a fixed area :** When sampling units are of fixed area, it is necessary to describe their size.

Smaller SU are more efficient than larger ones, because the larger the No. of SU observed more is the precision. Hence, smaller the SU is better in forests with more heterogeneity but more cost involved as a whole as compared to less number of larger sampling units.

A working rule adopted in Europe is that size of the SU should be large enough to include at least 20 measurable trees.

2. **Sampling units having a shape:** The usual shapes of SU followed in India are :

a) **Plots :** Square, rectangular, circular and polygonal

i) **Square and Rectangular :** Plots are most commonly used in India. Because of easy demarcation and lay out. Suited to plantations raised in rows. Usual size is ***0.1 ha and some times also follow 1.0 ha***

ii) **Circular plots :** Laying out of these plots is very easy on level ground once its centre and radius is fixed. It has the minimum perimeter for a given area as compare to any other geometric shape and thus has the minimum number of border line trees.

Size- 0.05 ha (12.62 m radius) and 0.1 ha (17.84 m radius)

Efficiency of the plot size is determined by formula **SE^2 x p**

Where, **SE is standard error** of the plot size

p is cost of inventory of plot.

b) **Strips:** Strips are laid across the forest from one end to other at a particular bearing at regular intervals and inventory of these strips made to serve as a sample.

Size: width is 20-40 m and length is convenient

The width and the distance between the strips determine the intensity of sampling.

$$I = \frac{W}{D} \times 100$$

I = Intensity of sampling

W = width of the strip in metres

D = Distance between the central line of the strips in metres

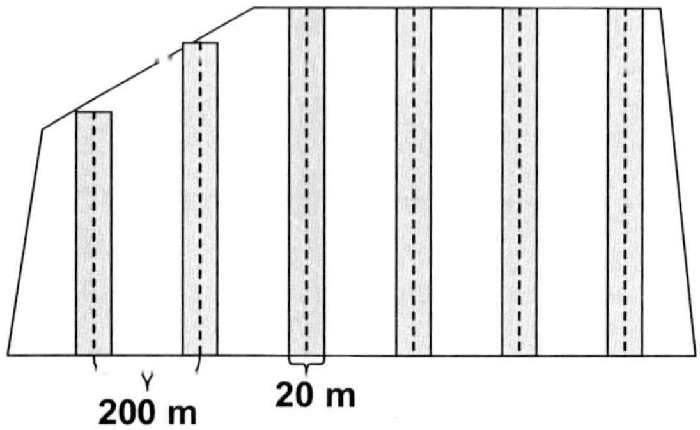

Fig. 14: Strip sampling

c) **Topographical units :** ***It is defined a sampling unit whose boundaries are predominantly topographical or natural features, such as nalas, streams, ridges, etc***. These are shown on maps and fixed exactly on ground. Even artificial features such as roads, inspection paths, block, compartment, sub-compartment boundaries also used as boundaries. Topographical Units are most frequently used as sampling units in hill forests, where other survey methods cannot be conveniently and accurately carried out.

Size – 12 to 24 ha

d) **Cluster :** The term 'cluster' is used to define a Sampling unit, which is in fact a ***group of smaller units***. The ***cluster is the statistical unit*** where as the ***smaller ones are only record units.***

Point sampling by using wedge prism

In earlier sampling methods discussed earlier, the sampling units may be either of fixed areas or be just points. Sampling units with fixed area was discussed earlier. But in this method, sampling from points or point sampling will be described.

Point sampling is the method of sampling in which the trees are measured from a single point.

In point sampling mainly two methods :

1. Horizontal Point Sampling (HPS) – Used to measure the basal area in m^2/ha directly. It was developed by *Bitterlich*
2. Vertical Point Sampling (VPS) - Used to measure the mean stand height. It was developed by *Hirata*

1. Horizontal Point Sampling (HPS)

In this method, Bitterlich proved that counting from a random point the number of trees whose breast height cross-section exceeds a certain critical angle, when multiplied by a constant factor gives an unbiased estimate of Basal **area per hectare.**

This method is also called as :

1. Angle count cruising
2. Pointless cruising
3. Variable plot cruising
4. Polyareal plot sampling
5. PPS (Probability Proportional to Size)

Terms used in Point Sampling

1. **Diopter :** This is a measure of the value of an angle expressed as its Sine. One diopter is approximately equivalent to an angle of **0.57^0** or **34.36** minutes

   Since Sin **0.57^0** = 1/100 = 1 diopter

2. **Basal Area Factor :** This is the multiplying factor, associated with any instrument.
3. **Plot Radius Factor :** This factor defines for each tree the radius of the circle within which the tree is tallied using an instrument with fixed critical angle. This factor is very useful in checking doubtful or borderline trees.
4. **Tree Factor :** It is the number of trees per hectare (or acre) represented by each tree tallied.

Uses of Horizontal Point Sampling (HPS): It is used for determination of :

1. Basal area per hectare = BAF x n

   Where 'n' is the number of trees tallied

2. Number of stem per hectare = $\frac{\text{Basal area factor of the prism}}{\text{Total basal area of the tally trees}}$
3. Volume per hectare = Basal area x Stand form height

Instruments used in Horizontal Point Sampling

1. Simple Angle Gauge
2. Wedge Prism
3. Spiegel Relaskop
4. Wide-Scale Relaskop
5. Tele Relaskop

□□□

Chapter 10

Yield Regulation and its Important Methods

Yield Regulation

"A term yield regulation is generally applied to the determination of the yield and the prescribed of means of realizing it". It means the fixing of working Plan Period in advance usually for a short period and the amount of timber or other produce which may be removed from the forest annually or periodically.

The management of forests for production and supply of wood requires continuous (or periodic) cutting of individual trees or crops of trees. Therefore, the chief object of forest management is stated as **regulation of production and supply i.e. yield.**

Functions of Yield Regulation

1. Calculation or determination of the amount of material or yield which may be removed annually or periodically from a forest over a stated period.
2. The construction of a cutting (felling) plan which determines the identity of the stands to be cut. Broadly, yield regulation is the estimation of possibility of the productive capacity of an area deciding as follows:
    a) How much be removed and how much be re-invested in the wood capital of the area,
    b) How much of the excess (from normal) wood capital could be removed in addition, and
    c) How much and from what portion of the G.S., the felling should be made.

The objects of the regulating yield :

i) To cut each crop or tree at maturity.

ii) To obtain maximum yield of the desired produce/\.

iii) To cut the same quantity of material annually or periodically (approximately).

iv) To limit the area to be felled to that which can be regenerated.

These objects can be quite easily achieved in the second and subsequent rotations but difficult in the first rotation.

The following three works are done in yield regulation :

i) Prescribing by calculation of the annual or periodic yield by volume,number of trees or by area.

ii) Prescribing the areas from which the prescribed yield will be taken out either according to an annual schedule or without it.

iii) Prescribing the rules of felling by which yield may be removed and the area may be successfully regenerated naturally.

Difficulties : In the first rotation, the difficulty arises due to the following:

i) In virgin forest, crops are generally over mature and decrepit, necessitating early removal. And the regeneration conditions are also not favourable.

ii) The crops are usually irregular, both in density and composition.

iii) Growth and composition data are not available for quite a few decades.

The yield is usually regulated for the period of the working plan, which is generally 10 years.

Definitions of some of the terms pertaining to yield

Yield : The volume or number of stems that can be removed annually or periodically or the area over which fellings may pass annually or periodically, consistent with the attainment of objects of management.

There are two types of yield in even aged forestry :

i) **Final yield:** (a) All the material that counts against the prescribed yield and which is derived from the main fellings in a regular forest. (b) As in the Yield Table, "it is the sum of the main crop and the subsidiary crop figures for the given crop age".

ii) **Intermediate yield**: "All the material from thinnings or operations proceeding the main felling in a regular forest, or its cash equivalent." (Syn - subsidiary crop).

Normal yield: "The yield from a normal forest".

Sustained yield: "The material that a forest can yield annually or periodically in perpetuity".

Total yield: "The standing volume of a crop including the total volume removed in thinnings since its establishment as a more or less even aged stand". Total yield is nothing but the sum of the final yield and intermediate yield.

Yield Capacity: "The total quantity of material per anum, of given species, that an area is capable of producing under normal conditions, so long as the factors of locality remain unchanged".

Yield Determination: The calculation of the amount of material which may be removed from a forest, annually or periodically over a stated period or of the annual or periodic area over which fellings may be made, consistent with the treatment prescribed.

Difference between Final yield and Intermediate yield

Sl.No.	Final yield	Intermediate yield
1.	This is the main yield derived from the main fellings in a regular forest.	This is the yield from cleanings, thinning and improvement fellings.
2.	The final yield (i.e. the removal of stands and their regeneration) controls the proportional distribution of age classes.	The intermediate yield from thinnings and other operations controls the economy by providing early returns and controlling the quality of timber.
3.	Silvicultural operations, such as cleanings and thinnings by well-timed removal of the suppressed and dominated stems do not decrease, but rather increase the final yield and improve the yield representing a bonus.	The intermediate yield may constitute anything from one-third to one half of the total yield.

Silvicultural systems in relation to yield

The following three broad types of systems will be recognized for the purpose of considering the effect of silvicultural systems on yield regulation :

i) **Clear felling** : resulting in regular, even aged forests, in which age gradations are recognized by area.

ii) **Regular Shelterwood** : resulting in regular even aged forests in which age classes are recognized by area.

iii) **Irregular Shelterwood and Selection** : resulting in irregular forests, in which neither age gradations nor age classes are recognizable by area.

Basis of yield regulation

The yield can, broadly be prescribed in three ways, *viz.* :

(i) By area, (ii) By volume or (iii) By area and volume combined.

1. In case of yield by area, the entire area, irrespective of the growing stock, forms the basis of calculation.
2. In case of yield by volume, the volume of growing stock, the increment or both volume of growing stock and its increment, may form the basis.

Methods of Yield Regulation

The following methods of yield calculation are classified according to the above parameters:

Sl.No	Basis	Method
A.	*Area only*	**A1 – Annual coupe by gross area** **A2 - Annual coupe by reduced area**
B.	*Volume only* (volume of Growing Stock)	**B1 – Von Mantel's Formula** **B2 – Howard's modification** **B3 – Simmons' modification** **B4 – Smythies modification** **B5 – Burma modification**
C.	*Area and Volume*	C1 – Permanent P.B. Method; allotment by: (i). Equalising area (ii). Equalising volume: Hartig's method (iii). Equalising area and volume C2 – Revocable P.B. Method **C3 – Single P.B. Method** C4 – Floating P.B. Method **C5–JUDEICH's Stand Selection (Management) Method**
D.	*Increment*	D1 – Increment Method D2 – Swiss Method **D3 – Biolley's "Check Method"**
E.	*Volume and Increment of whole Growing Stock*	E1 – Formula Methods (comparison of actual and normal G.S) (i).Austrian **(ii).Heyer's** (iii). Hundeshagen's (iv). Karl's v. Breymann's E2 – Hufnagl's Method (Variation I and II) **E3 – (i) French Method of 1883** (ii) 1894 Modification or Melard's Method (Regeneration Area Method) (iii) Smythies Modification (iv) Chaturvedi's Modification E4 – Hufnagl's Diameter Class Method E5 – Brandis Diameter Class Method (or the Indian Method) E6 – Volume Unit Method **E7 – Smythies Safe guarding Formula** (or UP Safe-guarding formula)

Note: Of the above methods B2, B3, B4, E5 and E7 are purely of Indian origin and deal with special situations and problems of Forest Management in Indian.

Yield Regulation Methods in Regular and Irregular Forests

Yield Regulation in Regular Forests

I. Yield Regulation in Clear Felling System

A. Yield Regulation Methods Based On "Area Only"

A_1 -Annual Coupes by Gross Area Method

This is the oldest and simplest form of regulating yield from a forest. This method is applicable to **coppice forests** and also to high forests (rotation is long and regeneration is normally seedling origin) worked on a system of clear felling and artificial regeneration as in Nilambur (Kerala), Bori and Betul (M.P.) teak plantation.

In India, this method is adopted in **coppice with standards and coppice with reserve systems**. It regulates the **final yield** in such a way that fellings in areas to be finally felled at rotation age and regenerated, without accounting **intermediate yield.**

Methodology

i) The area of the forest or the **felling series** (A ha) is divided into a number of **annual coupes** equal to the number of years in the rotation (r) and one coupe felled every year equal to (A/r) ha in area.

ii) The sequence of annual coupes is laid down in the working plan and shown on the map, and also demarcated on the ground as well. But there should be no objection to felling a coupe (nearly mature but damaged by fire) in advance of its prescribed date and making suitable adjustments in the felling order.

iii) This method of yield regulation will ensure equal sustained yield in the second and subsequent rotations. Annual coupes formed which are equal in the area on the ground are known as **equi-extensive coupes.**

A typical example of this case is illustrated in figure (in case of NGS) as follows:

The simplest method of achieving the objective of sustained yield is to maintain a complete succession of equal areas of crops of all ages from one year old upto the age of maturity (say 10 years) and remove the 10 years old wood annually and plant up the area again.

This matured wood represent the increment of the whole forest and difficulty of removing the annual increment from each unit area, say one hectare, is overcome by removing accumulated production of 10 hectare on 1/ 10th part of the total area, as illustrated in the figure given below :

Such series of trees or crops of all ages, from seedling to maturity, so as to enable the removal of the oldest is known as a *"Complete series of age gradations".*

As the forest in the above example has equal area of every age in it, an equal area will be available for felling at maturity. The establishment of such a series of age-gradations is one form of the crop necessary for ***"Sustained Yield Management"*** and for maintaining it in perpetuity. Such a forest provides a conceptual picture of *"Normal Forest"*.

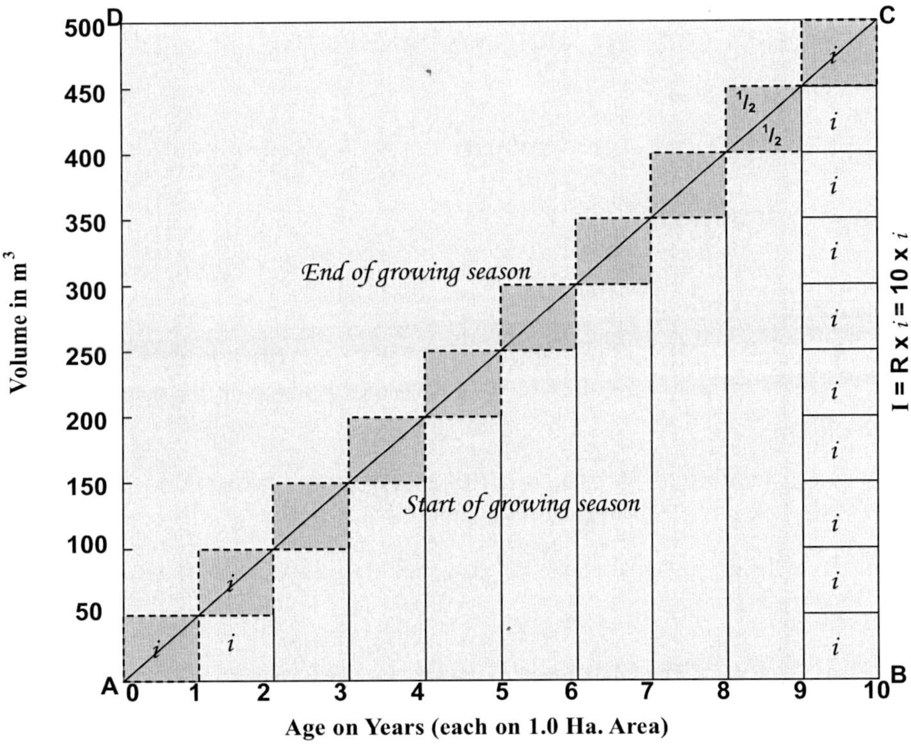

Fig. Theoretical Normal Growing Stock (NGS) in a series of 'R' (10) equal age gradations (one ha each).

B. A_2 - Annual Coupes by Reduced Area Method

Methodology

i) **Reduction factors** should be applied for equalizing annual yields and areas allotted to each coupe made **equi-productive** rather than equi-extensive (since the density and site quality may vary from coupe to coupe).

ii) **Reduction for density** is usually made (as this variation may be only a **temporary feature**) and full stocking may be expected after regeneration operations and this factor will not affect future yields.

iii) **Yield variation** due to site quality may be a **permanent feature** of the locality which is taken into account by determining and applying suitable reduction factors before formation of equi-productive coupes.

Advantages of Yield Regulation by Area Method:

a) It is easy to apply

b) It leads to absolute regularity of age gradations

Disadvantages

a) It is very rigid, every change of rotation will necessitate re-division of the coupes.

b) Prescribe fellings without considerations of the crop condition.

Limitations

a) In unmanaged forests, it is not possible to layout equi-productive coupes.

b) In mixed natural forests, regeneration by area is only a crude method.

B. Yield Regulation Methods Based on "Volume of Growing Stock"

B1-Von Mantel's Formula

Let AB represents units of area each occupied by a wood differing by one year from the preceding and the volume standing on these area be represented by a number of equal rectangles, each equivalent to one year's increment.

Thus, if the annual increment in each wood is represented by the rectangle I, the volume of each age gradation will be represented by i, 2i, 3i..............(r-1)i, ri, where "r" is the rotation. The total of these rectangles will be i+2i+3i+...........+(r-1)i + ri will represent the total growing stock at the end of the growing season before the oldest wood have been felled.

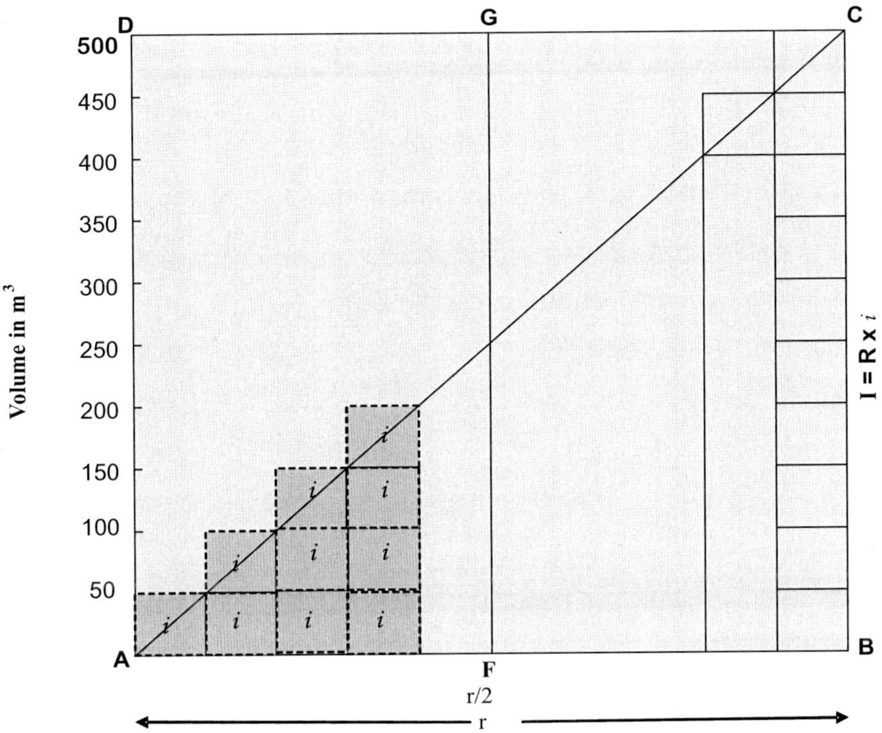

The line AC divides the rectangles representing current years' growth all over the age gradations into halves. The lower halves representing increment until the mid-growing season. Thus, D ABC represents growing stock at the mid growing season (summer growing stock).

∴ Growing Stock = Area of D ABC

= ½ AB x BC

= ½ r x I (where I = r x i)

∴GS = I x r/2 (summer growing stock)

I = 2 GS / r

$$\textbf{Increment} = \frac{\text{Twice the Growing Stock}}{\text{Rotation}}$$

$$\therefore \textbf{Annual Yield} = \frac{\text{Twice the Growing Stock}}{\text{Rotation}}$$

This formula is known as **"Von Mantel's formula"** (sometimes known as "**Formula of Glorious Simplicity**").

Accepting the above figure as correctly representing the growing stock, the following statements holds good :

1. Yield during rotation = Twice the growing stock (the above formula holds good with this statement).
2. During a rotation, half the increment is felled during that rotation and the other half goes to the new growing stock. According to second statement, **GS = I x (r/2),** where I = one year increment laid on over the whole forest, So that

Yield = 2 GS = GS + GS

Substitute GS = (I/2) x r

Yield = GS + (I x r/2) = GS + ½ increment during the rotation

The other half of the increment going to new growing stock. In other words, during a rotation, half the yield is represented by the growing stock at the commencement of the rotation and half by the increment during the rotation.

According to Von Mantel's formula,

Summer Growing Stock = 1 GFBC = D ABC = (I x r/2)

In the autumn (third season), immediately before the oldest wood is felled, the growing stock will represented by the full rectangles and therefore, the D ABC must be added to the Ds above the diagonal AC. i.e. r x i/2 = I/2 (where rxi=I)

∴ **The Autumn Growing Stock = (Ix r/2) + (I/2)**

In the spring season (first season), when the oldest wood has been felled and no further growth has taken place, so "I" must be deducted from the autumn growing stock.

∴ **The Spring Growing Stock = (Ix r/2) - (I/2)**

For practical purpose, the simpler formula for the summer (mid-season) is used.

Advantages of Von Mantel's formula

1. It is simple in application and requires determination of growing stock and rotation only.
2. It regulates the yield according to actual GS. Overstocked forests will be heavily felled and under-stocked forests lightly felled.

3. It is useful as a preliminary step in yield regulation, especially in irregular forests.
4. It gives conservative yield and helps in enrichment of the GS.

Disadvantages of Von Mantel's formula

1. The formula gives only the final yield and does not take the intermediate thinning into account.
2. It is inelastic because the surplus or deficit in the GS is spread over half the rotation.
3. It involves complete enumeration of the GS, which is not always practicable.
4. It neglects the age class distribution and rate of growth of the crop.
5. It gives only the final yield and is useful where natural forests are being brought under regulation.
6. The assumption that all age gradations put on equal increment throughout is wrong.

Examples for Von Mantel's formula

Find the yield by Von Mantel's formula from the following data with a rotation period of 120 years :

GS diameter class (cm)	Volume (m^3)
1-20	2000
21-30	1700
31-40	2000
41-50	1600
51-60	1500
>60	2000
Total =	**10800**

According to Von Mantel's formula,

$$\text{Annual yield} = \frac{\text{Twice the growing stock}}{\text{Rotation}}$$

$$= \frac{2\ GS}{R} = \frac{2 \times 10800}{120} = 180\ m3$$

$\therefore$ **Annual yield = 180 m³**

B_2 – Howard's Modification

Howard's modification was evolved to meet the special case of selection forests in which ***enumerations were carried out to half the exploitation girth***. It was assumed that the girth was directly proportional to the age. The only data required is as follows:

a) A decision of the rotation corresponding to the exploitable girth.

b) The determination of the girth corresponding to half the rotation. In the absence of more accurate data, this can be assumed to be half the exploitable girth.

c) The enumeration of trees down to half the rotation age.

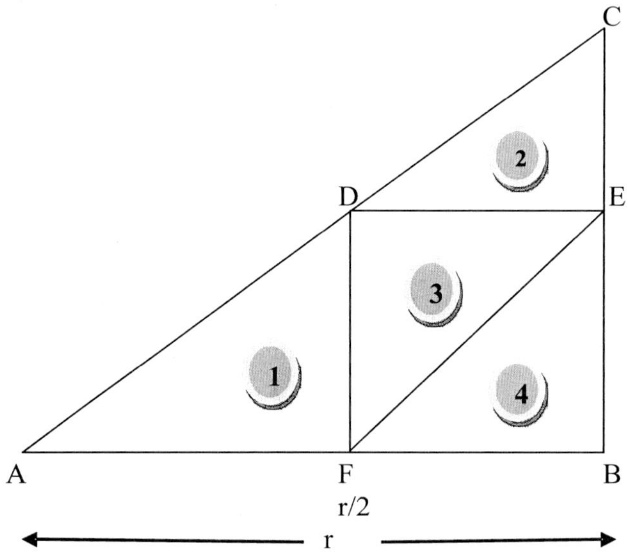

D ABC represents the total growing stock of forest on a rotation of "r" years. The figure BCDF represents the volume of growing stock which has been **enumerated down to half the rotation.** The enumerated portion is ¾ of the total growing stock (triangles marked 1, 2, 3 and 4 are equal).

Let V = the volume of enumerated GS = ¾ of total GS

$\therefore$ The total volume of the growing stock = V x $^4/_3$ – – – – – –(i)

Substituting (i) in Von Mantel's formula i,e. I = 2GS / r

$$\therefore Y = \frac{2x(4V/3)}{r} = \frac{8V}{3r}$$

$$\therefore Y = \frac{V}{(3/8)r}$$ This formula is known as ***"Howard's Modification"***

The difficulty in its application is that the limit of enumeration will change every time that the rotation is changed. The limit will also change with any change in the quality class.

B_3 – Simmon's Modification

A general formula **applicable to all fractional enumerations of the growing stock** was evolved by Simmons. It applies to cases where volume measurements include the complete poles of the trees enumerated.

Let G = Volume of the growing stock

V = Volume enumerated and measured

a = Volume not enumerated

$$n = \frac{\text{Rotation}}{\text{Age of the oldest gradation in "a"}} = \frac{r}{x}$$

Where x = Age down to which enumerations are made

r = Rotation

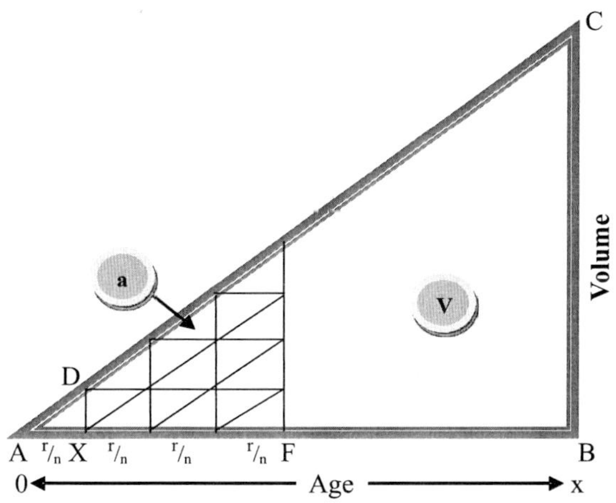

The rotation being divided into "n" parts and corresponding volumes of each part are in arithmetic progression series as shown in figure.

In the above figure, D ABC represents normal growing stock. Divide the rotation into "n" parts, erect perpendiculars and draw parallel as shown in figure.

Figure DXBC = V = Volume enumerated

D AXD = a = Volume not enumerated

D ABC = G = Volume of the growing stock

∴ Total GS = Summation of volume G

[We know that sum of AP series $S = (^n/_2)\ \{a+(2n-1)a\} = n^2a$]

∴ D ABC = $a+3a+5a+7a+\ldots\ldots+(2n-1)a = a + (a+2a) + (a+2x2a) + (a+3x2a) + \ldots\ldots + [a+(n-1)2a]$

$= (^n/_2)\ [a+(2n-1)a]$

$= \frac{1}{2}\, n\ [a+2an-a]$

$= \frac{1}{2}\, n \times 2an$

∴ GS = DABC = n^2a ———————— (a)

Now V =G-a = $n^2a - a$ (substitute $G = n^2a$)

V = a (n^2-1) ———————— (b)

From equations (a) and (b) $G : V :: n^2a : (n^2-1)a$

∴ **G x** $(n^2-1)a = V \times n^2a$

$$\therefore \mathbf{G} = \frac{Vn^2}{n^2-1} \quad \text{———————— (c)}$$

Substitute equation (c) in Von Mantel's formula i.e $Y = {}^{2GS}/_r$

$$\textbf{Annual yield} = {}^{2GS}/_r = \frac{2n^2V}{r(n^2-1)} \quad \text{———————————— (i)}$$

This formula can also be expressed in terms of "r" and "x", since $n = {}^r/_x$

$$\textbf{Annual yield} = {}^{2GS}/_r = \frac{2n^2V}{r(n^2-1)} = \frac{2(r/x)^2V}{r(r/x)2\ -1}$$

$$\mathbf{Y} = \frac{2rV}{r^2 - x^2} = \frac{V}{½ r [1 - (x^2/r^2)]}$$

It can be shown that Howard's formula is a special case of this general formula, where **x = ½ r**

Substituting the value of "x" i.e. put x=½ **r** in equation (ii), we get the annual yield as,

$$Y = \frac{2rV}{r^2 - x^2} = \frac{2Vr}{r2 - (r2/4)} = \frac{4 \times 2Vr}{4r^2 - r^2} = \frac{8Vr}{3r^2} = \frac{8V}{3r}$$

∴ **Y = $^{8V}/_{3r}$** – – – – This is nothing but **Howard's formula**

For example : The GS was enumerated down to age "x" AX = $^{r}/_{n}$

Take r = 120 years and X = 20 years, then n = 120 / 20 = 6 parts

It means that rotation is divided into 6 parts and GS is enumerated down to $^{1}/_{6}$ th of the exploitable girth / diameter, corresponding to $^{1}/_{6}$ th rotation i.e. 20 years. If the rotation is divided into "n" parts, then each $^{r}/_{n}$.

Solve the following problems by Simmon's formula :

1. Find out the annual yield by Simmon's formula, when GS down to diameter equivalent to an age of 20 years enumerated and measured i.e. x = 20 years, with a rotation of 100 years and the volume enumerated and measured is 2400 m^3.

Solution : r = rotation = 100 years

n = GS down to diameter equivalent to an age of 20 years enumerated and measured

i.e. x = 20 years then n = r/x = 100/20 = 5 (rotation is divided into 5 parts)

V = volume enumerated and measured = 2400 m^3

Applying the Simmon's formula (i),

$$Y = \text{Annual yield} = {}^{2GS}/_{r} = \frac{2\,n^2 \times V}{r(n^2-1)} = \frac{2x5^2}{100(5^2-1)} = \frac{50}{100x24}$$

∴ **Y = 50 m^3**

Applying the Simmon's formula (ii),

$$Y = \frac{2r\,V}{r^2 - x^2} = \frac{V}{\frac{1}{2} r\,[1-(x^2/r^2)]}$$

$$= \frac{2x100x2400}{100^2 - 20^2} = \frac{200x2400}{9600} \qquad \therefore \mathbf{Y = 50\ m^3}$$

2. Find out the annual yield by Simmon's formula, when enumeration and volume measurement made down to 20 cm diameter, corresponding to 40 years age. Volume measured is 12000 m^3 with a rotation of 120 years and corresponding diameter is equal to 60 cm.

B_4 – Smythies Modification

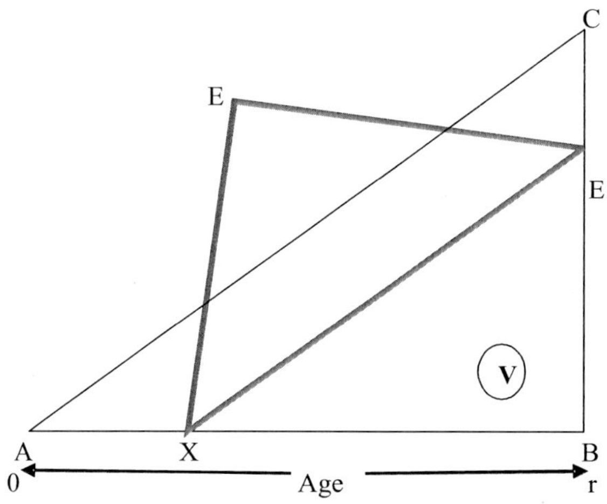

Let V = volume of GS enumerated and measured (Δ **XBD**)

r = rotation

X = Age down to which enumeration and measurement is done (corresponding to the girth / diameter down to which the volume is measured).

In the figure, Δ ABC represents the normal GS triangle. If XD is drawn parallel to AC, the rectangle EXBD will be completed. Then part of the GS neither enumerated nor measured is represented by figure AXDC and the enumerated and measured GS, V is represented by Δ XBD.

The yield in (r-x) years = Rectangle EXBD

= Twice the Δ XBD

= 2V

$\therefore$ **The annual yield Y =** $\dfrac{2V}{(r-x)}$ – – – *This is **Smythies Modification** of Von Mantel's formula*

This presupposes the existence of normal GS below the age "x" to supply the yield during the remaining "x" years of rotation, which is a risky assumption.

Important Note : The volume which Smythies fits into Von Mantel's formula is only timber which is not only excludes crops below a certain diameter but also the portion of the tree (in volume calculation) which is below that diameter (in India, standard timber limit is down to 20 cm diameter over bark).

B_5 – Burma Modification

Like Howard's Modification, Burma Modification was also evolved as a special case in which **enumeration and measurement of the GS** was done down to **$^1/_3$rd rotation** (corresponding to $^1/_3$ rd exploitable girth/diameter as assumed), instead of half the rotation in Howard's Modification.

Let V = volume of GS measured down to $^r/_3$ years

r = rotation

This can be proved geometrically as Howard's, or derived from Simmon's general formula:

We know Simmon's Modification as

$$\text{Annual yield} = Y = \frac{2\,n^2\ V}{r(n^2-1)} \text{ ---------------- (i)}$$

$$Y = \frac{2r\ V}{r^2-x^2} = \frac{V}{½\, r\,[1-(x2/r2)]} \text{ ----------------- (ii)}$$

where,

$$n = \frac{\text{Rotation}}{\text{Age of the oldest gradation in "a"}} = \frac{r}{x}$$

x = Age down to which enumerations are made

r = Rotation

In this special case n = 3 then $x = {}^{r}/_{3}$

Substituting values of "x" in equation (i), we get,

$$\text{Annual yield} = Y = \frac{2x9xV}{r(9-1)} = \frac{9V}{4r} \quad \therefore \mathbf{Y} = \frac{9V}{4r}$$

Again substituting values of "x" in equation (ii), we get,

$$\text{Annual yield} = Y = \frac{2\,V\,r}{r^2 - (r^2/9)} = \frac{9V}{4r} \quad \therefore \mathbf{Y} = \frac{9V}{4r}$$

C. Yield Regulation Methods Based On "Area and Volume"

C_5 – Judeich's Stand Selection (Management) Method

This method was practiced by **Judeich** in Germany. **The essence of this method is the careful selection of mature stands** (maturity being technical, financial or silvicultural depending on the object of management) and the allotment of the proportionate area of such stands to be felled and regenerated during the Working Plan (WP) period.

The procedure is as follows :

1. The forest is divided into a number of components of suitable size.
2. The compartments are inspected and described with reference to the treatment they require during the next working plan period (say 10 years).
3. The rotation and working plan period are fixed.
4. The compartments are selected for felling and regeneration during WP period on the following principles:

a) Stands which must be felled to meet the necessary silvicultural or protective necessities.

b) Mature and over mature stands (maturity being technical, financial or silvicultural depending on the object of management).

c) Stands of doubtful maturity, whose felling may be desirable for reasons of convenience.

e.g. One occurring between two mature stands.

5. The size of the mean annual coupe and the area to be felled during the WP period is determined. i.e $[(^{FS}/_{R}) \times P]$.
6. If the total area of the compartments selected for felling under statement 4(a), (b) and (c) is within, say 10% of the mean periodic coupe as calculated in statement (5) above, no further adjustment is necessary. If it is larger than this, then some of the areas brought in under statement 4(iii) may be omitted. If it is smaller than the calculated minimum area, then some more compartments, even though not quite mature, will have to be included.
7. The annual yield by volume may be prescribed by dividing the total standing volume in the compartments taken up for fellings (with or without an allowance for increment) by the period.

Advantages

1. The method is simple and elastic, working is firmly based on the actual condition of the stand.
2. It can be freely applied to all regular forests, even if abnormal.

Disadvantages

1. Crops may become mixed, as regards age class distribution, owing to freedom allowed in selecting them for felling.
2. Sustained yield may not be possible, if too much freedom is given in selection of stands (crops) for felling on entirely on silvicultural considerations.

Illustration of Judeich's Stand Selection Method

The size of the mean annual coupe is obtained by the formula $[(^{FS}/_{R}) \times P]$, here, FS = Area of the felling series

R = Rotation

P = Working Plan Period

The sum total of the areas selected on the basis of maturity and ability to regenerate can be ± 10% of the calculated area. If it is less or more than the permissible limit, then relatively larger or lesser areas are taken and at the end normal distribution is achieved.

For example

Suppose a forest is 1600 ha in area i.e. FS = 1600 ha

Rotation has been fixed at 80 years i.e R = 80 years

Working Plan period is 10 years i.e P = 10 years

The forest is composed of:

300 ha of 1-20 age classes

250 ha of 21-40 age classes

500 ha of 41-60 age classes

550 ha of 61-80 age classes

If the age class distribution were normal i.e. each age class had 400 ha of area, then in one working plan period is equal to $[(^{FS}/_{R}) \times P]$ i.e $(^{1600}/_{80}) \times 10$ = 200ha would have formed the regeneration PB.

But as there is a greater proportion of higher age classes, in the first working plan period, lesser area 300 ha is taken and it is gradually reduced to 250 ha and 200 ha in the second and third working plan periods to reach approximate normality as shown in the following table :

Age class	Area in ha				
	Normal	Actual	After 10 years	After 20 years	After 30 years
1-20	400	300	150+300=450 **(i)**	225+250=475 **(v)**	237.5+200=438
21-40	400	250	15+125=275 **(ii)**	225+138=363 **(vi)**	237.5+181.5=418
41-60	400	500	125+250=375 **(iii)**	137.5+187.5=325	181.5+162.5=344
61-80	400	550	250+275=525 **(iv)**	187.5+262.5=450	162.5+225=388 =400 (Appr. normality)

Explanation for the above table as how the figures have been calculated

i) Half of the actual class will go after 10 years to the higher class, but the other half will remain in it and 300 ha will come to it from regeneration PB. (part of present 61-80 age class).

ii) Half of lower class i.e. 150 ha and half of the actual of this class i.e. 125 ha.

iii) Half of the lower class i.e. 125 ha and half of the actual of this class i.e. 250 ha.

iv) Half of the lower class i.e. 250 ha and the remaining 275 ha after transfer of 300 ha for regeneration. In the second working plan period only 250 ha will be regenerated. So, the area figures in the various age classes will be as under.

v) Half of the present class i.e. 225 ha + 250 ha regenerated

vi) Half of lower class i.e. 225 ha and half of the present class i.e.138 ha

In order to find out current yield, the volume of the compartments selected for regeneration felling (with or without increment) is divided by the period.

- The advantage of this method is that it is simple and elastic.
- It keeps the condition of the crop fully in view.
- It is applicable to all regular forests even when they may be abnormal.

Volume and Increment method after allotment of area under Periodic Blocks (PBs)

The fixed area method is applicable in clear felling system where annual coupes are regenerated in one year. So, the yield of annual coupe is obtained by the following formula :

$$\textbf{Annual yield} = \frac{\text{Volume of P.B.I.+(Annual Increment in PBI during the period}/_{2})}{\text{Period}}$$

$$Ya = \frac{V + {}^{P}/_{2}}{P}$$ ------This is called as "***Cotta's formula***"

(Single Periodic Method)

Where, Ya = Annual yield

V = Volume of PBI

P = Period

i = Annual increment in PBI

Sometimes, increment is not added in calculating yield with object of increasing the growing stock or for serving as reserve against damages, such as fire, insect, diseases, etc.

In this method, in order to find out yield, the exploitation period is calculated by the following formula:

$$\textbf{Exploitation Period} = \frac{\text{Area of floating PB}}{\text{Area of felling series}} \text{xRotation}$$

Yield Regulation Method based on growing stock and increment

Heyer's formula

According to this method, annual yield is calculated by **Heyer's formula:**

$$Y = Ia + \frac{(Va - Vn)}{X}$$

Where, Y = Annual yield

Ia = Actual annul increment

Va = Actual growing stock

Vn = Normal growing stock

X = No. of years in which surplus or deficit is to be adjusted

For this formula, increment is taken to be the total of actual mean annual increment of the whole forest, "Va" is obtained from enumeration and "Vn" from the yield table, "X" is decided on the basis of local conditions (i.e. it is elastic).

Advantages of Heyer's formula

1. It is elastic because there is a wide choice as regards the period over which the surplus or deficit is distributed.

2. The ideal of the NGS is kept clearly before the Working Plan Officer.
3. Applicable to both regular and irregular forests and it clearly distinguishes between capital (GS) and income (increment).
4. Its main use is as a check on other methods.

Disadvantages of Heyer's formula

1. Artificial and tricky and may lead to anomalous results, as it disregasrds age classes distribution.
2. It ignores area and age. It is an office method rather than a field method.

D. Yield Regulation Methods Based on "Increment"

D3 - Biolley's "Check method"

This concept originates from Guraud which has later modified by Biolley. This method is based on measurement of increment. This method is emphasized more on silviclture and age class distribution inside the forest.

5 cm diameter classes down to 17.5 cm diameter at 6-10 yr interval. These are formed in three groups. And from these groups increment is calculated by using the formulae:

Total increment I= V2+N - V1

Where V1= Volume of GS at initial

V2= Volume of GS at final

N=Volume of wood removed during this period

In this calculation, there may be excess calculation of increment due to the presence of new recruitment during the period.

Passage or recruitmtent of trees from one diameter class to another is of three kinds, viz. :

i) From one diameter clas to the next higher class within the same group.
ii) From higher diameter class of one group to the lower diameter class of the next higher group.

iii) From the un-enumerated diameter class (optional group) to the lowest of the enumerated class.

Increment is calculated for each group, and only those trees are enumerated in next cycle (second inventory), which bear scribe mark. As for the recruitment, only the increase in the volume of recruited trees should be recorded as increment and not their full volume. Since there is no satisfactory method of assessing this increment, it was considered appropriate that calculations of increment are based based on the trees which were already enumerated in the previous enumeration. The recruirtment would be adjusted in the lower groups and their increment ignored. Hence, it is preferable to substract the whole volume of recruirtment from the total increment during the measurement interval.

Thus, it should be subtracted to get actual increment as follows:

Increment Z = V2 - V1 + N - P

Where Z = Increment

V_2 = Present GS volume – second inventory

V_1 = GS volume n years ago – first inventory

N = Volume of trees cut

P = The volume new recruitment i.e. volume of recruitment in "n" years (from lower storey to main stand)

It can also be expressed as follows: **Increment = GS_2 – GS_1 + Fellings – Recruitment**

There are various ways of determining "P" as follows :

i) By recording all trees that do not bear scribe marks separately in second inventory (which were not measured in first inventory), these trees will be of the lowest class/category.

ii) It can also be determined arithmetically.

In **Biolley's** method, fellings are made strictly on silvicultural considerations, and in all age grouls and not in the *Large Group* only.

Yield prediction serves as a check against over felling, the increment being calculated on the number of trees that existed in the previous enumeration, and excluding the recruitment to that group.

Annual Increment = Z/n = $[(V_2 + N) - (V_1 + P)] / n$

Where n is the interval period for enumeration.

In order to adjust the deficit or excess of GS in a forest further modification is introduced as follows:

Annual Increment Y = Z/n= $[(V_2 + N) - (V_1 + P)]/n \pm (Ga - Gn)/A$

Where Ga is actual GS

Gn is Normal GS and

A is period of adjustment.

Biolley's Check Method leads an irregular forest gradually to normal. Optimum GS and size class distribution is checked by periodical total enumeration. There is neither rotation, nor any exploitable diameter. Trees of any size may be removed, provided their removal benefits the remaining crop in improving the increment or size class distribution. This method was found to be successful in the hands of experienced foresters, who had intimate knowledge of their forests.

E. Yield Regulation Methods Based On "Volume and Increment" (by diameter classes)

E3 - French method of 1883 or Melard method

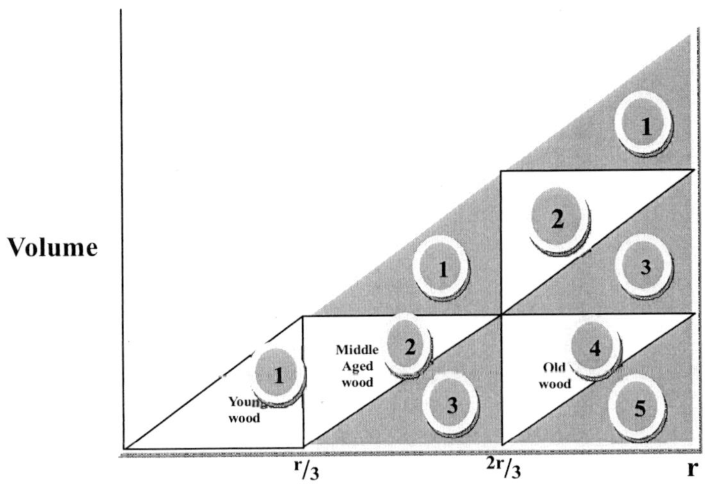

This method depends on the fact that in a normal forest, which is fully stocked and has the correct proportion of age classes. The volumes of the oldest third, the middle third and the youngest third are in the proportion of 5:3:1 and in order to attain normality, this proportion should always be aimed at. The calculation is based linear relationship between age and volume as shown in the above diagram.

This method was originally applied for selection and irregular forests of tolerant species.

Let V_o = Volume of old wood

V_m = Volume of middle wood

I_o = Increment per unit per annum old wood

I_m = Increment per unit per annum middle wood

r = Mean age at which it is estimated matured trees will be felled

n = A factor varying according to circumstances

Annual yield $Y = \{[V_o / (r/3)] + [(V_o \times I_o) / 2]\} + [1/n\ (V_m \times I_m)]$

The first portion of the formula provides for the removal of the oldest woods plus the correct portion of the increment during a period equal to one third of the rotation in which time, they will be replaced by the middle by the middle aged wood. The later portion provides for the removal in thinning of that portion on the increment of the middle wood which will not be required to replace the old wood.

If the old wood is in excess and $(V_o/V_n) > (5/3)$, then in practice, a certain adjustment is made by transferring some trees from the old class to the middle age class, or if the volume of old is in deficit and $(V_o/V_n) < (5/3)$, transfer is made in the opposite direction by shifting some trees from middle aged class to the old class. This means that the removal of old trees is either retarded or accelerated. Before any transefer is made, it should be considered whether the attainment of theoretical ratio is of sufficient value to warrant such an exchange.

When the forest is abnormal, the usual practice was as follows:

A forest of 100 ha contain contain 22,000 m^3 of old wood and 11,000 m^3 of middle wood in place of the normal quantities of 20,000 and 12,000 m^3.

Wood	Growing Stock in m^3			
	Actual	Normal	Surplus	Deficit
Old wood	22000	20000	2000	--
Middle wood	11000	12000	--	1000
Total	33000	32000	2000	1000

Total surplus 2000 - 1000 = 1000

Thus, there is a surplus GS of 1000 m^3 which may be removed during the period, but there is deficit of 1000 m^3 in the volume of the middle wood, which before applying the formula, must be made good by transferring to it the smallest diameter classes of the large wood upto 1000 m^3. Thus, the yield of large wood is reduced but the total yield remains higher than it would have been if the forest were normal with no surplus growing stock. In actual operations, trees of the diameter of the transferred classes will be treated as immature, thus building up the medium class to normal.

If on the contrary, there were only 16000 m^3 of old wood and 13000 m^3 of middle wood, there would be a total deficit of 3000 m^3 and of 4000 m^3 in the large wood class.

Wood	Growing Stock in m^3			
	Actual	Normal	Surplus	Deficit
Old wood	16000	20000	--	4000
Middle wood	13000	12000	1000	--
Total	29000	32000	1000	4000

Total deficit 4000 – 1000 = 3000 m^3

The old wood class would be brought upto 17000 m^3 by a transfer of the medium class of the 1000 m^3 surplus in that class. Thus, the yield of old wood is increased but the total yield remains less than is forest were normal. In actual operations, trees of the transferred classes will in this case be treated as mature. Thus, the surplus of medium wood will be reduced and since less than the total normal yield is cut, the volume of old wood will be increased.

Essential silvicultural requirements must not be neglected in the fellings and consequently, the exent to which these transfers can be made will depend on the nature of forest in each case. These transfers should not be considered an essential part of the method.

When marking for fellings, thinning and improvement, fellings are first marked and the volume of these plus that of any windfalls is deducted from the possibility, the balanced is then marked in final fellings.

Advantages of French method of 1883

1. The yield is in accordance with the condition of the forest.
2. The method leads to the forest over to normality
3. The method is elastic and accurate and has worked well in practice.

Disadvantages French method of 1883

1. Trees have to be enumerated down to one third of rotation age.

E_7 – Smythies Safeguarding Formula

Smythies evolved this formula for calculating yield of forests managed by selection system in UP. Later on, it began to be applied to most of the selection forests and PB. Inter areas of conversion system in UP and MP.

According to this formula, **Annual yield** $= \frac{X}{(I + {}^{x}/_{2})} \times 100 \pm A\%$

Where, x = No. of trees of class II that will pass into exploitable class I during the felling cycle and is calculated by $x = ({}^{f}/_{t})\ (II - Z\%II)$

f = Felling cycle

t = Time taken by II class trees to pass into class I

Z = No. of class II trees that die in t years

I = No. of class I trees

II = No. of class II trees

A = the arbitrary number by which calculated yield can be increased or decreased depending on the condition of the crop.

In order to apply this formula, the Working Plan Officer (WPO) has to fix up exploitable diameter.

e.g. Find out the yield of fir spruce from the following data by Smythies Safeguarding Formula :

Class I trees = 66,138 out of which 20,000 are over matured.

Class II trees = 36,499

Felling cycle (f) = 10 years, t = 25 years, Z = 25%

Solution : According to Smythies Safeguarding Formula,

$$\textbf{Annual yield} = \frac{x}{(I + {}^{x}/_{2})} x100 \pm A\%$$

Where, x = No. of trees of class II that will pass into exploitable class I during the felling cycle and is calculated by $\boldsymbol{x = ({}^{f}/_{t})\ (II - Z\%II)}$

f = Felling cycle = 10 years

t = Time taken by II class trees to pass into class I = 25 years

Z = No. of class II trees that die in t years = 25%

I = No. of class I trees = 66,138

II = No. of class II trees = 36,499

A = the arbitrary number by which calculated yield can be increased or decreased depending on the condition of the crop = +10

$\therefore\ x = ({}^{f}/_{t})\ (II - Z\%II)$

$= {}^{10}/_{25}$ (I36499 -25% of 36499)

= 0.40 (36499 - 9125)

= 0.40 x 27374

= 10949.60 $\therefore$ $\boldsymbol{x = 10950}$

Then, **Annual yield** $= \dfrac{x}{(I + {}^{x}/_{2})} x100 \pm A\%$

$$= \frac{10950}{66138 + ({}^{10950}/_{2})} x100 \pm A\%$$

$$= \frac{10950}{71613} x100 \pm A\%$$

Annual yield = 15.29 ± A %

As about ${}^{1}/_{3}$ rd of the class I trees are over mature, **"A" will be taken as + 10,** which is a arbitrary number

$\therefore$ **Yield = 15.29 + 10 = 25.29 %**

❑❑❑

Chapter 11

Working Plan and its Importance

Definition: Working plan is *"a written scheme of management aiming at continuity of policy and action and controlling the treatment of a forest"*. It is synonymously called as "**Instrument of Forest Management**" or "**Management Plan**".

Characteristics of Good Working plan

1. It should be simple and brief, exact and definite for the subordinate staff to follow the prescriptions.
2. It should be based on thorough knowledge of the tract to be dealt with.
3. It should aim at achieving realistic objectives, workable in practice and not idealistic objectives.
4. It should avoid limiting the discretion of the executive staff to an irrational degree, particularly in silviculture matters.
5. It should recognize practical difficulties in respect of marketing and transport problems, limitations of the technical abilities of the staff, co-ordination of the administrative resources in men, money and equipment.
6. It should provide a work of experience, containing all relevant information and a foundation on which all subsequent management plans can be built up.

Objectives of working plan

The primary objective of a meaningful plan is the attaining ***"Maximum benefit to the greatest number of people for all time"***. This ideal condition is afforded by maintaining forests as ***Normal Forest.***

Working plan objective should be the creation of an ideal condition of the forest which meets the aims of the management.

But the aim of forest officer should be in that direction – that of *bringing his forest as near to the normal forest state as may be as possible and keeping in that condition.*

Steps in Working Plan Preparation

Broadly working plan preparation involves :

1. Survey and assessment of the past results, present facts, resources and constraints
2. Analysis of facts for long term plan
3. Short-term plan in conformity with a long-term plan
4. Provision of control of prescriptions, for maintenance of records and collection of data/facts

Working plan period is the period for which detailed prescriptions are laid down in a working plan. It is at present ***10 years.***

Annual Plan of Operations (APO)

Annual Plan of Operation is ***"a tabular statement showing the order and extent of all works to be carried out during the year".***

Such a plan is based on the prescriptions of the working plan where it exists, otherwise on general silvicultural principles as modified by financial prescriptions/provisions.

Preparation of Working Plan

1. Preliminary working plan report

Preliminary working plan report examines the results of past working and decides how far the prescriptions of the previous working plan should be followed and where and in which direction modifications are necessary.

2. First Preliminary Report

It is the preliminary re-connaissance report on the operation of the current working plan. This briefly reviews for each working circle; the results of management, success or failure of fast prescriptions and suggestions for changes.

In case of new working plan, the preliminary report will contain a short description of forest concerned, facts relating to their management, treatments recommended and a sketch map showing the proposed working circles.

In respect of changes in management, generally only tentative proposals are made pending collection of further information by the WPO (Working Plan Officer) during the course of first years field work.

This report also indicates the information to be collected, the maps to be prepared, the type and intensity of enumerations to be carried out and so on.

3. Second Preliminary Report

In some times, a second preliminary report is prepared by the WPO (Working Plan Officer) after the first seasons of field work. In this report, **Part II** of the WP is written up as complete as possible, chapter by chapter, using the standard paragraph headings in their proper order and making it fully self-contained.

4. Field Work

1. Working Season

The WPO should commence the field work immediately after the rainy season and normally continue upto summer. In hilly divisions, the work should be continued till June.

2. Examination of territorial units

The WPO should examine the blocks, compartments and sub-compartments are properly demarcated and adequately sub-divided for the new plan.

3. Compartment description

The WPO will bring all the descriptions of compartments upto date, by incorporating all important changes brought about on account of various factors. Descriptions should be concise and convey an adequate idea regarding composition, quality, age, density and general characteristics of the growing stock.

To obtain a good general idea about the compartment, it is advisable to traverse it in two diametrically opposite directions. The minuteness of description will depend on the method of adopted and the object in view :

a) **Boundaries :** These are checked with entries in the compartment histories or the demarcation register and any discrepancy or encroachments are brought to the notice of territorial staff.

b) **Rock and Soil :** Important facts about soil should be expressed in a few words, describing the underlying rock surface, composition and depth.

c) **Age classes :** This is unimportant in selection forests. In uniform forests, the over wood should be allotted to definite age classes.

d) **Quality :** Measuring the heights and diameters at least **10 dominant** trees in each compartment or sub-compartment assesses the quality of crop; selected trees should be collectively representing the average for the whole area.

e) **Density of stocking :** This is estimated ocularly by inspection and checked with enumeration results. Estimates of quality and density are important, if the yield regulation is based on area and is to be reduced for quality and stocking.

f) **Regeneration :** The adequacy or otherwise of young regeneration and also its condition should be mentioned.

4. Stock Mapping

Stock Map is ***"the map showing distribution of different forests or stand types which have a bearing on management, with information about their composition, age class, etc".***

Detailed descriptions of compartments are tedious and bulky in case of large areas. It would be very difficult to get an idea about the forests even if it is written up with due care. A graphic representation of the nature and composition of the forest (i.e. Stock Map) would probably give a better idea of its condition and contents and could be prepared with much less trouble.

Details reflected in stock maps would depend on the intensity of management and crop composition.

Broadly the main categories to be distinguished are :

a) Crop composition
b) Density
c) Quality
d) Age class
e) Regeneration

For all practical purposes, stock maps show the principle species, their purity and/or mixture, quality, density, age classification by a predetermined pattern of colours, hatchings, symbols, figures, etc.

Preparation of Maps by W.P.O

i) **Management Maps (scale - 1:50,000):** These maps show new Working Circles, Felling Series, Periodic Blocks and other details of management.

ii) **Stock Maps (scale - 1:15000):** These maps give the distribution forest types and main forest species, non-forest areas, blanks, etc.

iii) **Regeneration Survey Map (scale - 1:5000 or 1:4000):** The result of regeneration survey is plotted on a large scale map with 1:5000 or 1:4000 scale for field use during marking, cultural operations, etc.

iv) **Working Plan Map (scale - 1:50,000):** These maps show all features which are reasonably permanent, such as physiographic features, territorial boundaries including pillars and their numbers, names of blocks, compartments, Forest Rest Houses (FRH), roads, railways and main features of the country around the reserved forests.

v) **Enumeration Map (scale - 1:50,000):** This map is prepared by WPO showing location of plots, strips, topographic units, compartments and sub-compartments actually enumerated.

vi) **Forest Type Map (scale - 1:50,000):** These maps show forest types. For each main group, the following colour scheme may be used :

Sl.No	Group designation	Colour
1	Tropical wet evergreen	Violet
2	Tropical semi evergreen	Purple
3	Tropical moist deciduous	Cobalt blue
4	Littoral and swamp forest	Prussian blue
5	Tropical dry deciduous	Yellow
6	Tropical thorn	Red
7	Tropical dry evergreen	Pink
8	Sub tropical broad leaved hill forests	Vermillion
9	Sub tropical pine	Orange
10	Sub tropical dry evergreen	Burnt umber
11	Northern wet temperate	Olive green
12	Himalayan moist temperate	Green
13	Himalayan dry temperate	Yellow
14	Sub alpine	Burnt sienna
15 & 16	Alpine	Sepia

vi) **Reference Map :** This map show main boundaries of the forests, ranges, roads, canals, FRHs, neighbouring towns and villages, etc. Scale of the map will depend on the size and shape of the division.

vii) **Soil Map :** This is a divisional map on a convenient scale showing broad soil types on the basis of data collected in the soil survey during the WP field work.

Note : A Register of the maps will be kept in the W.P. Office.

5. Writing up the Working Plan

A working plan is a comprehensive reference document for the concerned forest area; as such it should contain all relevant statistics and data in a very concise form.

It is necessary to reproduce for ready reference all government orders pertaining to grant of rights and concessions to local people, regulation of grazing, etc. as also the legal position of the forests.

In modern working plans, there should be more stress on the ecological, environmental and socio-economic aspects, watershed management, recreational forestry, etc. rather than on mere commercial timber exploitation.

The Working Plan should consist of **two parts :**

Part-I dealing with the factual information about the area

Part-II dealing with the prescriptive part (future management) followed by appendices

In addition, the WPO will also update the compartment Histories and stock maps and prepare control forms.

Control and Records

System of control : The WPO will prepare a draft set of control forms to control all operations prescribed and suggested in his W.P. These forms will be submitted to CF (WP) for approval and preparation of final copies. The deviations got approved by the CF (WP) or CCF.

Control Forms : Are prescribed to control the sequence of operations, tending operations, plantations and artificial regeneration, revenue and expenditure.

Compartment histories : The WPO should bring all sets of compartment histories to date and hand over back to the DFO (T).

Plantation Journal : The WPO should prescribe the maintenance of separate *Plantation Journal* for each plantation in an appropriate form.

Fire Records : The details of areas burnt, damage caused, etc. will be recorded in "Fire Records" along with the sketch maps of the areas burnt. DFO (T) sends reports to the CF / CCF as per instructions.

Climate Register : Observations of temperature and rainfall, depth of wells and water table, floods, drought, storms are recorded in this register.

Flowering of bamboos and seed years of principal species: These observations are recorded in a separate register.

Deforestation and Afforestation Records : These observations are recorded in a separate register.

Game Record : The observations regarding regulations of wildlife, notifications for creation wildlife parks and sanctuaries are maintained in a separate register.

Cattle Census : The observations on census conducted are recorded in a separate register.

Standard Format of Writing Up of the Working Plan

Introduction : Glossary of Botanical Terms and List of Common Animals and Birds

Part-I

Summary of facts on which the proposals are based :

Chapter I : The Tract Dealt With

- Name and situations
- Configuration of the ground
- Geology: Rock and Soil
- Climate
- Water supply
- Distribution and Area
- State of Boundaries
- Legal position
- Rights and concessions

Chapter II: Flora and Fauna

Part A – Forest Flora

- Occurrence and distribution of the species
- Composition and condition of the crop
- General description of the growing stock
- Injuries to which the crop is liable

Part B – Forest Fauna

I. General description

a) Animals

i) Game animals: carnivores, Herbivores

ii) Non-game animals

b) Birds: Game birds, land birds and aquatic birds

c) Reptiles

d) Fishes

II. Injuries to which the fauna is liable

III Protection and management of the fauna

Chapter III. Utilization of the Produce

- Agricultural customs and wants of the population
- Markets and marketable products
- Lines of export
- Methods of exploitation and their cost
- Past and current prices

Chapter IV. Staff and Labour Supply

Chapter V. Past Systems and Management

- General history of the forests
- Past systems of the management and their results
- Special works of improvement and their results
- Past yield
- Past revenue and expenditure

Chapter VI. Statastics of Growth and Yield

Part-II

Future management discussed and prescribed.

Chapter I. Basis of Proposals

- General objects of management
- Method of treatment to be adopted
- Working circles, their area and distribution, reasons for their constitution

- Block and Compartments
- Period of Working Plan and necessary for intermediate revision

Chapter II. Working Plan for the .... Working Circle

- General constitution
- General chapter of the vegetation
- Blocks and Compartments
- Felling Series and Cutting Sections
- Special objects of management
- Area and allotment
- Analysis and valuation of the maps
  - Stock Maps
  - Quality and Age classes
  - Density
  - Enumeration and their results
- Silvicultural systems
- Rotation and conversion period
- Exploitable diameters
- Reducing factors and reducing areas
- Felling cycle
- Division into periods and allotment to periodic blocks
- Calculation of the yield
- Table of fellings
- Method of executing the fellings
- Subsidiary silvicultural operations and their economics
  - General operations
  - Clearings and Thinnings
- Supplementary fellings
- Artificial regeneration and their economics
  - Treatment of existing plantations
  - Nursery techniques

- New plantations and method of establishment, etc.
- Choice of species
- Fencing and tending

- Other regulations
  - Fire protection and control burning
  - Grazing
  - Exercise of rights and concessions
- Economic analysis
- Effect of prescriptions on the environment and the ecosystem

Chapter III, IV, V *etc.* – One Chapter for Each Working Circle

Chapter .... Raw Material for Forest Industries

Chapter .... Wildlife Management

Chapter......... Watershed Management and Soil Conservation

Chapter......... Multiple use Forestry-outdoor Recreation and Environmental Conservation

Chapter .... Miscellaneous Regulations

(Prescribed and suggested)

- Petty fellings
- Deviations
- Roads, paths and bridges
- Buildings
- Water supply
- Telephones
- Fire protection
- Maintenance of boundaries
- Rights and concessions
- Survey and maps
- Research plots
- Lopping schemes

- Medical facilities
- Development of industries

Chapter .... Establishment and Labour

Chapter .... Control and Records

- System of control
- Control forms
- Compartment histories
- Plantation journals
- Divisional note book
- Fire records
- Forest records

Chapter .... Financial Forecast and Cost of the Plan

- Past yield
- Future yield
- Past revenue and expenditure
- Future revenue and expenditure
- Summary of the financial forecast
- Cost of enumeration
- Cost of the working plan

Chapter .... Summary of Prescriptions

Appendices: - Estate area statement

- Stock maps
- Result of enumeration and estimation of growing stock
- Status of the regeneration
- Compartment history forms
- Results of socio-economic survey.

❑❑❑

Chapter 12

Joint Forest Planning and Management (JFPM)

Joint Forest Management (JFM)

The Joint Forest Management (JFM) seeks to develop partnerships between local community institutions (as managers) and state forest departments (as owners) for sustainable management and joint benefit sharing public forest lands (usually degraded).

The National Forest Policy, 1988 envisages people's involvement in the development and protection of forests. It has also been felt that forest management programmes need to be reoriented in such a manner that they respond to rural communities needs and that the forest produce, fuel wood, minor forest produce, timber, etc. are available to the villagers preferentially, apart from a share in the proceeds, so that village communities are motivated to identify themselves with the development and protection of forests.

The official ground for JFM was prepared by the National Forest Policy, 1988. They reversed the forest management aspects by creating massive peoples movement, with involvement of local people in achieving forest management objectives. This was followed on **1st June, 1990** by circular ***(Letter No. 6-21/1981, dated 1-6-1990)*** from the Secretary to the Government of India, Ministry of Environment and Forests, New Delhi to the forest secretaries of all states and union territories providing guidelines for the "Involvement of village communities and voluntary agencies in the regeneration of degraded forests.

Objective of JFM

The primary objective of JFM is "involvement of people in the protection and management to check the speed of deforestation and to rehabilitate the degraded forest for multiple benefits to the society and local communities".

Origin

- The early experiment of JFM concept was started in 1970's (1971 -72) itself in ***Arabari village*** of **Midnapur district** (West Bengal) on degraded **Sal** forests.
- In 1976-77, it was initiated in ***Sukhomajri village*** of Haryana.
- In 1980-1990, the ***Jhabua experiment*** in the **Madhya Pradesh** in unique example for JFM concept.

Joint Forest Planning and Management (JFPM) in Karnataka

JFPM is a comprehensive scheme of the Karnataka Forest Department (KFD) to partner with and involve local village communities in the conservation and sustainable management of forests.

This involves the formation of Village Forest Committees (VFCs) to formally enter into partnership agreements with the forest department for planning and implementing various forest protection, conservation and development programmes.

This is done based on the Joint Forest Management Plan (JFMP) that the villagers evolve in collaboration with the forest department and various government and non-government agencies.

Why was JFPM initiated?

Over the decades there has been an alarming decrease in forest cover in India. This was due to continuous encroachment and destruction of forests for agriculture, timber, mining, industrial development, water resources development, power generation, urban development, etc. Forest management, being oriented towards exploitation of forests for their commercial value, excluded the involvement of local communities and neglected their interests. This disturbed the strong sense of ownership and protection of forests that existed amongst local communities, and made their survival difficult due to decreased access to forest resources.

In the mean time, over-exploitation of forest resources, encroachment, illicit tree felling, poaching of wild animals, forest fires, smuggling of timber and overgrazing have increased resulting in the destruction and degradation of forests. Despite stringent forest protection law, increase in staff, communication networking and intensive patrolling the situation has not improved. Also, there is an alarming increase in the number of conflicts between the local communities and the forest department.

It is now being realized that the Forest Department staff, spread thinly over hundreds of square kilometres, simply cannot adequately protect forests from further destruction and degradation. A new forest management approach involves local communities and provides them benefits for protecting and improving forests is essential. This will have positive impact on the social and economic situation, and improve the extent and quality of our forests. JFPM embodies this new approach.

How the Government policies support the JFPM?

The National Forest Policy (NFP), 1988, envisages involvement of the people in the protection and development of forests. Government of India, Ministry of Environment and Forests, in letter dated ***1st June, 1990*** issued guidelines to the State Governments for involving Village Communities and Voluntary agencies in the regeneration of degraded forest lands and outlined the approach of initiating JFM.

Karnataka is one of the earliest states to issue a Government Order (G.O) No. AHFF 232 FAP 86, Bangalore dated ***12th April, 1993*** for the implementation of the JFPM scheme.

Which areas come under JFPM?

1. Degraded forest lands, where the ***canopy density is 0.25 and less.***
2. Reserved forests that are pre-dominately inhabited by the tribal people or in the vicinity of areas, where forest dependent tribal people live or which they traditionally depend upon for their livelihood or which they culturally identify themselves with, may also be subjected to JFPM involving tribal irrespective of the density of the canopy cover of the forests.
3. Government wastelands, C&D class lands, gomal lands, unclassified lands and other lands under the control of the Revenue department transferred for the purpose of JFPM to the Forest Department.
4. Roadsides, canal banks and tank foreshores and other non-forest lands under the control of Karnataka Forest Department (KFD).

Whether the protected areas (PA's) come under JFPM?

National parks and Wildlife sanctuaries do not come under JFPM. However, ***Eco Development Committees (EDC's)*** could be formed for PA's where there is no sharing of forest produce.

"The state forests which are pre-dominately inhabited by tribal population or where the forest department tribals living in and around the state forests are traditionally dependent upon the forests for their livelihood and cultural identity such forests, irrespective of the density of the canopy cover of the forests, may also be subjected to the Joint Forest Planning and Management".

What is the method of disposal of forest produce and sharing pattern?

The beneficiaries identified through the VFC will be entitled to grasses, leaves and fuel wood free of coat, from the JFPM areas of forests as well as other non-forest lands, upon fulfillment of the prescribed conditions. The beneficiaries shall also be entitled for lops and tops and pruning free of cost. The distribution of such produce will be supervised by the managing committee of the VFC. The managing committee shall ensure a fair and equitable distribution of the above forest produce to all the right holders. The committee may work out its own principles and mechanism for distribution of produce with a view of meeting the needs of the local people.

Regarding the disposal of Minor forest produce/fruits, timber and fuel wood, the requirement of the local village should be treated as a first charge on such final produce. The surplus, after meeting the demands of the concerned villages, shall be disposed off by the VFC through open public auction.

As it would be difficult to determine exactly the local needs of the villagers in absolute terms, 50 per cent of the MFP, fruits, timber and final harvest shall until further orders be made available for local sale through VFC's to meet the needs of the local villagers at rates to be fixed by the Forest Department form time to time. The balance 50 per cent of the MFP, fruits, timber and final harvest will be disposed of through public auction.

The proceeds arising from local sale by the VFC as well as those arising from the disposal through auction, after deducting all the expenditure incurred on the final harvest and auction, shall be shared between the Government, beneficiaries and the VFC in the ratio's mentioned below :

As for as the degraded forest lands and non-forest Government wastelands belonging to the Revenue Department are concerned, the sharing would be on the following pattern:

50 per cent to Government

25 per cent to the beneficiaries through the VFC as per the rules to be framed for the purpose; and

25 per cent to a special fund to be called Village Forest Development Fund (VFDF). This fund will be operated by the VFC as per rules to be framed by the Government in consultation with the Principal Chief Conservator of Forests (PCCF).

Impacts of JFPM

The JFPM programme has led to several positive impacts like :

1. **Improvement in the condition of the forests :** This is corroborated by the fact that the past few years the over all forest cover of the country has increased by *3896 sq. km and dense cover by 10098 sq. km* and incidence of illicit felling has been declined. Reports reveals that prolific growth of under storey vegetation in many instances, has led to increased biodiversity and relatively rapid increase in the wild herbivore populations.
2. **Increase in income :** The committees have benefitted from the employment generated under JFPM projects through micro-planning, sale of non-timber forest products and bamboo yield, etc. Many VFCs have sustained the level of community funds, which are used for local developmental activities and personal loans, thus lessening the bondage of money lenders.
3. **Reduction in encroachment :** In many places, JFPM has helped reduce area under illegal encroachments.
4. **Involvement of NGOs :** The JFPM programme has led to a considerable involvement of NGOs and community based organizations through the degree of involvement.
5. **Change in attitude and relationship :** One of the most significant impacts of JFPM programme has been the change in the attitude

of local committees and officials towards each other and towards forests. It was unthinkable in pre-JFPM days that Divisional Forest Officer will sit and discuss with villagers while now even top forest management is easily accessible to villagers, as department has accepted the role of facilitator.

Constraints in effective implementation of JFPM

1. Lack of co-ordination between local people and forest department, forest department and NGO's and vice versa.
2. Gender inequality – non involvement of women in JFPM activities.
3. Community problems - Caste, Status, Tribes, Class and internal hierarchies.
4. Non effective involvement of peoples in the programme.
5. Lack of awareness about importance of forest among peoples.
6. Inefficient Forest Department people in motivating people about JFPM and its importance.
7. Lack of motivating village leaders.
8. Insufficient funds for effective implementation.
9. Inter and intra village equity issues.
10. Focus on forest protection for timber production rather than need based forest management.

Future approach

The JFPM has to be managed in future with the following objectives :

1. Suitable silvicultural practices especially the raising nurseries like use of mulches, clonal propagation, etc.
2. Quick growing species to be developed
3. Suitable model of multi-tier plantation to be developed and demonstrated
4. The high yielding varieties of NTFPs to be propagated and demonstrated
5. Multiple uses, high yielding varieties of fuel wood, fodder, and fruit bearing species, are to be planted for improving the economic condition of the people.

Salient features of Joint Forest Planning and Management in Karnataka

Order	N. AHFF 232 FAP86, Bangalore on 2nd April, 1993
Definition	Community POarticipation by formation of Village Forest Committee for planning, implementation, protection, harvest and sharing of produce
Objective	Protection, maintenance, regeneration and community need based management of forest
Management	VFCs should be registered under Karnataka Societies Act. Interested members from the village should form the promoter's committee frm the General Body and work out by laws.
Membership	Open to all households residing in the notified area or jurisdiction of the VFC by paying Rs. 2, for SC/ST Rs. 1/-
Managing Commiittee	15 mermbers comprise Managing Committee. 11 (Chairman, women-2, SC/ST-2, Artisans-1, Land less Labour-1 and General-4) are elected by General bdy and 4 are ex-officio members. Section Forester will be ex-oficio Secretary from Karnataka Forest Department.
Election of Managing Committee	General body to elect 10 members and Chairman. Local Revenue Inspector will be the presiding officer to conduct the election for VFC
Tenure of Managing Committee & Meetings	Five years. It should meet once in a quarter of a year
Functions of Managing Committee	(1) Planning, (2) Implementation of the approved Joint Forest Planning and Management (JFPM), (3) Sharing of the produce, (4) Carrying out day-to-day affairs; protection and conservation.
JFPM Area	Forest having less than 25% of canopy and other Govt. lands. This area is not sold/leased/handed over to the VFC but the beneficiaries have usufructory rights over the produce.
Sharing of produce	(1) Free access to leaves and fodder, (2) Harvested produce is shared between the Forest Department and VFC in a 50:50 ratio. Out of its 50% share, the VFC credits 25% to the Village Forest Development Fund, the rest of the produce is distributed to VFC members or credited to Village Development Fund.
Memorandum of Understanding Financial Assistance	Signed between the VFC (Managing Committee) and the Forest Department. The village Forest Development Fund will be created from revenue generated from sales proceeds and membership fees. Forest Department will provide initial expenditure.
Decision-Making	VFC, jointly with the Forest Department, decides about planting of trees and the species to be planted, based on their requirement.

Access to usufructory rights	Households in the jurisdiction are eligible to enter the forest to collect the produce like fruits, grass, twigs and branches for bonafide use
Women's participation	Women are members or co-members of the VFC. Out of the 10 elected members of the Managing Committee, at least two should be women.
Maintenance of records	The Secretary (Forester or Guard with SSLC qualification) is responsible for maintaining account, minutes and funds of the VFC.
Supervision	Forest Department officers of rank DCF and above should attend Managing Committee meetings of alol VFCs, at least once in 6 months.
JFPM Plan	Prepared by the Managing Committee in consultation with the Forest Department and approved by the General Body. Final approval by the DCF.
Role of NGOs	NGOs can act as promoters, but cannot claim benefits for participation.
Employment generation	To execute the JFPM plans local labour can be employed on a priority basis, and wages paid according to department norms.

Chapter 13

Microplan and its Application

Meaning of the terms used in "Microplan Preparation" (as defined)

i) **"Microplan"** means the scheme of management of a village forest.

ii) **"Sarpanch"** means the Sarpanch of a Forest Panchayat.

iii) **"Village community"** means such persons as are registered in the electoral rolls relating to village.

iv) **"Village committee"** means a Village Forest Committee or Forest Panchayat.

v) **"Village Forest Committee"** means a committee constituted under sub-section (6) of Section 29 of the United Provinces Panchayat Raj Act, 1947 for the purposes of these rules.

vi) **"Village Forest"** means a village forest referred to in Section 28 of the Act.

Preparation of Microplan and Annual Implementation Plan

A microplan for a period of five years shall be prepared for the management and protection of a village forest by the Village Committee with the assistance of forest officials, in such manner, as may be directed by the Forest Department. The microplan shall be placed before the village community for its approval before it is finally sanctioned by the Divisional Committee constituted under Rule 7.

The Village Committee shall prepare every year an Annual Implementation Plan in Form 2 for the management and development of village forest on the basis of the sanctioned microplan and submit it to the Range Committee constituted under Rule 7. The Range Committee shall place the Annual Implementation Plan before the Divisional Committee on or before the first day of September in every year.

Constitution and Functions of Various Committees

I. There shall be a Range Committee for village forests in each range

The **Range Committee** shall consist of the following members:

1. Pramukh of the concerned Kshetra Panchayat - **Ex officio Chairman.**
2. One member from amongst women Pradhans of the Gram Panchayats in the concerned Khand nominate dby the Pramukh of the concerned Kshetra Panchayat - **Member.**
3. One member from amongst Pradhans of the Gram Panchayats in the concerned Khand belonging to the Scheduled Castes / Scheduled Tribes nominated by the Pramukh of the concerned Kshetra Panchayat - **Member.**
4. One member from amongst Pradhans of the Gram Panchayats in the concerned Khand nominated by the Pramukh of the concerned Kshetra Panchayat - **Member.**
5. One member nominated by the Divisional Forest Officer from amongst residents of the range - **Member.**
6. Range Forest officer of the Range - **Member Secretary.**

There shall be a Divisional Committee for village forests in each division.

II. The Divisional Committee shall consist of the following members:

1. Divisional Forest Officer of the Division - **Chairman**
2. One person from amongst residents of the Division nominated by Adhyaksha, Zila Panchayat - **Member.**
3. The Assistant Conservator of Forests/Sub -Divisional Officer in-charge of the spearhead team - **Member.**
4. One person from amongst member of voluntary organisations nominated by the Divisional Forest Officer - **Member**
5. One officer from amongst Assistant Conservators of Forests/Sub-Divisional Officers in the Division nominated by the Divisional Forest Officer - **Member - Secretary.**

The Range Committee shall meet at least **once in every month** and the Divisional Committee shall meet at least **once in every four months**. The quorum of the meeting shall be **one-third of the**

members. For attending a meeting, only the bus fare will be admissible to non-official members from the place of their residence to the place of the meeting. All expenditure in regard thereto shall be incurred from the budget of the microplan.

The duties /Responsibilities of the Range Committee:

1. Examine and consolidate the Annual Plan for the Village Forest in the Range.
2. Inspect, supervise and verify the works done by the Village Committee.
3. Inspect account book and other records maintained by the Village Committee and take assistance of the concerned Range Officer.
4. Ensure that all the Village Committees in the Range are discharging the duties and exercising the powers assigned to them properly, equitably and justly. In case of any default, the Range Committee shall intervene promptly and report the matter to the Divisional Forest Officer.
5. Submit budget proposals to the Divisional Committee in accordance with the instructions issued by State Government in this behalf.
6. Discharge such other duties as may be assigned by the Divisional Forest Officer.

The duties / Responsibilities of the the Divisional Committee:

1. Examine and approve the microplan for the village forest;
2. Supervise and monitor the works of Village Committees and Range Committees;
3. Perform such other functions as may be directed by the Divisional Forest Officer and the State Government.

Procedure for Transaction of Business of Village Committee, Range Committee and Divisional Committee

A Village Committee shall meet at least once in every month at such time and place, as may be appointed by the **Chairman of the Village Committee**

i) All matters which come up before a village committee, Range Committee or Divisional Committee shall be decided by a majority of the members present and by voting.

ii) The Chairman of Village Committee, Range Committee or Divisional Committee, as the case may be, and in his absence, a member duly elected in this behalf by the members present in the meeting, shall preside over the meetings of the village committee, Range Committee or Divisional Committee, as the case may be.

iii) A prior notice of at least seven days of the meeting of a village committee, and of fifteen days for the meeting of the Range Committee and Divisional Committee, shall be given to the members of the concerned Committee.

iv) Two third members shall form quorum of the village committee.

v) All the decisions of a village committee, Range Committee or Divisional Committee shall be recorded in a minute book to be kept for the purpose.

Funds

For the management of the village forest under these rules, the Village Committee shall arrange funds. As far as possible, the funds shall be arranged from the Government and non-Government sources including contributions by the village community and through the income under Rule 11. Whenever the Government provides fund for the management of the village forest, it shall be released in installments by the Divisional Forest Officer in accordance with the orders of the Government issued in this behalf from time-to-time.

Operation of Accounts

The funds referred to in Rule 8 and all other money received shall be deposited in the name of the concerned Village Committee in a Nationalized Bank, Scheduled Bank, Co-operative Bank or Post Office and shall be operated jointly by the Chairman and Member – Secretary of the Village Committee.

All withdrawals from the Bank shall be made with the prior approval of the village committee and details of the amount withdrawn and the expenditure incurred shall be placed before the Village Community in its next meeting.

The procedure for incurring expenditure and its accounting shall be in accordance with the orders issued by the State Government from time-to-time.

Accounts and Audit

The village committee shall maintain proper accounts and other relevant records and prepare an annual statement of accounts in accordance with the directions of the Government.

The accounts of a Village Committee shall be audited by the Director of Accounts and local bodies.

Allotment of Income

The apportionment of the income out of sale of forest produce, and through fees, permits, compensation and other means under these rules shall be made in the following manner :

1. The share of the village community in the income after deducting the cost of investment and after meeting rights and privileges shall be fifty per cent subject to the maximum of Rs. 50,000 in a year calculated from the date of the agreement referred to in Rule 3;
2. Provided that not more than fifty per cent of the share of the income of the village community shall be distributed to the members of the village community and remaining fifty per cent amount shall be spent on the community works including recycling of funds for the management of village forest;
3. After allotment of the income to the village community under Clause (i) the rest of the income shall be allotted to the owner of the land;
4. Provided that half of the amount referred to in this clause shall be spent for the development of the village forest.

❑❑❑

Chapter 14

Sustainable Forest Management (SFM)

A definition of sustainable tropical forest management for wood production

It is important to define the meaning of the term **sustainable management of tropical forests,** where it is applied to the production of wood. A study undertaken for the International Tropical Timber Organization led to a definition having these primary considerations:

i) Sustainable forest management should be practiced on an operational and not an experimental scale.

ii) It should embrace a balanced and comprehensive range of management activities that include working plans, yield prediction and control and other technical requirements.

iii) It should include the wider political, social and economic criteria without which sustainability is probably unattainable.

iv) **Criteria :** Criteria define the essential factors of forest management against which forest sustainability may be assessed. Each criterion relates to a key management factor which may be described by one or more qualitative, quantitative or descriptive indicators.

v) **Indicators :** Through measurement and monitoring of selected indicators, the effects of forest management action, or inaction, can be assessed and evaluated and action adjusted to ensure that forest management objectives are more likely to be achieved.

Criteria and Indicators for Sustainable Forest Management

Criteria and indicators for sustainable management at national and the forest level

Criteria and indicators are tools which can be used to define, implement and monitor Sustainable forest management in the broadest sense of the term, nationally and at the forest level.

Features of the ITTO Guidelines Concerning Sustainable Forest Management at National and Forest Levels

A. National Level

1. Policy and Legislation

i) Forest policy
ii) National forest inventory
iii) Permanent forest estate
iv) Forest ownership
v) National forest service

B. Forest Level

1. Planning

i) Static and dynamic inventory
ii) Setting of management objectives
iii) Choice of silvicultural concept
iv) Yield regulation
v) Annual allowable cut
vi) Management inventory
vii) Mapping
viii) Preparation of working plans
ix) Environmental impact assessment

2. Harvesting

i) Pre-harvest prescriptions
ii) Roads
iii) Extraction
iv) Post-harvest stand management

3. Protection

i) Control of access
ii) Fire protection
iii) Use of chemicals

4. Legal Arrangements

i) Concession agreements

ii) Salvage permits

iii) Logging permits on private or customary land

5. Monitoring and Research

i) Yield control and silviculture

ii) Environmental impact studies

Sustainable Forest Management (SFM)

Sustainable forest management (SFM) is the management of forests according to the principles of sustainable development. Sustainable forest management uses very broad social, economic and environmental goals. A range of forestry institutions now practice various forms of sustainable forest management and a broad range of methods and tools are available that have been tested over time.

Definition

Sustainable forest management is defined as **"The stewardship and use of forests and forest lands in a way, and at a rate, that maintains their biodiversity, productivity, regeneration capacity, vitality and their potential to fulfill, now and in the future, relevant ecological, economic and social functions, at local, national, and global levels, and that does not cause damage to other ecosystems".**

In simpler terms, the ***concept can be described as the attainment of balance – balance between society's increasing demands for forest products and benefits, and the preservation of forest health and diversity***. This balance is critical to the survival of forests, and to the prosperity of forest-dependent communities.

There appears to be growing international consensus on the key elements of sustainable forest management. Seven common thematic areas of sustainable forest management have emerged based on the criteria of the nine ongoing regional and international criteria and indicators initiatives.

The seven thematic areas are:

- Extent of forest resources
- Biological diversity

- Forest health and vitality
- Productive functions and forest resources
- Protective functions of forest resources
- Socio-economic functions
- Legal, policy and institutional framework.

This consensus on common thematic areas (or criteria) effectively provides a common, implicit definition of sustainable forest management. **The seven thematic areas were acknowledged by the international forest community at the fourth session of the United Nations Forum on Forests and the 16th session of the Committee on Forestry**. These thematic areas have since been enshrined in the **Non-Legally Binding Instrument on All Types of Forests** as a reference framework for sustainable forest management to help achieve the purpose of the instrument.

On January 5, 2012, the Montreal Process, Forest Europe, the International Tropical Timber Organization, and the Food and Agriculture Organization of the United Nations, acknowledging the seven thematic areas, endorsed a joint statement of collaboration to improve global forest related data collection and reporting and avoiding the proliferation of monitoring requirements and associated reporting burdens.

Definitions and Basic Principles of Sustainable Forest Management In Relation to Criteria and Indicators

Afforestation : The establishment of trees by sowing, planting or natural regeneration on areas from which trees have always or very long been absent.

Assessment : The process by which information about forest management is collected with a view to establishing, within a defined framework of expectations, the current status and probable future direction of interactions between human beings and forests, using certain criteria and indicators.

Biological diversity : The variability among living organisms from all sources including, *inter alia,* terrestrial, marine and other aquatic ecosystems and the ecological complexes of which they are part; this includes diversity within species, between species and of ecosystems.

Biomass : The total aboveground living organic matter in trees expressed as oven dry tons per unit area. It is referred to as biomass density when expressed as mass per unit area, e.g. tons per hectare. Excludes stumps and roots (belowground biomass), foliage, flowers and seeds. Different procedures in estimating biomass will be followed for the different vegetation types.

Conservation forest : Areas set aside by law or some other ruling for conservation purposes, for example: national parks, biological reserves, water reservoirs.

Criterion : A category of conditions or process by which sustainable forest management can be assessed. A criterion is characterized by a set of related indicators, which are monitored periodically to assess change (Montreal Process, 1995).

A criterion describes the different sides of sustainability on a conceptual level. It is a distinguishing element or set of conditions or processes by which a forest characteristic or management measure is judged (Pan-European Forest Process, 1994).

Deforestation : A non-temporary change of land use from forest to other land use or depletion of forest crown cover to less than 10 per cent. Clear cuts (even with stump removal), if shortly followed by reforestation for forestry purposes are not considered deforestation.

Degradation : Changes within the forest class (from closed to open forest), which negatively affect the stand or site and, in particular, that lower the biological productivity capacity and diversity.

Desertification : Land degradation in arid, semi-arid and dry sub-humid areas resulting from various factors, including climate variations and human activities.

Ecosystem : A community of plant and animal species and micro-organisms, considered together as a functional system which includes the complex, ever changing relations that exist among plants, animals and microbes, including man, and their environment. The term is used in identifying a certain forest site type (e.g. health forest). The term 'habitat' is used in a general sense for the place, where an organism is found (FAO, 1989).

Exotic (introduced) species : Any species growing or living outside its natural range of occurrence. Normally, this refers to species purposely or accidentally introduced into countries or regions they do not historically occur.

Exploitable forest : A forest on which there are no legal, economic or technical restrictions on wood and non-wood production. It includes areas where, although there are no such restrictions, harvesting is not currently taking place; for example, areas included in long-term utilization plans.

Forest : Land with tree crown cover (or equivalent stocking level) of more than 10 per cent and area of more than 0.5 ha. The trees should be able to reach a minimum height of 5 m at maturity in situ. May consist either of closed forest formations, where trees of various storeys and undergrowth cover a high proportion of the ground, or of open forest formations with a continuous vegetation cover in which tree crown cover exceeds 10 per cent. Young natural stands and all plantations established for forestry purposes which have yet to reach a crown density of 10 per cent or tree height of 5m are included under forest, as are areas normally forming part of the forest area which are temporarily unstocked as a result of human intervention or natural causes but which are expected to revert to forest. Includes: Forest nurseries and seed orchards that constitute an integral part of the forest; forest roads, cleared tracts, firebreaks and other small open areas within the forest; forest in national parks, nature reserves and other protected areas such as those of special environmental, scientific, historical, cultural or spiritual interest; windbreaks and shelterbelts of trees with an area of more than 0.5 ha and a width of more than 20 m. Rubber wood plantations and cork oak stands are included. **Excludes:** Land predominantly used for agricultural practices.

Forestry : Activities related to the management of forests and other wooded land for the production and supply of wood and/or other goods and services.

Forest degradation : Impoverishment of standing woody material mainly caused by human activities, such as over-grazing, over-exploitation (for firewood in particular), repeated fires, or due attacks by insects, diseases, plant parasites or other natural causes such as cyclones. Very often degradation does not show up so much in decrease of woody vegetation but rather as a gradual reduction in biomass, changes in species composition and soil degradation.

Forest ecosystem : An ecological system composed of interacting biotic and abiotic components of the environment in which trees are a major constituent, such that their canopies cover 20 per cent or more of the area.

Forest goods and products : Wood and non-wood forest products obtained from forests.

Forest land : Countries have defined forest land differently and, as such, a single definition is not possible here. When reporting, each country should provide its own definition for forestland.

Forest management unit : A clearly demarcated area of land covered pre-dominantly by forests, managed to a set of explicit objectives and according to a long-term forest management plan. A forest management unit may cover several hundred hectares to fractions of. The entire area of the forest management unit will have to be clearly demarcated on the ground and usually also on a map. Under the broad objectives to which the entire management unit is subjected, sub-units may be managed under different and separate management regimes.

Forest services : Environmental services (e.g. conservation of soil, water, biological diversity; micro and macro climatic effects; nutrient cycling) and socio-cultural services other than those provided by the production of wood and non-wood products (e.g. recreation and tourism, protection of cultural, aesthetic and scientific values) provided by forests.

Forest type : Classification of forestland based on species forming a plurality of live-tree stocking. Type (e.g. low forest, multi-layered forest, even-aged forest, etc.) is determined on the basis of species plurality of all live trees that contribute to stocking (Pan-European Forest Process, 1994).

Function : The set of processes that results from interactions among biotic and abiotic components of the ecosystem. Four classes of processes are important:

i) processes that affect the rate and total quantity of energy;

ii) processes that affect the rate and total quantity of nutrient cycling;

iii) processes that influence ecosystem services important to human beings; and

iv) processes that affect the life and diversity of living organisms over both short and long-time periods

Growing stock : The living tree component of the standing volume.

Guideline : A recommendation that leads or directs a course of action to achieve a certain goal.

Indicator : The fulfillment of a criterion is evaluated by using indicators. A typical indicator is a measure of an aspect of the criterion or a measurable quantitative, qualitative or descriptive variable which when compared to previous measurements demonstrates changes or trends. The indicator has to be judged on a scale of acceptable standards of performance which may vary widely from region-to-region and from time-to-time. Some aspects of criteria cannot be quantified. Their fulfillment can only be judged through the existence and effective implementation of a regulatory framework.

By repeatedly measuring the fulfillment of the criteria, countries can evaluate whether forest management is moving towards or away from sustainability. Also, they can be used as a tool for reporting on the implementation of the commitments made and thus whether the objectives set are being met.

Monitoring : Based on repeated data collection, periodic and systematic measurement and assessment of changes in indicators.

Natural forest : A forest that has evolved and reproduced itself naturally from organisms previously established, and that has not been significantly altered by human activity.

Non-wood forest products : Goods of biological origin other than wood, derived from forests, other wooded land and trees outside forests.

Other wooded land: Land either with a tree crown cover (or equivalent stocking level) of 5-10 per cent of trees able to reach a height of 5 m at maturity in situ; or a crown cover (or equivalent stocking level) of more than 10 per cent of trees not able to reach a height of 5 m at maturity in situ (e.g. dwarf or stunted trees) and shrub or bush cover. **Excludes :** Areas having the tree, shrub or bush cover specified above but of less than 0.5 ha and width of 20 m, which are classed under "other land". Land pre-dominantly used for agricultural practices. It excludes land occupied by "trees outside the forest".

Plantation forests : Forest stands established by planting or/and seeding in the process of afforestation or reforestation. They are either of introduced species (all planted stands), or intensively managed stands of indigenous species which meet all the following criteria: one or two species at plantation, even age class, regular spacing. **Excludes :** Stands which were established as plantations but which have been without intensive management for a significant period of time. These should be considered semi-natural.

Principle : A fundamental law or rule as a guide to action; a rule of conduct; a fundamental motive or reason for action, especially one consciously recognized and followed. A principle is commonly formulated around a core concept based on social ethics, values, and tradition as well as on scientific knowledge. Usually principles can be expressed concisely and crisply, for example, sustainable development principle, sustained yield principle, sovereignty principle, polluter pays principle, and a set of forest principles negotiated at the World Summit (CSCE Seminar and Montreal Process, 1993).

Production forest : A forest managed to harvest forest products and to sustain the bioproductivity of the system.

Productive forest : An area of forest capable of producing wood for more than a certain predicted amount, e.g. the increment volume is more than 1 m^3/ha/year in the foreseeable future.

Protected area : As defined by the International Union of Nature Conservation (IUCN) a protected area is an area of land and/or sea, especially dedicated to the protection and maintenance of biological diversity, and of natural and associated cultural resources, managed through legal or other effective means.

Protection forest : A forest that is generally situated on broken ground, or ground subjected to periodic or permanent floods, and therefore, rendered physically non-productive and difficult to manage, with the exception of the lands included in the category below.

Reforestation : Artificial establishment of forests on land which carried forestry before and involving the replacement of the indigenous tree species by a new and essential different species or genetic variety.

Regeneration : Re-establishment of a forest stand by natural or artificial means following the removal of the previous stand by felling or as a result of natural causes, e.g. fire or storm.

Shrub and brush land : Woody perennial plants, generally of more than 0.5 m and less than 5 m height, and often without a definite stem and crown. "Trees outside the forest" are excluded.

Sustainable development : The management and conservation of the natural resources base, and the orientation of technological and institutional change in such a manner as to ensure the attainment and continued satisfaction of human needs for present and future generations. Such sustainable development (in agriculture, forestry and fisheries sectors) conserves land, water, plant and animal genetic resources, is environmentally viable and socially acceptable.

Sustainable forest management : It is the stewardship and use of forests and forest lands in a way, an at a rate, that maintains their biological diversity, productivity, regeneration capacity, vitality and their potential to fulfill, now and in the future, relevant ecological economic and social functions, at local, national and global levels, and that does not cause damage on other ecosystems.

Tree: A woody perennial with a single main stem, or in the case of coppice with several stems, having a more or less definite crown. Includes bamboo, palms and other woody plants meeting the above criterion. The definition excludes non-forest fruit tree species.

Trees outside forests : Trees on land other than forest or other wooded land. **Includes :** Trees on land that meets the definitions of forest and of other wooded land except that the area is less than 0.5 ha and the width is less than 20 m; scattered trees in permanent meadows and pastures; permanent tree crops, such as fruit tree orchards and coconut palm plantations; trees in parks and gardens, around buildings, in hedgerows and in lines along streets, roads, railways, rivers, streams and canals; trees in shelterbelts and windbreaks of less than 20 m in width and 0.5 ha in area.

Unexploitable forest: Forest and other wooded land on which there are legal, economic or technical restrictions on wood and non-wood production. **Includes:** a) forest and other wooded land with severe legal restrictions on wood production, e.g. national parks, nature reserves and other protected areas, such as those of special scientific, historical or cultural interests; b) forest and other wooded land where physical productivity is too low or harvesting and transportation costs to the nearest market are too high to warrant wood harvesting.

Unproductive forest : A forest which is not regularly managed, yielding timber less than a certain amount, e.g. the increment volume is less than 1 m^3/ha/year in the foreseeable future.

Vegetation type : Mixture of vegetation covering a forest site. Used in identifying a certain forest site type, e.g. heath forest (Ministerial Conference on the Protection of European Forests and the Pan-European Forest Process; Geneva, 09/1994).

❑❑❑

Chapter 15

Community Forest Management

Modern tools in Forest Management. Introduction to the concept of forestry as a common property resource - Community Forest Management and forest development through NGOs, civil societies, citizen groups.

Community forestry

Community forestry is an evolving branch of forestry whereby the local community plays a significant role in forest management and land use decision-making by themselves in the facilitating support of government as well as change agents. It involves the participation and collaboration of various stakeholders including community, government and non-government organisations (NGO's). The level of involvement of each of these groups is dependent on the specific community forest project, the management system in use and the region. It gained prominence in the mid-1970s and examples of community forestry can now be seen in many countries including Nepal, Indonesia, Korea, Brazil, India and North America.

Overview

Community forestry is a branch of forestry that deals with the communal management of forests for generating income from timber and non-timber forest products as forms of goods while in other hand regulating ecosystem, downstream settlements benefits from watershed conservation, carbon sequestration and aesthetic values as in forms of services . It has been considered one of the most promising options of combining forest conservation with rural development and community empowerment and poverty reduction objectives. Community forestry is defined by the Food and Agricultural Organization of the United Nations as "any situation that intimately involves local people in forestry activity". Community forestry exists when the local community in an area plays a significant role in land use decision-making and when the community is satisfied with its involvement and benefits from the management of the surrounding forest and its resources.

Community forestry is first implemented through the establishment of a legal and institutional framework including the revision of legal norms and regulations for forest management, the development of National Forest Plans and the strengthening of decentralization processes to sub national levels of government. The second principal line of action is the implementation of pilot projects to demonstrate the feasibility of the community forestry framework. However, a study by the Overseas Development Institute shows that the technical, managerial and financial requirements stipulated by the framework are often incompatible with local realities and interests. A successful legal and institutional framework will incorporate the strengthening of existing institutions and enable the dissemination of locally appropriate practices as well as the local capacity for regulation and control.

In a 2016, review of community-based forestry, FAO estimated that almost one-third of the world's forest area is under some form of community-based management.

History

Community forestry first came to prominence in the mid-1970s and has continued to evolve over the last few decades in a growing number of countries. The availability of forest resources are often greatly reduced for use by the local people due to increasing pressures to cultivate the land, reliance on the forest resources are also affected by economic and political changes. The evolution of community forestry in Nepal dates back to the late 1970s and was first instilled as an attempt to improve the management of forest resources and address environmental issues that were of great concern with the countries failing centralized forest policy. Over the past two decades, community forestry has been applied successfully in many developing countries, with its main goal being the alleviation of poverty amongst local forest communities and forest conservation. More recently, community forestry has been implemented in developing countries and it has been successful in its aims of sustainable forest management, climate change adaptation plan of action, and securing socio-economic benefits for local communities.

Stakeholders

There is a large variety of stakeholders involved when considering community forestry. Participation from some of the various levels of community, government and non-government organisations (NGO's) are essential in the project's success. While specific stakeholders vary between different community forestry projects the primary stakeholder groups are as follows:

Local Community

- Communities living adjacent to or within the forest
- Traditional authorities
- Community-based organisations (forest users groups, etc.)
- Community representatives / local councils

Government

- State Government
- National Government
- Departments of Agriculture, Forestry, Environment, etc. (specific the country and/or region)

NGO's

- Environmental/conservation groups
- Commercial forestry industries
- Industries reliant on forests (i.e. harvestable products other than wood, e.g. game meat)
- Tourism industry
- Animal welfare groups

Natural Ecosystem

Stakeholders of community forestry have a vested interest to establish sustainable practices, whether this be to develop and maintain a regular income, ensure that forests are sufficiently protected to ensure their longevity or to reduce illegal activities and manage the area in such a way to promote tourism and conservation. In this situation, stakeholders came to conclusion to handover forest resources to local communities for conserving, managing and utilization by their own decision. Despite significant development, continued improvement in the collaboration between local governments and forest communities seems to be a key point for better community forest management. A wide range of futures scenarios have been put upto help the environmental decision process.

Challenges

A study conducted in the Brazilian Amazon determined that there are a number of challenges that must be faced, when developing a sustainable management strategy for community forestry. These challenges are outlined in Table 2 and Figure 1 shows the impact each management challenge has on other obstacles. The model is segregated into two phases: the *development phase* during which several enabling factors (land ownership, organisational capacity, technical knowledge and capital) are needed to obtain a legal management permit and secondly the *operational phase,* where factors (clandestine loggers, access to markets, infrastructure and managerial skills) influence the successfulness of the management program. Each of the challenges outlined in Table 1 must be addressed in order for a self-sustaining community forestry management program to be established.

Land ownership	It is not uncommon for small settlements living traditionally to lack clear title to the forests and lands, as such their rights to harvest the land may come into dispute. Formal recognition of land ownership or rights to use is needed for legal forest management. In Nepal, there is still confusion to communities about their tenure into services, such as income from trading of carbon sequestration come from forestry resources. Government wants to hold revenue raised from trading of carbon but communities claim that it is our property due tobe managed by us.
Organizational capacity	Organizational capacity refers to the community's competence to organize a forest management program.
Capital	A community will require start-up capital to invest in the required infrastructure, equipment, and to hire a forester to organise and oversee management plans.
Technical knowledge	While it is common for community members have a thorough understanding of forest ecology in a natural and historical sense, they often lack the technical knowledge and legal certification required to manage forest resources legally.

Best practices

For a conservation program within a Community forest to succeed, community involvement is imperative. Governments with interest in forest conservation introduce statewide policies and legislations which have historically failed to deliver the desired outcomes, such as in China, Nepal and Peru. Moreover, no single stakeholder by itself can ensure the success of such a program.

Community Forestry and wildlife Conservation

Though there is little research on the role of community forestry to wildlife conservation, some empirical studies suggests that it help in wildife conservation. It is done by decreasing the human disturbance, increasing regeneration of forest and increasing of ground cover.

Nepal

Common land in Nepal is owned by the state which often does not have the capacity to monitor and manage the area. This often leads to the over use of the resources by the community due to lack of incentives. To overcome this, programs involving community participation were introduced and 'Forest User Groups' (FUG) formed to manage the forests resources without giving them ownership of the land. Community forest management system in Nepal becomes one of the successful program out of 8 around world that is recognized on Rio 20+. This has resulted in better outcomes in the region.

Indonesia

Villagers from three communities in Bantaeng district in Indonesia, with the assistance of a funded project obtained a Forest management license and secured a 35-years lease on their local forest. With the incentive to preserve their source of income, the villagers have had a positive impact on forest conservation. This is now viewed as a reference model for the Ministry of Forestry's future projects.

Korea

Farmers enter into a profit sharing contract with the 'Village Forestry Association' (VFA) to form a co-operative which assists farmers with reforestation in keeping with the legislation. VFA, though loosely linked to the Office of Forestry enjoys a degree of autonomy facilitating community participation. This system demonstrates the desirable mix of top-down and bottom-up planning ensuring government control as well as effective reforestation through active community participation.

Management system

As it is unlikely for any two areas to have identical socio-economic and environmental conditions, there is no blueprint management plan that would provide a blanket solution to all the problems. Based on research over several years in Nepal, it was noted that to have and effective management system, we need to identify variables which would affect the success of the system and group them into the following five sets:

i) Attributes of the resource system,

ii) Attributes of the user group,

iii) Attributes of the governance system,

iv) Attributes relating to interactions between the user group and resource, and

v) Attributes relating to interactions between the governance system and the resource.

In some cases, it is unrealistic to expect progress in a community level management of forest activities, as often conflict arise with respect to land use and benefit sharing within the community. Such issues can be overcome by recognising that a community level of management may not be the most effective management technique. Instead, adopting the following approach will provide a solution :

i) Management by smaller work groups within the community, sharing common interest in the resources.

ii) A clear management plan with specific benefit sharing arrangement within the work group.

iii) Develop management systems which are within the expertise of the working group.

Faith communities are increasingly participating in efforts to promote ecological sustainability. Whereas the last 50–100 years has seen them lease out their territory to industry, they are beginning to reclaim and restore this land. Their recognition amongst local and national authorities have allowed community forestry schemes to develop and there have been several highly successful efforts across Cambodia, which have been extended to Vietnam and Laos. In September 2010, Buddhists monks were awarded the UNDP's Equator Prize for their ongoing conservation work. This comprises the establishment of tree nurseries, seedling distribution, ordination activities, composting schemes and a vegetable garden. They are using this work to promote sustainable living and conservation throughout three districts; the pilot project, launched in 1997, in Kratie consists of a six pagoda network that covers 1,461 hectares (3,610 acres). The site has become a valuable source of information and environmental education as well as a base for the local community. Villagers regularly hold panel discussions about how they can go on to best take advantage of what the natural forest has to offer without destroying it.

Incentives

Farm forest for household use

i) Preserving the source of community's livelihood

ii) Maintaining soil integrity by preventing erosion.

iii) Use of fuel wood and fodder- Planting trees to provide fuel wood as well as fodder for cattle can be encouraged in ways that do not conflict with cash crops and food production. e.g. The Neem tree was introduced in West Africa and is now the most widely grown tree in the drier parts of the continent. It was easily cultivated and provides the farmers with good timber, fuel and shade.

iv) Developing nursery networks through support activities which assist with subsidies. This encourages entrepreneurship to produce tree planting stock for sale.

Farm forests for markets

Tree growing can take on the characteristics of a crop, where there is a market for wood products, such as poles, fuel wood and, pulp for production of paper. Companies tie-up with farmers for supply of these products giving a steady source of income to the farming community. For example, in Philippines, over 3000 farmers cultivate trees for pulp production for an industry that provides a market as well as a minimum price for the product, and Cooperatives of Village Forestry Association in Korea have helped local communities cater to a growing market in forest products, such as timber and mushrooms.

References

1. Agrawal, A., Chhatre, A, and Hardin, R. (2008). 'Changing Governance of the World's Forest'. *Science* 320: 1460–1462
2. Balakathiresan, S., 1986, Essentials of Forest Management, Nataraj Publishers, Dehra Dun (India).
3. Bhattacharya P., Kandya A.K. and Krishna Kumar., 2008, Joint Forest Management in India, Aavishkar Publisher, Jaipur (India).
4. Desai, V., 1991, Forest Management in India - Issues and Problems. Himalaya Pub. House, Bombay (India).
5. Edmunds, D. and Wollenberg, E., 2003, Essentials of Forest Management, Natraj Publishers, Dehra Dun (India).
6. Evans, K., De Jong, W., and Cronkleton, P. (2008) "*Future Scenarios as a Tool for Collaboration in Forest Communities". ''S.A.P.I.EN.S.'' '''1''' (2)". Sapiens.revues.org. 1 October, 2008. Retrieved 30 November, 2011.*
7. *Glossary of Forestry Terms in British Columbia" (pdf). Ministry of Forests and Range (Canada). March 2008.*
8. Jerome L Cutter., 1983, Timber Management: A Quantitative Approach. John Wiley and Sons.
9. Lutz, E and Caldcott (1999) Decentralisation and biodiversity conservation, A World bank symposium. Washington: The World Bank.
10. *Mozgeris, G. (2008) "The continuous field view of representing forest geographically: from cartographic representation towards improved management planning". ''S.A.P.I.EN.S.'' ''1'' (2)". Sapiens.revues.org.*
11. Mozgeris, G. (2008) "The continuous field view of representing forest geographically: from cartographic representation towards improved management planning". *S.A.P.I.EN.S.* 1(2)
12. Philip Joseph Burton, 2003. *Towards sustainable management of the boreal forest* 1039 pages
13. Philipp S. Duncker 1, Susana M. Barreiro 2, Geerten M. Hengeveld 3, Torgny Lind 4, William L. Mason 5, Slawomir Ambrozy 6 and Heinrich Spiecker. Classification of Forest Management Approaches: A New Conceptual Framework and Its Applicability to European Forestry.

14. Ram Prakash and L. S. Khanna. Theory and Practice of Silvicultural Systems
15. Ramprakash., 1986, Forest Management, IBD, Dehradun (India).
16. Recknagel, A. and Bentley. J., 1988, Forest Management. IBD, Dehra Dun (India).
17. Ribott, (1990). 'Accountable representation and power in Participatory and decentralized environmental management', *Unasylva* 50(4).
18. Shindler, Bruce; Lori A. Cramer (January 1999). "Shifting Public Values for Forest Management: Making Sense of Wicked Problems". Western Journal of Applied Forestry (Society of American Foresters) 14 (1): 28–34. ISSN 0885-6095.
19. Trivedi, P, R. and Sudarshan, K, N., 1996, Forest Management. Discovery publications, New Delhi (India).

Young, Raymond (1982). Introduction to Forest Science. John Wiley & sons. p. 207. ISBN 0471064386.

❑❑❑

Chapter 16

Model Questions Bank and IFS Question Papers

Q. Choose The Correct Answer for the Following

1. The Karnataka is one of the earliest states to issue G.O on adopting JFPM in the year:

   a) 1999   b) 2003

   c) 1993   d) 2009

2. In a situation, where the volume of growing stock is found more than expected is:

   a) Over stocked   b) Under stocked

   c) Normal stocked   d) None

3. An age class with one year as the interval is called:

   a) Age class   b) Regular age

   c) Age gradation   d) Irregular age

4. The increase in growth that takes place in a particular year is:

   a) PAI   b) CAI

   c) MAI   d) FMAI

5. Thinning operation carried out in regular forest is:

   a) Annual yield   b) Intermittent yield

   c) Periodic yield   d) Sustained yield

6. Forest may be managed primarily for the purpose of:

   a) Productive   b) Protective

   c) Both a & b   d) None

7. Shorter rotations are financially attractive for:
   a) Public owner's b) Private owner's
   c) Both a & b d) None
8. The rotation which is most profitable is called as:
   a) Economic b) Physical
   c) Technical d) Silvicultural
9. Annual yield is equal to the twice the G.S. divided by the rotation period is:
   a) Von-mantel's b) Heyer's
   c) Cotta d) Brandie's
10. Conversion of inferior forest to more valuable by:
    a) Multi planting b) Mono planting
    c) Enrichment planting d) Single planting
11. In gross area method, the felling series is divided into a number of:
    a) Periodic blocks b) Rotation
    c) Annual coupes d) Felling series
12. The increment in the growth, yield / volume, quality and price of individual trees or crops during a given period is called as:
    a) Increment b) MAI
    c) PAI d) CAI
13. The sum (by no or volume) of all the trees growing in a forest or specified part of it is:
    a) Actual stock b) Normal stock
    c) Growing stock d) None
14. The material that a forest can yield annual or periodically in perpetually is:
    a) Annual yield b) Sustained yield
    c) Periodic yield d) None

15. The period which a forest crop takes between its formation and final felling is known as:

a) Rotation b) Yield regulation

c) Technical rotation d) Total yield

16. This term generally applied to the determination of the yield and the prescribed means of realizing it:

a) Normal yield b) Yield regulation

c) Total yield d) Annual yield

17. A species retains its satisfactory vigour of growth and reproduction on a given site in this rotation:

a) Silvicultural b) Physical

c) Financial d) Technical

18. The practical application of scientific, technical and economic principles of forestry is called as:

a) Forest Economics b) Forest Management

c) Forest Mensuration d) Forest Biology

19. The forest, which must be preserved for the physical & climatic consideration is called as:

a) Social Forestry b) Farm Forestry

c) Protection Forestry d) Agro forestry

20. In a situation, where the volume of growing stock is found less than expected is:

a) Over stocked b) Under stocked

c) Normal stocked d) None

21. The total volume of trees in a fully stocked forest with normal distribution of age classes for a given rotation is called as:

a) Actual Growing Stock b) Normal Growing Stock

c) Total Growing Stock d) All of these

22. The time that elapses between successive main fellings on the same area is called as:

a) Felling period b) Felling time

c) Felling series d) Felling cycle

23. The period during which a change from one silvicultural system to another is effected is called as:

a) Conversion period b) Regeneration period
c) Rotation period d) None

24. The increase in girth, diameter, basal area, height, volume, quality and price of individual trees or crops during a given period is called as:

a) Increment b) CAI
c) PAI d) MAI

25. The period between seeding felling and final felling on a particular area is:

a) Regeneration interval b) Regeneration period
c) Regeneration Block d) All

26. Forest renders the benefits as :

a) Tangible benefits b) Intangible benefits
c) Both a & b d) Commercial benefits

27. The material that a forest can yield annually or periodically in perpetuity is called as:

a) Sustained yield b) Normal yield
c) Total yield d) Annual yield

28. The period which a forest crop takes between its formation and final felling is known as:

a) Rotation b) Silvicultural Rotation
c) Technical Rotation d) Total Yield

29. Pressler's law of increment percent for the year "r", when MAI culminates, can be expressed by the formula:

a) $p = [(V-v)/(V+v)]x(200/n)$ b) $p=100/r$
c) $p = 400/(nD)$ d) None

30. The rotation through which a species retain satisfactory vigour of growth and reproduction on a given site is:

a) Silvicultural b) Physical
c) Financial d) Technical

31. A general formula applicable to all fractional enumerations of the growing stock was evolved by:

a) Von Mantel b) Simmons

c) Howard d) Smythies

32. The Normal Growing Stock of a Eucalyptus plantation worked on 10 years rotation on 10 ha area, one ha under each gradation with the volume of 10 year gradation being 500 m^3 is:

a) 2150 m^3 b) 2050 m^3

c) 2500 m^3 d) 3500 m^3

33. The most important factor/s in which conditions are likely to differ while preparing Yield Tables (sample plots) from data collected on normally stocked forests is / are:

a) Density b) Quality

c) Density & Quality d) None

34. All the material from thinnings or operations preceding the main felling in regular forest or its cash equivalent is known as:

a) Final yield b) Normal Yield

c) Total yield d) Intermediate yield

35. This formula applies only to the special cases in which enumeration is carried out down to the diameter corresponding to half the rotation:

a) Simmons b) Smythies

c) Von Mantel d) Howard

36. The rotation which yields the highest average annual gross or net revenue irrespective of the capital value of the forest is called as:

a) Financial or Economic Rotation

b) Technical Rotation

c) Rotation of Maximum Volume Production

d) Rotation of Highest Income

37. This law states that "in a fully stocked selection forest, the number of stems falls off from one diameter class to the next diameter class in geometrical progression":

a) Mungar's b) Howard's
c) De Liocourt's d) Fischer's

38. The German Forester who advocated the concept of progressive yield is:

a) Hartig b) Heyer
c) Von Mantel d) De Liocourt

39. The regular, continuous supply of the desired produce to the fullest capacity of the forest is:

a) Final yield b) Normal Yield
c) Sustained yield d) Intermediate yield

40. According to this formula, the annual yield is equal to twice the G.S. divided by the rotation period:

a) Von Mantel's b) Simmons's
c) Heyer's d) Smythie's

41. The increase in girth, diameter, basal area, height, volume, quality and price of individual trees or crops during a given period is called as:

a) Increment b) CAI
c) PAI d) MAI

42. A term generally applied to the determination of the yield and the prescribed means of realizing it is known as :

a) Normal yield b) Yield regulation
c) Total yield d) Annual yield

43. The period between seeding felling and final felling on a particular area is:

a) Regeneration interval b) Regeneration period
c) Regeneration duration d) None

44. According to this formula, the annual yield is equal to twice the G.S. divided by the rotation period:

a) Von Mantel's b) Simmons's
c) Heyer's d) Smythie's

45. The Normal Growing Stock of a Eucalyptus plantation worked on 10 years rotation on 10 ha area, one ha under each gradation with the volume of 10 year gradation being 500 m^3 is:

a) 2150 m^3 b) 2050 m^3

c) 2500 m^3 d) 3500 m^3

46. The most important factor/s in which conditions are likely to differ while preparing Yield Tables (sample plots) from data collected on normally stocked forests is/are:

a) Density b) Quality

c) Both d) None

47. Forest renders the benefits as :

a) Tangible benefits b) Intangible benefits

c) Both d) None

48. These maps show the new Working Circles, Felling Series, Periodic Blocks and other details of management:

a) Working Plan Maps b) Management Maps

c) Stock Maps d) Reference Maps

49. The tree that occupies more than its fair share of growing space in a wood land is:

a) Buttressed tree b) Wolf tree

c) Fluting tree d) None

50. The rotation through which a species retain satisfactory vigour of growth and reproduction on a given site is:

a) Silvicultural b) Physical

c) Financial d) Technical

51. Forest department has constituted _____ no of VFCs in the state during the past 13 years.

a) 3887 b) 1887

c) 2887 d) 4887

52. The Karnataka is one of the earliest states to issue G.O on adopting JFPM in the year:

a) 1983 b) 2003

c) 1993 d) 2013

53. In a situation, where the volume of growing stock is found more than expected is:

a) Over stocked b) Under stocked

c) Normal stocked d) None

54. An age class with one year as the interval is called as:

a) Age class b) Regular age

c) Age gradation d) Irregular age

55. The time elapsing between two successive felling on the same area is:

a) Felling period b) Felling time

c) Felling cycle d) Felling series

56. The increase in growth that takes place in a particular year is:

a) PAI b) CAI

c) MAI d) FMAI

57. Thinning operation carried out in regular forest is:

a) Annual yield b) Intermittent yield

c) Periodic yield d) Sustained yield

58. Forest may be managed primarily for the purpose of:

a) Productive b) Protective

c) Both a & b d) None

59. Shorter rotations are financially attractive for:

a) Public owners b) Private owners

c) Both a & b d) None

60. The type of rotation which is most profitable is called as:

a) Economic b) Physical

c) Technical d) Silvicultural

61. The formula "Annual yield = 2 GS / Rotation " refers to:

a) Von-Mantel's b) Heyer's

c) Cotta's d) Brandie's

62. Conversion of inferior forest to more valuable by:

a) Multi planting b) Mono planting

c) Enrichment planting d) Single planting

63. In gross area method, the felling series is divided into a number of:

a) Periodic blocks b) Rotation

c) Annual coupes d) Felling series

64. A general formula applicable to all fractional enumerations of the G.S. was evolved by:

a) Simmon's b) Brandie's

c) Heyer's d) Smythie's

65. The main task/s broadly involved in management of forests is/are:

a) Control of composition and structure of the growing stock

b) Harvesting and marketing of forest produce

c) Administration of forest property and personnel

d) All of these

66. This type map shows the distribution of different forests or stand types which have a bearing on management, with information about their composition, age class, etc.:

a) Working Plan map b) Stock map

c) Management map d) Forest type map

67. The map showing the results of fire protection and prepared according to the directions from special Chief Conservator of Forests (CCF) is_______________

a) Regeneration survey map b) Enumeration map

c) Control map d) Working Plan map

68. A sub-division of Felling Series formed with the object of regulating cuttings in some special manner is called as:

a) Cutting Section b) Coupe

c) Periodic Block d) None

69. This is defined as "part or parts of forest set aside to be regenerated or otherwise treated during a special period".

a) Coupe b) Cutting Section
c) Periodic block d) Working circle

70. The ratio of sample population to the whole population is called ___________

a) Sample plot b) Sample enumeration
c) Sampling unit d) Sampling intensity

71. Instrument of Forest Management is:

a) Working Plan b) Working Circle
c) JFPM d) None

72. ___________is defined as the practice of forestry for the simultaneous or sequential use of a forest area for two or more purposes.

a) Multiple Use Forestry b) Intensive Forestry
c) Botha & b d) Plantation Forestry

73. The condition when only one periodic block is allotted at each working plan revision is known as:

a) Floating PB b) Fixed PB
c) Permanent PB d) All of these

74. The condition when all the Periodic Blocks are allotted and retain their territorial identity at working plan revision is known as:

a) Floating PB b) Single PB
c) Fixed PB d) None

75. The principle of maximum ___________has been the backbone of forest management:

a) Normal yield b) Progressive yield
c) Total yield d) Sustained yield

76. Pre requisite/s for Sustained Yield management is/are:

a) Normal age class gradations
b) Normal Increment
c) Normal growing stock
d) All of these

77. The simplest method of achieving the objective sustained yield is to maintain a complete succession of ____________ of crops of all ages from one year old upto the age of maturity.

a) Equal areas
b) Unequal areas
c) Small areas
d) Large areas

78. This concept states that "raising the productivity of soil, and of the crop, by silvicultural treatments, judicious tending, and enrichment of the forest by changing the crop composition and by replacement of the original inferior forest by valuable species":

a) Sustained yield
b) Normal yield
c) Progressive yield
d) All of these

79. Continuous supply with required/needed products is achieved by:

a) Sustained yield
b) Normal yield
c) Final yield
d) Progressive yield

80. The type of rotation applied in case of "Wood based industries that have their own forests and plantations" is:

a) Technical rotation
b) Rotation of maximum volume production
c) Financial rotation
d) Rotation of maximum income

81. The type of Rotations controlling the financial returns are:

a) Financial rotation and Technical rotation
b) Rotation of maximum income and Rotation of maximum volume production
c) Rotation of maximum income and Silvicultural rotation
d) Rotation of maximum income and Financial rotation

82. Rotations which control the output of material, forest products in form, size and quantity are:

a) Silvicultural rotation and Rotation of maximum volume production

b) Technical rotation and Rotation of maximum volume production

c) Financial rotation and Technical rotation

d) Rotation of maximum income and Silvicultural rotation

83. The Karnataka is one of the earliest states to issue G.O. on adopting JFPM in the year:

a) 1999 b) 2003

c) 1993 d) 2009

84. _______________ is the main territorial division of forest, generally bounded by natural features and bearing a local proper name.

a) Block b) Compartment

c) Sub compartment d) Coupe

85. In Chir pine forests, rotation period is 120 years and regeneration period is 30 years, then the number of periodic blocks are _______________

a) One b) Two

c) Three d) Four

86. If 100 years is the rotation and 10 years the Felling Cycle, then there will be ______ felling coupes, each being one tenth of the Felling Series and worked at intervals of __________ years.

a) 10, 10 b) 10, 20

c) 15, 10 d) 10, 15

87. Who is the Head of Forest Force (HOFF) in Administrative (organizational) classification of forests of State?

a) IGF b) PCCF

c) MOEF d) CCF

88. The principle of maximum ____________________ has been the backbone of forest management:

a) Progressive yield b) Yield Regulation

c) Sustained yield d) Normal yield

89. The rotation which yields the highest average annual gross or net revenue irrespective of the capital value of the forest is _______________

a) Technical rotation

b) Rotation of maximum volume production

c) Financial rotation

d) Rotation of highest income

90. The simplest method of achieving the objective sustained yield is to maintain a complete succession of ____________ of crops of all ages from one year old up to the age of maturity.

a) Equal areas b) Unequal areas

c) Small areas d) Large areas

91. The condition when all the Periodic Blocks are allotted and retain their territorial identity at working plan revision is known as:

a) Floating PB b) Single PB

c) Fixed PB d) All of these

92. The ratio of sample population to the whole population is called _____________

a) Sample plot b) Sample enumeration

c) Sampling unit d) Sampling intensity

93. According to this formula the annual yield is equal to twice the G.S. divided by the rotation period:

a) Von Mantel's b) Simmons's

c) Heyer's d) Smythie's

94. In gross area method, the felling series is divided into a number of:

a) Periodic blocks b) Rotation

c) Annual coupes d) Felling series

95. The period during which a change from one silvicultural system to another is effected is called as:

a) Conversion period b) Regeneration period

c) Rotation period d) None

96. This law states that "in a fully stocked selection forest, the number of stems falls off from one diameter class to the next diameter class in geometrical progression":

a) Mungar's b) Howard's

c) De Liocourt's d) Fischer's

97. The period between seeding felling and final felling on a particular area is:

a) Regeneration interval b) Regeneration period

c) Regeneration Block d) All

98. A general formula applicable to all fractional enumerations of the growing stock was evolved by:

a) Von Mantel b) Simmons

c) Howard d) Smythies

99. This formula applies only to the special cases in which enumeration is carried out down to the diameter corresponding to half the rotation:

a) Simmons b) Smythies

c) Von Mantel d) Howard

100. The rotation which yields the highest average annual gross or net revenue irrespective of the capital value of the forest is called as:

a) Financial or Economic Rotation

b) Technical Rotation

c) Rotation of Maximum Volume Production

d) Rotation of Highest Income

101. The German Forester who advocated the concept of progressive yield is:

a) Hartig b) Heyer

c) Von Mantel d) De Liocourt

102. These maps show the new Working Circles, Felling Series, Periodic Blocks and other details of management:

a) Working Plan Maps b) Management Maps

c) Stock Maps d) Reference Maps

Q. Match The Following

Set I

Part A	Part B
1. Rotation	a) D.F.O.
2. Regeneration period	b) 1976
3. Site improvement	c) Production resin
4. JFPM	d) Normal even aged
5. Instrument of forest Management	e) Immature stand
6. Thinning	f) Working plan
7. Regular forest	g) NFP, 1988
8. Special objective	h) Manures and fertilizers
9. National Commission on Agriculture	i) Whole periodic block
10. Kingpin of forest administration	j) Harvesting age

Set II

Part A	Part B
1. Functional classification of Forests	a) Sampling intensity
2. Main territorial division of the forest	b) Cluster
3. Forest capital	c) Reserved forests
4. Ideal Forest	d) CAI
5. Group of smaller units	e) Block
6. Sampling fraction	f) Protection forests
7. Highest Net Returns	g) Growing stock
8. Legal classification of Forests	h) Economic Rotation
9. Increment in a particular year	i) Cutting Section
10. A sub division of Felling Series	j) Normal Forest

Set III

Part A	Part B
1. First Forest Policy	a) Working Plan
2. Stock map	b) Microplan
3. Head of State Forest Department	c) 1980
4. Annual felling area	d) Sustained yield
5. Scheme of management of a village forest	e) Distribution of different forests
6. Written scheme of forest management	f) 1894
7. Highest Net Returns	g) P.C.C.F
8. Forest Conservation Act	h) Economic Rotation
9. Maximum capacity of the forest	i) 1865
10. First Forest Act	j) Coupe

Set IV

Part A	Part B
1. Functional classification of Forests	a) Working Plan
2. Main territorial division of the forest	b) Equi-productive coupes
3. Yield regulation gross area method	c) Principle of Dynamic
4. Ideal Forest	d) The principle of maximum sustained yield
5. Progressive yield	e) Block
6. Instrument of Forest Management	f) NFP, 1952
7. Faustmann's formula	g) Principle of Static
8. Sustained yield	h) Economic Rotation
9. Backbone of Forest Management	i) IFA, 1927
10. Legal Classification of forests	j) Normal Forest

Set V

Part A	Part B
1. Reduction Factors	a) The principle of maximum sustained yield
2. Total yield	b) Burma modification
3. Formula of glorious simplicity	c) Increment percent
4. Financial Rotation	d) Whole of a PB
5. GS of one-third rotation	e) Von Mantel's formula
6. Backbone of Forest Management	f) Density and Quality
7. Yield regulation gross area method	g) Howard's modification
8. Increment and Volume	h) Final and intermediate yield
9. Regeneration Period	i) Equi-extensive coupes
10. GS of half the rotation	j) Based on soil expectation value

Set VI

Part A (Basis)	Part B (Method)
1. Area only	a) Judeich's selection method
2. Volume only	b) Biolley's "Check method"
3. Area and Volume	c) Smythie's safe guarding formula.
4. Increment	d) Von Mantel's formula
5. Volume and Increment	e) Simmons modification
6. GS down to 1/3rd rotation	f) Reduced area method
7. Reduction factors	g) Smythies modification
8. GS at half the rotation	h) Burma modification
9. GS of timber excluding crops below certain diameter	i) Annual coupe by gross area method
10. Fractional enumeration of GS	j) 1Howard modification

Q. Fill in the Blanks With Correct Answer

1. Trinity of norms of the Normal Forests are a.____________________, b.___________________________, c.____________________________________
2. Pre-requisite of the sustained yield is _________________________.
3. Forest renders __________________ and ______________________benefits.
4. Indian forests under the state ownership accounts to ______________%.
5. One of the objectives of the normal forest management is ______________________.
6. __________________ rotation has no relevance to economic forestry.
7. _______________ is the sum of all the trees growing in the forest.
8. The material that a forest can yield annually in perpetuity is_____________
9. ______________ is the kind of rotation which is adopted in industrial enterprises
10. The concept dealing with the attainment of balance between society's increasing demands for forest products and benefits, and the preservation of forest health and diversity is known as _______________.
11. "Village Forest" means a village forest referred to in Section 28 of the _________________ Act.
12. Supply under sustained yield management is _____________________.
13. Total number of all the trees growing in the forest is called as _____________________.
14. Rotation is mainly applicable to _____________________forest.
15. The time that elapses between successive main fellings in the same area is called ____________________.
16. The type of Rotation which coincides with natural lease of life of species on given site is called as ____________________.
17. ____________________is the smallest permanent working plan unit of management.
18. An age class with one year as the interval is called as _______________.
19. 1._____________________, 2._____________________, 3.______________________ are territorial classification types.
20. Forests are divided into Blocks, Compartments and Sub-compartments for ____________________and ______________________ works.
21. Supply under sustained yield management is _______________________.

22. When MAI reaches maximum and starts falling off at that junction it meets CAI, this point of intersection is called as ______________.
23. Expand BCFT__________________.
24. The average annual increment for any short period is called as ______________________________.
25. _____ Law explains that the percentage reduction in the stem number from one diameter class to the next diameter class is constant.
26. The type of rotation applied in case of "Wood based Industries that have their own forests and plantations" is ________________.
27. __________________ yield is economically more suitable (Sustained yield / Progressive yield).
28. The average NGS at the middle of the growing season in a Eucalyptus plantation worked on 10 year rotation on 10 ha area and one ha under each gradation with the volume of 10 year gradation being 600 m^3 is _______________.
29. The time that elapses between successive main fellings on the same area is called as ____________________.
30. The period during which a change from one silvicultural system to another is effected is called as _______________________.
31. If 100 years is the rotation and 10 years the Felling Cycle, then there will be _________ felling coupes, each being one-tenth of the Felling Series and worked at intervals of ____________ years.
32. The total volume of trees in a fully stocked forest with normal distribution of age classes for a given rotation is called as ________.
33. Criteria and indicators are tools which can be used to define, implement and monitor ____________________ in the broadest sense of the term, nationally and at the forest level.
34. The expression giving percentage relationship between increment and the volume producing it, is known as________________.
35. The increase in girth, diameter, basal area, height, volume, quality and price of individual trees or crops during a given period is called as _________________.
36. ______________ is the per cent ratio of *"Normal Yield"* to the *"Normal Growing Stock"*.
37. The diameter or girth decided upon as the normal size for felling in order to fulfill the objects of management is known as ____________.
38. The material that a forest can yield annually or periodically in perpetuity is called as __________________.

39. The period which a forest crop takes between its formation and final felling is known as ________________.

40. ________________ law of increment percent for the year "r", when MAI culminates, can be expressed by the formula {P = 100/r}.

41. The rotation through which a species retain satisfactory vigour of growth and reproduction on a given site is ________________.

42. The NFP, 1952 suggested to keep a minimum of 1/3rd of the country's total land area under forests, with ________% in Himalayas and hilly tracts and ________% in the plains.

43. Under regular shelter wood or uniform system of natural regeneration, ________________takes place the age gradations and ________________takes place the annual coupe, each containing the one age class instead of one age gradation.

44. ____________ is main territorial division of forest, generally bounded by natural features and bearing a local proper name.

45. ________________ rotation is suitable for adoption where the total quantity of material is important but not the size or specification.

46. ________________ is the total volume of stands in a forest with normal age classes and a normal increment.

47. Who is the Head of Forest Force (HOFF) in Administrative (organizational) classification of forests of State? ______________.

48. The Sample size in the total forest area of 1000 ha with a sampling intensity of 10% is ___________ ha.

49. The concept of progressive yield is advocated by a German Forester ________________.

50. The rotation which yields the highest average annual gross or net revenue irrespective of the capital value of the forest is ____________.

51. The type of Rotations controlling the output of material, forest products in form, size and quantity are ________________ and ________________ Law states that the percentage reduction in the stem number from one diameter class to the next diameter class is constant.

52. A sub division of Felling Series formed with the object of regulating cuttings in some special manner in Management (Silvicultural) Classification is ________________ felling area usually one of an annual series unless otherwise stated, preferably numbered with

roman numerals I, II, III, *etc* in Management (Silvicultural) Classification is ________________.

53. Under Territorial classification, forests are divided into i. ________, ii. __________ and iii.________ for executive and protective works.

54. The period required to regenerate the whole of a Periodic Block is called as ____________________________

55. ____________________________ Rotation is important from the overall national point of view.

56. A general formula applicable to all fractional enumerations of the growing stock was evolved by________________.

57. All the material from thinnings or operations preceding the main felling in regular forest or its cash equivalent is known as____________________yield.

58. __________________(Name of scientist) formula applies only to the special cases in which enumeration is carried out down to the diameter corresponding to half the rotation.

59. ________________map (type) shows the distribution of different forests or stand types which have a bearing on management, with information about their composition, age class, etc.

60. A sub division of Felling Series formed with the object of regulating cuttings in some special manner is called as ________________.

61. ________________is defined as "part or parts of forest set aside to be regenerated or otherwise treated during a special period".

62. The map showing the results of fire protection and prepared according to the directions from special Chief Conservator of Forests (CCF) is____________________.

63. The ratio of sample population to the whole population expressed in percentage is called ______________________.

64. The condition of PB when only one periodic block is allotted at each working plan revision is known as________________.

65. The simplest method of achieving the objective ______________ is to maintain a complete succession of equal areas of crops of all ages from one year old upto the age of maturity.

66. This concept of ____________________ yield states that "raising the productivity of soil, and of the crop, by silvicultural treatments, judicious tending, and enrichment of the forest by changing the crop composition and by replacement of the original inferior forest by valuable species".

67. The condition PB when all the Periodic Blocks are allotted and retain their territorial identity at working plan revision is known as ________________.

68. The type of rotation applied in case of "Wood based industries that have their own forests and plantations" is ________________.

69. The sampling intensities used for tropical wet evergreen forests and tropical moist deciduous forests are ______ % and ______% respectively.

70. The most important factors (reduced or modification factors) in which conditions are likely to differ while preparing Yield Tables (sample plots) from data collected on normally stocked forests are ______________ and ______________.

71. The type of Rotations controlling the financial returns are ______________ and ______________.

72. Forest inventory is synonymous with the term __________ in North America and ______________in India.

73. The rotation which yields largest volume per unit area per annum and used frequently with combination of other rotation is ________.

Q. State True or False

1. To obtain sustained yield, forest must be abnormal.(F)
2. SFM is management of forests according to the principles of sustainable development. (T)
3. SFM was developed by the Ministerial Conference on the Protection of Forests in India (F)
4. In JFPM, micro plans are prepared by local communities in association with the KFD. (T)
5. Compartment is the main territorial division of forest, generally bounded by natural features and bearing a local proper name. (F)
6. {(Area of F.S x W.P. Period) ÷ Area to be felled} = Rotation period. (T)
7. {(Regeneration Pd. x Area of F.S) ÷ Area under P.B} = Rotation period. (T)
8. Sub-compartment is the smallest permanent W.P unit of management. (F)
9. Number of stems in ideal selection forests inversely related to average dbh. (T)

10. Forestry enterprise is a short-term investment than agriculture. (F)
11. Technical rotation is adapted particularly by industrial firm. (T)
12. The rotation period, for the maximum volume production is slightly longer in richer sites as compared to poorer sites. (F)
13. The rotation which is more profitable is called as economic rotation. (T)
14. Normal forest is purely an artificial conception. (T)
15. In sustained yield concept, forest is regarded as an investment, the capital is safe. (T)
16. A forest which corresponds in every way to the objects of management is normal forest. (T)
17. Forests may be managed primarily for protective and productive purpose. (T)
18. Shorter rotations are financially attractive for privet owners. (T)
19. Rotation of highest income/revenue is calculated without interest or irrespective of the times, when the items of income or expenditure occur. (T)
20. Sub-compartment is the smallest permanent W.P. unit of management. (F)
21. Forestry enterprise is a short term investment than agriculture. (F)
22. Technical rotation is adapted particularly by industrial firm. (T)
23. The principle of maximum sustained yield is the back bone of Forest Management. (T)
24. Periodic Annual Increment is the increment which a tree or crop puts on a single year. (F)
25. Shorter the regeneration period - wider the age classes - then it is more uneven aged stand. (F)
26. Forestry is a long-term investment and there is a long interval between the formation and harvesting of forest crops. (T)
27. Volume per hectare = Basal area x Stand form height. (T)
28. CAI is not uniform throughout the life of a tree or stand but it rises to a maximum and gradually decreases. (T)
29. Longer the regeneration period - Wider age classes - then less even aged (T)
30. The chief object of forest management is stated as regulation of production and supply of yield. (T)

31. De Licourt's Law says the percentage reduction in the stem number from one diameter class to the next diameter class is variable. (F)

Q. Answer the Following in One or Two Sentences

1. Forest management
2. Normal forest
3. SFM
4. JFPM
5. Working plan
6. Sustained yield
7. Increment.
8. Rotation
9. M.A.I.
10. Under-stocked
11. Over-stocked
12. Age-gradation
13. Age class
14. Growing stock
15. PAI
16. CAI
17. Micro plan
18. Cutting Section
19. Production period
20. Compartment
21. Exploitable size
22. Felling Series
23. Forest type
24. Increment percent
25. Working Circle
26. Utilization Percent
27. Yield Capacity
28. Regeneration period
29. Coupe
30. Felling cycle
31. Periodic Block
32. Conversion Period
33. Production Period
34. Technical Rotation
35. Yield Capacity
36. NGS

Q. Answer the Following in Brief

1. Scope of forest management.
2. Silvicultural rotation. Attributes of normal forest.
3. Micro plan.
4. Scope of working plan
5. JFPM in Karnataka.
6. Progressive yield.
7. Criteria and indicators of SFM.
8. What is De-Liocourt's law and write its formula?
9. Write the duties and responsibilities of VFC's.
10. What is Flurry's constant? Why it is evolved?
11. Technical Rotation
12. Types of Yield
13. Define normal forest and list the basic attributes of normal forest?
14. Rotation of maximum volume production
15. Advantages of sustained yield
16. Kinds of abnormality found in the forest
17. Write the scope of working plan.

18. Define yield determination and differentiate between the Final yield and Intermediate yield.
19. Differentiate between Sustained Yield (SY) and Progressive Yield (PY).
20. Differentiate between the Final yield and Intermediate yield.
21. Define yield regulation and write the functions of yield regulation.
22. List out the different type of maps prepared by W.P.O.
23. Write the criteria and indicators of SFM.
24. Write in brief about the methods to determine the actual growing stock.
25. Write the duties and responsibilities of VFC's
26. Write the hierarchy of the State Forest Department (administrative unit and officer incharge)
27. Explain the concept and principles of Sustained Yield.
28. What is Working Plan? Write its objectives.
29. Define the increment and give an account on CAI and MAI with graphical representation.
30. Write in brief about the annual coupes by reduced area method. What are the advantages and disadvantages of yield regulation by area?
31. Explain in brief the territorial and silvicultural classification under forest organization.
32. Explain the determination of Normal Growing Stock in clear felling system based MAI method.
33. What is the Rotation? Explain the types of rotation.
34. Explain the concept of Normal Forest.
35. Explain the concept and principles of sustained yield.
36. What is working plan? Write its objectives.
37. Write in detail about the kinds of abnormalities.

Q. Answer the Following

1. Explain the concept and principle of sustained yield and write its advantages.
2. Define normal forest. What are the basic features of normality and kinds of abnormalities?

3. Define rotation? List the different rotations and factors affecting length of rotation.
4. Explain Von Mantel's formula and write its merits and demerits.
5. What is yield regulation and what are the principles and objectives of yield regulation?
6. Explain diagrammatically the relationship between CAI and MAI.
7. Explain the concept and principle of sustained yield and write its advantages.
8. Define increment? Explain different expression of increment.
9. Justify the statement that "working plan" is a tool for forest management and what do you mean by working plan?
10. Define the increment and give an account on CAI and MAI with graphical representation.
11. Define yield regulation and write the functions of yield regulation.
12. Explain the determination of Normal Growing Stock in clear felling system based on MAI method.
13. Write in brief about the annual coupes by Gross Area method. What are the advantages and disadvantages of yield regulation by area?
14. Explain Von Mantel's formula and write its merits and demerits
15. Define the rotation and explain the different types of rotation.
16. What is Normal Forest? What are the basic features of normality and kinds of abnormalities?
17. Explain the determination of Normal Growing Stock in clear felling system based MAI method.
18. What is the Rotation? Explain the types of rotation.
19. Explain the concept of Normal Forest.
20. Explain the concept and principles of sustained yield.
21. What is working plan? Write its objcctives.
22. Write in detail about the kinds of abnormalities.

Indian Forest Service (IFS)
Question Papers (2000-2007)
IFS 2007 Forestry: Paper - I

Section A

1. Answer any four of the following (answer should not exceed 150 words for each question) :

   a) Discuss the silvicultural system for managing mangrove forests of India. (10)

   b) How are forests managed under the clear felling system? (10)

   c) Neem (*Azadirachta indica*) is a tree for solving global problems. Justify the statement. (10)

   d) Classify the methods of regeneration of forests. How will you select the trees for seed collection? (10)

   e) Discuss the importance of exotics in Indian Forestry. (10)

2. a) Discuss the impact of deforestation on ecological aspects. (20)

   b) Why is thinning necessary in forest crops? Discuss in brief the various methods of thinning. (20)

3. a) Discuss the salient features of shelterwood system of forest management with its merits and demerits. (20)

   b) Discuss the impact of forests on the climate of a locality. How do forests affect soil and water conservation? (20)

4. Describe the silviculture of any four of the following species :

   a) *Pinus roxburghii* (10)

   b) *Tectona grandis* (10)

   c) *Eucalyptus tereticornis* (10)

   (d) *Terminalia tomentosa* (10)

   (e) *Prosopis juliflora*. (10)

Section B

5. Answer any four of the following (answer should not exceed 150 words for each question) :

a) Describe environmental impact assessment tool in forestry. (10)

b) Describe the ethnic communities of India. Give their contribution to ethnobotany. (10)

c) What is gene conservation? Discuss in brief the different methods of *ex situ* conservation of forest species. (10)

d) Describe the importance and future scope of medicinal and aromatic plants in India. (10)

e) Define Joint Forest Management (JFM). Discuss the role of NGOs in effective implementation of management plans. (10)

6. a) Discuss different agroforestry systems under different agroecological zones. (20)

   b) Discuss briefly the role of forests in control of air, water and noise pollution. (20)

7. a) Explain the importance of watershed management in rural development. Discuss the factors affecting watershed management in detail. (20)

   b) What is a progeny test? Discuss the various objectives of progeny testing in tree improvement. (20)

8. Write short notes on any four of the following:

   a) Carbon sequestration (10)

   b) Clonal seed orchards (10)

   c) Hi-tech nursery (10)

   d) Ozone layer depletion (10)

   e) Wind-breaks and shelter-bells. (10)

Paper - II

Section A

1. Attempt any four questions from the following (not more than 150 words for each) :

   a) How is the remote sensing used in monitoring forest cover ? (10)

b) Write in brief on Topographic Surveys in Forestry. (10)

c) What is the importance of estimating form factor of a tree ? Write common formula used to estimate the form factor. (10)

d) Discuss how yield can be regulated in regular forests with clear felling system. (10)

e) What are the main objects of preparation of Divisional working plans for the forest plantations? (10)

2. a) Explain with diagram how annual yield of a forest is regulated by using Von Mentel's method. Provide formulae wherever necessary. (20)

   b) Show the relationship between Current Annual Increment (CAI) and Mean Annual Increment (MAI) of a forest stand. (10)

   c) Describe working principles of Christen's Hypsomcter in tree height measurement. (10)

3. a) To compute volume of standing trees which parameters are required to be measured ? Write instruments used and brief procedure of their handling. (20)

   b) After introduction of Joint Forest Management (JFM) scheme in different States, Forestry Administration is nearer to the people. Substantiate the statement with examples. (10)

   c) How age of the trees can be determined in which annual rings are not clearly observed ? (10)

4. a) What are the major principles of designing roads in the remote forest area? Provide diagrams, wherever necessary. (20)

   b) Write in brief on different types of timber bridges commonly constructed in interior areas of forest. (10)

Section B

5. Attempt any four from the following (not more than 150 words each) :

   a) Why herbaria and arboreta are pre-requisites for Dendrology? (10)

   b) Write in brief on important conservation projects for wild animals in India. (10)

c) What are the important features of Demand and Supply Curve? On what factors of Demand and Supply of Forest produce depend ? (10)

d) What is rotational grazing?What are its advantages?Under what situations this is followed?(10)

e) Write properties and uses of Turpentine oil and Lac. (10)

6. a) Describe general scenario of marketing and Trade of timber and Non-Timber Forest Products (NTFP) through various agencies in India. (20)

b) List important modern harvesting practices adopted in forest plantations. (10)

c) What is shifting cultivation? List adverse effects of shifting cultivation on forests. (10)

7. a) What is Succession ? Describe primary and secondary succession along with examples. How the succession is studied in Natural Forests ? (20)

b) Which are the defects in National Forest Policy of 1894 and 1952? (10)

c) What are various causes for large scale drying of Shisham (**Dalbergia sisso**) in Northern India? How can you effectively manage Shisham plantation in the back drop said problem? (10)

8. a) What is controlled burning ? Under Indian conditions how is it advantageous to prevent occurrence of wild fire in a forest? During which season it is followed? (20)

b) Tiger census raises question mark in Indian wildlife management. Give your view points. How can you effectively tackle the problem? (10)

c) Timber Identification is pre-requisite to check adulteration in the timber market. Give reasons. (10)

IFS Forestry 2006

Paper - I

Section A

1. Answer any four of the following (answer should not exceed 150 words for each question):

a) What are the factors that adversely affect natural regeneration of tree species? (10)

b) Explain raising of quality tree nursery stock in containers. (10)

c) Give an account of silvicultural management of Teak plantations. (10)

d) What is ordinary thinning? Explain briefly different grades of ordinary thinning. (10)

e) Explain in brief different methods of vegetative propagation in tree species. (10)

2. a) Explain the selection system and its application to Sal forests. (20)

   b) Explain the kinds and pattern of fellings in uniform system. (20)

3. a) How degraded mangrove formations can be rehabilitated? (20)

   b) Discuss afforestation of cold deserts with suitable tree species. (20)

4. Describe silviculture of the following species:

   a) *Dalbergia sissoo* (10)

   b) *Tectona grandis* (10)

   c) *Acacia nilotica* (10)

   d) *Dendrocalamus strictus* (10)

Section B

5. Answer any four of the following (answer should not exceed 150 words for each question):

   a) Describe agro-forestry systems under any two agro-climatic zones of India. (10)

   b) What are multipurpose tree species? Explain with examples. (10)

   c) Write a brief note on India's experience with joint forest management (JFM) in last fifteen years. (10)

d) Forests are key to tribal economy Justify. (10)

e) Saline and alkaline soils can be reclaimed by afforestation. Explain. (10)

6. a) Explain different kinds of soil erosion, thee causes and management of soil eroded areas. (20)

   b) Explain integrated watershed management approach. (20)

7. a) How forests and tree plantations help in environmental conservation? (20)

   b) Write a note on Environmental Impact Assessment (EIA). (20)

8. Write notes on:

   a) Provenance testing of tree species. (10)

   b) Sea production areas. (10)

   c) Heritability and genetic gain. (10)

   d) Progeny testing. (10)

Paper - II

Section A

1. Attempt any four from the following (not more than 150 words each):

   a) What is the relationship between Mean Annual Increment (MAT) and Current Annual Increment (CAI) for a Normal Forest? (10)

   b) What are the reasons for loss of Biodiversity? How is the loss of Biodiversity overcome? (10)

   c) Discuss the concept and use of Horizontal Point Sampling when wedge prism is used. (10)

   d) What are the advantages of GIS over traditional forest management? (10)

   e) Write various steps involved in formulation of village forest committees. How do these committees help in J.P.F.M.? (10)

2. a) Write the procedure to measure height of a tree in the following situations: when (i) observer's eye is above the top of the tree. (ii) observer's eye is below the base of the tree. (20)

b) Describe Normal Forest concept for Commercial Plantations. (10)

c) What is the importance of Prismatic Compass in Forest Surveys? (10)

3. a) What are working plans? How are they prepared and used for planting and enumeration of forest stands in a Forest Division? (20)

b) Describe Stump analysis method of determining growth of trees. (10)

c) Describe the role of working plans in nature conservation. (10)

4. a) Under what circumstances are Chain Survey and Plane Table Survey used in Forestry ? Write in brief on the procedure for any one survey. (20)

b) Distinguish between Silvicultural Rotation and Rotation of the maximum volume production. (10)

c) What are the salient differences between Local volume table and General volume table? (10)

Section B

5. Attempt any four from the following (not more than 150 words each):

a) Name different types of nutrient cycling which occur in tropical forest ecosystems. Give examples. (10)

b) In the present context, what is the role of rotational and controlled grazing to overcome damage due to grazing animals? (10)

c) Write the Processing and Sale procedure for Katha and Lac. (10)

d) Explain the application of Indian Penal Code in Forestry. (10)

e) Which are the important defects observed in stored timber? (10)

6. a) Enlist insect pests and diseases of Forest Nurseries. Briefly explain the methods to prevent and control both of them. (20)

b) List different types of air pollutants. What are their effects on growth and productivity of forests? (10)

c) Why are cases of encroachment of forest area still observed in the forests nearby human settlement? How is the damage report framed? (10)

7. a) Why is it necessary to take up Cost: Benefit analysis of Forest Plantations? Describe the main points to be taken into consideration while conducting Cost: Benefit analysis of short rotation commercial species and traditional timber species. (20)

b) What are the salient features of the National Forest Policy, 1988? (10)

c) Define Climax. State different theories of climax. Which are the different types of climaxes that are found? (10)

8. a) What is Composite Wood? Write raw material, manufacturing process, marketing and uses of the most commonly used composite wood in India. (20)

b) What are ecosystem energetics? Describe the energy flow in forest ecosystem. (10)

c) What is the role of Land depots and Water depots in commercial storage of forest products? (10)

IFS Forestry 2005

Paper - I

Section A

1. Answer any four of the following (answer should not exceed 150 words for each question): (10 x 4 = 40)

a) What are the conditions necessary for establishment of a tree nursery?

b) What do you understand by aerial seeding? Discuss briefly its success and failures in the Indian context.

c) Enumerate different tree species found in the Mangrove forest and explain with examples.

d) Give an account on the management of Eucalyptus or Poplar plantation.

e) What are the different grafting their ecological adaptations methods used for forest tree species?

2. a) What is the difference between Coppice with standards system and the shelter wood Coppice system? (20)

   b) Describe the Indian irregular shelter wood system with examples of its application in tropical rain forests. (20)

3. a) Explain 'thinning' operation with respect to teak plantation. (20)

   b) Describe different kinds and pattern of feelings. (20)

4. Describe the silviculture of the following species:

   a) Anthocephalus cadamba (10)

   b) Hardwickia binata (10)

   c) Gmelina arborea (10)

   d) Populus deltoides (10)

Section B

5. Answer any four of the following (Answer should not exceed 150 words for each question): (10 × 4 = 40)

   a) Enumerate different Agro forestry systems with models.

   b) What is the role of tree species in watershed management?

   c) What is the role of NGOs in JFM activities?

   d) What is 'acid rain'? – Explain.

   e) Discuss briefly about the role of NTFP in Indian economy. (20)

6. a) Describe a model of Silvipasture. (20)

   b) Suggest suitable tree species for different soil types. (20)

7. a) How industrial pollution can be controlled with suitable tree species? (20)

   b) Write an account on coastal afforestation. (20)

8. Write notes on:

   a) Urban forestry (10)

   6) ICRAF (10)

   c) Industrial Agroforestry (10)

   d) Leaf fodder trees. (10)

PAPER - II

Section A

1. Attempt any four questions from the following (not more than 150 words for each): (10×4=40)

   a) Explain the concept of normal growing stock in clear felling system.

   b) Describe types of maps prepared for divisional working plans.

   c) Discuss role of Current Annual Increment (CAI) and Mean Annual Increment (MAI) in fixation of rotation.

   d) Write general principles of usufructs sharing under joint forest management.

   e) Describe different types of mortar and its function in building construction.

2. a) How measuring is carried out in chain survey when an obstacle coming in chain line can be chained across but not seen across? (20)

   b) What is quarter girth formula? How it is used for calculation of volume of a log? (10)

   c) Discuss electromagnetic spectrum and mention the band with spectral range used in remote sensing. (10)

3. a) Describe types of bonds in brick masonry works and explain general rule for good brick bonding. (20)

   b) Write the concept and principle of horizontal point sampling. (10)

   c) How annual yield is calculated in a forest managed under uniform system of management? (10)

4. a) Describe method of measuring height of a tree situated on sloping ground in such a way that observer's eye lies between top and base of tree. (20)

   b) What do you mean by alpha and beta diversity, and how they are measured? (10)

   c) What is Geographic Information System (GIS)? Describe role of GIS for natural resources Management. (10)

Section B

5. Attempt any four from the following (not more than 150 words each):

   a) What are ecological pyramids? Describe any one of them. (10)

   b) Describe procedure of declaration of reserved forests mentioning important sections of the India Forest Act, 1927. (10)

   c) Explain general rules followed during felling of trees in a forest. (10)

   d) Describe the damages caused to the forests by grazing and browsing animals. (10)

   e) Discuss objectives and methods of forest valuation. (10)

6. a) Explain the principles on the basis of which Champion and Seth have classified forest types of India. (20)

   b) What are gums? List some important gums of India along with the names of source tree. (10)

   c) Describe significance of clonal parks in forestry. (10)

7. a) Mention the salient features of National Forest Policy, 1988 and discuss its superiority over National Forest Policy, 1894. (20)

   b) What is shifting cultivation? How it is practiced in hilly areas? (10)

   c) Discuss role of cost-benefit analysis in forestry sector. (10)

8. a) Curiosity medicinal plants on the basis of plant parts used and explain general rules for collection of medicinal plants. (20)

   b) Discuss types of preservatives available for preservation of timber. (10)

   c) Discuss methodologies of census of wild animals. (10)

IFS 2004 Forestry

Paper - I

Section A

1. Answer any four of the following (answer should not exceed more than 150 words for each question): (10 x 4 = 40)

a) What is the criteria to select number of clones and their deployment in plantation forestry?

b) How willow cultivation is life line in cold desert areas of the country?

c) Describe storage behaviour of recalcitrant seeds and name seven tree species producing seeds of this category.

d) Why do forest plantations fail?

e) Describe the storage methods of recalcitrant seeds and name seven tree species which fall under this category.

f) Importance and method of tree introduction.

2. a) Discuss the term site quality and describe the basis of its classification. (20)

   b) What are different uses of vegetative propagation ? Name the five different examples of topophysis. (20)

3. a) Describe briefly clear felling system with its merits and demerits. (20)

   b) Write the importance of mangrove forests and methods of rehabilitation of degraded mangrove forests. (20)

4. Describe the silviculture of any four species: (10 x 4 = 40)

   a) Gmelina arborea.

   b) Cedrus deodara

   c) Santalum album

   d) Populus spp.

   e) Tectona grandis.

Section B

5. Answer any four of the following (Answer should not exceed more than 150 words for each question) : (10 x 4 = 40)

   a) Describe the different methods of plus tree selection in uneven aged forests.

   b) Explain about water pollution and methods of their control with main emphasis on phytoremediation.

   c) Suggest practical methods for the reclamation of saline and alkaline soils.

d) What do you mean by ethno botany, its importance and practice in nature conservation by tribal people?

e) Write a note on Environmental Impact Assessment.

f) Why the provenance testing is prerequisite before taking genetic improvement of any given species? How it can be done?

6. a) Describe the role of NGOs in JFM with special reference to biodiversity conservation. Justify with suitable example. (20)

b) What do you mean by shifting cultivation and improved fallows and its management under agro forestry system? (20)

7. a) Describe the basis of land classification in brief for watershed management. (20)

b) Explain the importance and different ways of carbon sequestration in terrestrial ecosystem.(20)

8. Write notes on any four of the following: (10 x 4 = 40)

a) Importance and types of Heritability. How it can be increased?

b) Specific combining ability and its utility in tree improvement.

c) Breeding value.

d) Acid rain.

e) Hybrid vigour and its utility in tree breeding.

Paper – II

Section A

1. Attempt any four questions from the following (not more than 150 words for each):(10x4=40)

a) Describe the method for calculation of normal growing stock from yield table.

b) Write significance of enumeration map in a divisional working plan.

c) Explain relationship between sustained yield and normal forest.

d) Discuss advantages of remote sensing technique in Forestry.

e) Write procedure for preparation of general volume table.

2. a) What are the different methods of Plain Table Survey ? Describe any one. (20)

   b) Explain form of a tree and discuss principle of Girder Theory. (10)

   c) What is biological diversity? Why Indian subcontinent is rich in biodiversity? (10)

3. a) Describe Biolley's check method of yield regulation in irregular forest (20)

   b) Discuss general specification of cement mortar. (10)

   c) Explain superiority of remote sensing over ground survey. (10)

4. a) Describe Austrian Assessment Method of yield regulation in regular forest. (20)

   b) What are the advantages and disadvantages of brick masonry work over stone masonry work? (10)

   c) Discuss the concept of Joint Forest Management and mention the advantages of Joint Forest Management over traditional forest management. (10)

Section B

5. Attempt any four from the following (not more than 150 words for each): (10 x 4 = 40)

   a) Describe biotic components of an ecosystem.

   b) Describe the process of typical succession in Xeric condition.

   c) Discuss extraction of forest timber by means of aerial ropeways.

   d) Describe concept and method of rotational grazing.

   e) Discuss the types of fencing applied to protect forestry crops.

6. a) Discuss artificial and natural systems of classification of plant species.(20)

   b) Describe primary as well as derived forest fires. (10)

   c) Discuss types of lac crop harvested in India. (10)

7. a) Compare and contrast National Forest Policy 1988 with that of 1952. (10)

b) Explain "damping off" diseases of forest nurseries and discuss its control method. (10)

c) Describe the procedures of sales of forest produces. (10)

8. a) What is Ethnobotany? How it helps in Indian systems of medicines? (20)

b) What is particle board? Mention common types of particle boards available in India.(10)

c) Describe natural defects of timber.(10)

IFS 2003 Forestry

Paper - I

Section A

1. Answer any four of the following:

(answer should not exceed 150 words for each question)

a) What are the different propagation methods used for commercially exploited trees? (10)

b) Briefly describe about the ecological status of "Shola-grassland" vegetation. (10)

c) Discuss briefly about the various measures for afforestation of cold desert and suitability of different tree species. (10)

d) Describe about the importance of mangroves in India. (10)

e) Write about the management of sal or teak plantation. (10)

2. a) Discuss briefly about the topographic factors influencing vegetations. (10)

b) Explain briefly the shelter wood coppice system. (20)

3. a) Explain about the effects of thinning on physiological and mensurational aspects of tree growth. (10)

b) Define "Conversion". Explain the reasons for conversion of silvicultural system. (10)

4. Describe the silviculture of the following species:

a) Shorea robusta (10) b) Tamarindus indica (10)

c) Azadirachta indica (10) d) Pinus roxburghi (10)

Section B

5. Answer any four of the following:

   (answer should not exceed 150 words for each question)

   a) Agroforestry is called 'Multiple land use system'.—Justify. (10)

   b) What are the merits and demerits of JFM? (10)

   c) Explain "Wastelands"—suggest suitable economically important tree species for wastelands afforestation. (10)

   d) How trees are playing a vital role in soil and water conservation? (10)

   e) Write the names of tree species and their characters in controlling "Noise pollution". (10)

6. a) What is 'home garden'? Explain with a model. (20)

   b) Write a brief account on tree seed technology. (20)

7. a) What are the causes and extinguishing methods for forest fire? (20)

   b) Discuss the tree improvement in teak or bamboo. (20)

8. Write notes on:

   a) Rayon (10)

   b) Beedi leaf (10)

   c) Clonal orchard (10)

   d) Mycorrhiza (10)

Paper - II

Section A

1. Attempt any four questions from the following (not more than 150 words for each):

   a) Define and explain the concept of normal forest. (10)

   b) Indicate the essential elements of forest working plan. (10)

   c) Why is Haga-Altimeter used and how is it used for measurement? (10)

   d) Explain the role of village forest in forest management. (10)

   e) How is forest surveying considered important in relation to chain surveying? (10)

2. Define management and indicate the concept and objectives of forest management. (40)

3. The concept of rotation in Forestry be indicated with definitions. Explain types of forest rotation.(40)

4. Forest productivity is dependent on the growth increment. Explain with definitions of increment referring current and annual increment with graphical representation. (40)

Section B

5. Attempt any four from the following (not more than 150 words for each):

   a) Explain the drawback of 1894 Forest Policy. (10)

   b) Indicate the formation of resin canal and extraction of oleoresin. (10)

   c) Explain with diagram, the extraction procedure of stump. (10)

   d) Discuss the methods involved in the production of Tendu leaves and explain how the leaves are processed for the market. (10)

   e) Explain how joint forest management is assisting in forest conservation? (10)

6. Why seasoning is essential ? Indicate general principles of seasoning. (40)

7. Explain Forest Act relating to reserve forest and indicate the benefits of the Act. (40)

8. How is pulp prepared from bamboo? Explain the steps for paper production. (40)

IFS 2002 Forestry

Paper - I

Section A

1. Answer any four of the following:

   a) Describe monoculture at gene and at species level. (10)

   b) Compare the silviculture of poplar (Populus deltoids) with Casuarinas equisetifolia. (10)

   c) Discuss the salient features of the management of mangrove forests in India. (10)

   d) Describe the influence of air and soil temperature on the growth of the plants. (10)

e) Highlight variations in the selection system of management. (10)

2. a) What do you understand by 'clonal' propagation? Maximum gain can be obtained through clonal propagation—Justify. (20)

   b) Discuss the objectives and methods of thinning followed in India. (20)

3. a) Describe in detail various coppice systems of forest management. (20)

   b) Discuss the forest types of cold desert ecosystems. (20)

4. Describe the silviculture of the following species: (40)

   i) Acacicz nilotica

   ii) Anogeissus latifolia

   iii) Cedrus deodara

   iv) Shorea robusta

Section B

5. Answer any four of the following:

   a) Discuss the evaluation of agro-forestry systems. (10)

   b) Define watershed management and its objectives. (10)

   c) What is progeny testing? Why is it important in tree breeding?

   d) What do you understand by 'carbon sequestration' and how can it be effectively managed? (10)

   e) What is the Joint Forest Management (J.F.M.)? What in your opinion are the bottlenecks in its effective implementation. (10)

6. a) Describe the development of degraded lands through silvi-pastoral system in India. (20)

   b) What should be the basis for the choice of species in agro-forestry systems? (20)

7. Write short notes on:

   a) Shelter-belts (10)

   b) VAM (10)

   c) Ozone depletion (10)

   d) Plugging of gully through tree planting (10)

8. a) What are the different selection methods in tree improvement? (10)

   b) Describe the selection and breeding for disease resistance in trees. (10)

   c) Enumerate various steps in the creation of 'clonal' seed orchards. (10)

   d) Distinguish between incomplete and complete pedigree mating designs. Why is factorial mating design preferred in tree breeding? (10)

Paper - II

Section A

1. Attempt any four questions from the following (not more then 150 words for each):

   a) Define normal growing stock. Discuss how normal growing stock yield table is determined in a clear felling system. (10)

   b) Discuss the concept of sustained yield in forestry. (10)

   c) Describe the use of aerial photography in forestry related activities. (10)

   d) Discuss the role of working plan in biodiversity conservation. (10)

   e) What is the importance of maps in forestry? Discuss stock maps. (10)

2. a) Define the term 'rotation'. Enumerate the various rotations followed in the stand management and discuss briefly any two of them. (20)

   b) Explain the yield regulation by gross area method. (10)

   c) Describe the principles of point sampling and list the conventionally used instruments in horizontal point sampling. (10)

3. a) Define normal forest. Elaborate the characteristics of normal forest. (20)

   b) Explain schematically the exact relationship between C.A.I. and M.A.I. in the forest stand managed under clear felling system. (10)

c) What is increment per cent ? Show how increment per cent is worked out by using Pressler's formula. (10)

4. a) What are the bases considered in the regulation of yield? List them with at least one method employed in each one of them. (20)

b) Describe the various types of maps used in the working plan. (10)

c) Discuss the importance of temporary and fair weather roads in the forests. (10)

Section B

5. Attempt any four from the following (not more than 150 words for each):

a) What is plant succession? Write down the causes of primary succession and discuss the stages of succession on new sites of temperate Himalaya. (10)

b) What are the main defects found in wood? Describe the defects due to abnormal growth. (10)

c) What is meant by encroachment in the forests? Discuss the factors responsible for encouraging encroachment. (10)

d) Discuss the importance of economic analysis in making forestry decisions. (10)

e) Discuss the legal provisions made under I.F.A. 1927 for protection against fire. (10)

6. a) Describe the revised classification of forest types of India as proposed by Champion and Seth (1968). Give two examples for each type. (20)

b) Differentiate between :

i) Gum and Resin

ii) Tans and Dyes

iii) Sapwood and Heart Wood

iv) Lac and Shellac

v) Floating and Rafting. (10)

c) What is shifting-cultivation ? Describe the various measures for control of this practice. (10)

7. a) What are the causes of forest fire? Discuss in brief the damages caused to forest by fire. (20)

b) "Plants are amongst the most important sources of medicines and drugs." – Discuss with suitable examples. (10)

c) What do you understand by demand? Discuss the various factors influencing the demand of forest products. (10)

8. a) What is meant by "Preservation of timber"? Why is it done ? Describe in brief the different wood preservation techniques. (20)

b) What are the sources of soil nitrogen in forest ecosystems? Give an account of nitrogen cycling in forest ecosystems. (10)

c) Discuss the basic objectives of National Forest Policy, 1988. (10)

IFS 2001 Forestry

Paper - I

Section A

1. Answer any four of the following:

a) Variations in stand density, such as induced by thinning, cause very large variations in diameter growth but remarkably little in height growth. Discuss. (10)

b) Discuss the relative merits of direct seeding and planting. (10)

c) Describe the 'volume method of regulation' of cut for sustained yield. (10)

d) Describe the different variations of shelterwood method of regeneration of even-aged stands. (10)

e) Discuss the relative merits of pure and mixed stands. (10)

2. a) Discuss the problems of stand establishment in cold areas. (20)

b) Describe the method of periods and periodic blocks for regeneration. (20)

3. a) Discuss the environmental effects of clear-cutting and harvesting. (20)

   b) Describe the various objectives of formulating a silvicultural system for a stand. (20)

4. Describe the silviculture of the following species in details: (40)

   a) Poplars

   b) Bamboos

   c) *Prosopic juliflora*

   d) Cedrus deodara

Section B

5. Answer any four of the following:

   a) Discuss the impact of fire on forest regeneration. (10)

   b) Describe the chemical composition of acid rain and its impact on forest vegetation. (10)

   c) Describe the general guidelines for the selection of plus trees from even-aged stands. (10)

   d) Write a note on integration of livestock in agro forestry practices. (10)

   e) Discuss the importance NTFPs in the life of tribals. (10)

6. a) Describe the different types of damage caused by wind erosion of soil. (13)

   b) How can forest trees be deployed for checking soil erosion by wind? (13)

   c) Write a note on rehabilitation of degraded areas through forestry. (14)

7. a) How do agro-forestry practices lead to increase in soil fertility? (20)

   b) Briefly describe the main agro forestry systems. (20)

8. a) Describe the types, sequence and time scale of species trials. Give object and features of each phase. (20)

   b) Give a detailed account of selection and management of seed stands in conifers. (20)

Paper - II

Section A

1. Attempt any four questions from the following (not more than 150 words for each):

   a) Describe the concept of normality in regular and regular forests. (10)

   b) What are the advantages of remote sensing in forestry? (10)

   c) What is the yield table? How is it used in determining rotation? (10)

   d) Discuss peculiar features of forestry practices. (10)

   e) What are the objectives of joint forest management? How does it differ from the traditional forest management? (10)

2. a) Describe Brandis diameter class method of yield regulation in an irregular forest. (20)

   b) Discuss the importance of form factor in calculation of standing volume of tree. (10)

   c) Describe the various reasons for having high biological diversity in tropics. (10)

3. a) Describe any two methods of volume measurement in a sample plot. (20)

   b) What are Culverts? How are they de signed? (10)

   c) Discuss the importance of soil expectation value in deciding economic rotation. (10)

4. a) Describe the method of survey by the use of a prismatic compass and its chain. (20)

   b) What is mortar? Describe the functions of mortar in building construction. (10)

   c) What is the lean on tree? How is it measured?(10)

Section B

5. Attempt any four from the following (not more than 150 words for each):

   a) Discuss the process of typical succession in riverine and coniferous forests. (10)

b) What are the objectives of seasoning? (10)

c) Describe the nursery disease of economically useful trees. (10)

d) Discuss the importance of cost-benefit analysis in forestry. (10)

e) Describe utilization of forest products in ayurvedic medicine with examples. (10)

6. a) How are forest fires classified ? Discuss the importance of fire lines. (20)

b) Describe collection and processing of bidi (tendu) (Diaspyros embryopteris, Pers) leaf. (10)

c) Describe different types of papers used in daily life. (10)

7. a) What is gum? Describe different types of gum obtained from trees. (20)

b) What is Vermin? How does it differ from game animals? (10)

c) Describe different kinds of non-timber forest products obtained from Indian forests. (10)

8. a) Write down the damages caused to the forests by grazing animals and discuss how rotational grazing helps in the protection of forests? (20)

b) Discuss the mechanism of drought resistance, drought tolerance and drought avoidance by plants to avoid water stress. (10)

c) Describe timber grading and state its importance. (10)

IFS 2000 Forestry

Paper-I

Section A

1. Answer any four of the following:

(answer should not exceed 150 words for each question)

a) Define vegetative propagation and discuss in detail the various techniques adapted in vegetative propagation. (10)

b) Define coppice and explain in detail coppice with standard system (use suitable example). (10)

c) What are tidal swamp forests? List the different forest types found in them along with their species composition. (10)

d) Differentiate between silvics and silviculture. (10)

e) Differentiate between evenaged and unevenaged stands. Discuss the merits and demerits of evenaged stands. (10)

2. a) Explain in the detail the silvicultural practices that ensure good natural regeneration in teak forests. (20)

 b) List the tending operations carried out in stand management and explain in detail various weeding methods adapted. (20)

3. Describe the silvicultural practices adapted in the stands of the following species:

 a) Azadirachta indica (10)

 b) Dalbergia sissoo (10)

 c) Pinus roxburghii (10)

 d) Santalum album (10)

4. a) Explain the concept of Forest site. (10)

 b) On which criteria the site quality in forests are measured? (10)

 c) Discuss its merits and limitations of the criterion adopted. (10)

Section B

5. Answer any four of the following:

 (answer should not exceed 150 words for each question)

 a) Differentiate between Taungya and alley cropping with suitable examples. (10)

 b) List the benefits derived from soil mycorrhizae. (10)

 c) List the different components of watershed and explain their role in micro-watershed management. (10)

 d) What are exotic species? Briefly describe the advantages and problems associated with exotic forestry. (10)

 e) Discuss the role of NGO's in popularizing the J.F.M. (10)

6. Classify the agro-forestry systems based on function, structure and nature of components. (40)

7. "The route cause of most of the environmental pollution is the increasing population"—justify the statement with facts and figures. (40)

8. a) What is indirect selection ? Explain in detail its role in breeding trees for pest and disease resistance. (20)

   b) Which are the different components of phenotypic variation? How are they important for a tree breeder? (20)

Paper-II

Section A

1. Attempt any four from the following:

   (Not more than 150 words for each)

   a) Describe the pre-requisites for a forest to become a normal forest. (10)

   b) 'Working Plan is a tool for the management of a forest.' Justify the statement. (10)

   c) Discuss the rotations that controls the financial returns. (10)

   d) What is the importance of reduced area method of calculating the annual yield? (10)

2. a) Discuss Smythies Safeguarding formula for fixing annual yield in a selection forest. (20)

   b) Write down the principles and formula for Von Mantel's method of yield regulation and its modifications. (10)

   c) How is yield regulated in a forest which is worked under uniform system of management? (10)

3. a) How the concept of joint forest management has been originated? What are the achievements of joint forest management? (20)

   b) What do you mean by biodiversity ? How is it assessed ? (10)

   c) Discuss stand table and its significance in forestry calculations. (10)

4. a) Describe the principle and technique for measuring height of a leaning tree. (20)

b) Discuss the technique of road alignment in a forest area. (10)

c) What are the differences between aerial photographs and maps? (10)

Section B

5. Attempt any four from the following:

(Not more than 150 words for each)

a) Describe different varieties of wood preservatives and write about the diffusion method of treatment. (10)

b) Give a concise account on extraction of Katha. (10)

c) Give an account of fibres derived from forest. (10)

d) What do you know about the Shellac? (10)

e) Write about the important roles played by wild animals on forest regeneration. (10)

6. a) Define composite wood and describe the process of plywood making. (20)

b) What are the common methods of selling forest produces and which method is most effective? (10)

c) Write a detail account on natural defects of timber. (10)

7. a) What constitute a fire environment? Discuss the mechanism of spread of forest fire. (20)

b) What are resins ? How are they classified? Describe with examples. (10)

c) Discuss the importance of wood seasoning and mention the principle involved in it. (10)

8. a) What are the objectives of forest valuation? Describe different methodologies for assessing forest goods and services. (20)

b) Describe the significance of establishing a herbarium. (10)

c) How is the shifting cultivation practised? Mention its disadvantages and control measures. (10)

❑❑❑

Appendices

Appendix - I

Forest Research Institute (FRI), Dehradun and Indian Council of Forestry Research and Education (ICFRE)

Forest Research Institute (FRI), Dehradun

The Forest Research Institute is an institute of the Indian Council of Forestry Research and Education and is a premier institution in the field of forestry research in India. It is located at Dehradun in Uttarakhand, and is one of the oldest institutions of its kind. In 1991, it was declared a deemed university by the University Grants Commission.

Established as Imperial Forest Research Institute in 1906, Forest Research Institute (FRI) Dehradun, is a premier institution under the Indian Council of Forestry Research and Education (ICFRE). Styled in Greeko Roman Architecture by C.G. Blomfield, the main building is a National Heritage which was inaugurated in 1929.

The Indian Council of Forestry Research and Education (ICFRE) is the apex body in the national forestry research system to develop a holistic forestry research through planning, promoting, educating and coordinating research education and extension of all aspects of forestry.

The following forestry research institutes and centres under the Council are responsible for undertaking research in their respective eco-climatic zones:

- Forest Research Institute, Dehradun
- Arid Forest Research Institute, Jodhpur
- Rain Forest Research Institute, Jorhat
- Institute of Wood Science and Technology, Bangalore

- Tropical Forestry Research Institute, Jabalpur
- Institute of Forest Genetics and Tree Breeding, Coimbatore
- Himalayan Forest Research Institute, Shimla
- Institute for Forest Productivity, Ranchi
- Centre of Social Forestry and Eco-rehabilitation, Allahabad
- Institute of Forestry Research & Human Resources Development, Chhindwara

In addition, the Indian Plywood Industries Research and Training Institute, Bangalore, an autonomous body of the Ministry, is a premier institution engaged in research and training activities on mechanical wood industries technology. The Indian Institute of Forest Management, Bhopal, an autonomous organization of the Ministry also undertakes training, research and consultancy in forest management.

Indian Council of Forestry Research and Education (ICFRE)

The Indian Council of Forestry Research and Education (ICFRE) is an autonomous organisation or governmental agency under the Ministry of Environment and Forests, Government of India. Headquartered in Dehradun, its functions are to conduct forestry research; transfer the technologies developed to the states of India and other user agencies; and to impart forestry education. The council has 9 research institutes and 4 advanced centres to cater to the research needs of different bio-geographical regions. These are located at Dehradun, Shimla, Ranchi, Jorhat, Jabalpur, Jodhpur, Bengaluru, Coimbatore, Allahabad, Chhindwara, Aizawl, Hyderabad and Agartala.

Type	**Autonomous Organisation**
Established	**1986**
Parent institution	**Ministry of Environment and Forests (India)**
President	**Maanas**
Director	**Maanas**
Location	**P.O. New Forest, Dehradun, Uttarakhand, India 248006** **30.345192°N 78.002193°ECoordinates: 30.345192°N 78.002193°E**
Campus	**Urban**
Acronym	**ICFRE**
Website	**www.icfre.org//**

History

ICFRE is the largest organization responsible for forestry research in India. ICFRE was created in 1986, under the Ministry of Environment and Forests (India), to direct and manage research and education in forestry sector in India. ICFRE is headed by a Director General with headquarters at Dehradun. ICFRE became an autonomous council under the Ministry in 1991.

Mandate

The mandate of the ICFRE is to organise, direct and manage research and education in the forestry sector, including in cooperation with FORTIP (UNDP/FAO Regional Forest Tree Improvement Project), UNDP and World Bank on economically important species. ICFRE established a National Bureau of Forest Genetic Resources (NBFGR).

Research perspective

- Conservation, protection, regeneration, rehabilitation and sustainable development of natural forest ecosystems.
- Revegetation of barren, waste, marginal and mined lands.
- Research on tree improvement.
- Enhancing productivity of wood and non-wood forest produce per unit of area per unit time by application of scientific and technological methods.
- Research on improved utilisation, recovery and processing of forest produce for value addition and employment generation.
- Ecological rehabilitation of all fragile ecosystems, such as mountains, mangroves, deserts, etc.
- Socio-economic and policy research for developing strategies towards attracting people's participation in forest management.

Research Institutes

Institute and their locations, sorted alphabetically					
Name	**Acronym**	**Established**	**City**	**Jurisdiction**	**Website**
Arid Forest Research Institute (AFRI)	AFRI	1988	Jodhpur	Rajasthan, Gujarat, Dadra and Nagar Haveli	afri.res.in
Forest Research Institute (FRI)	FRI	1906	Dehradun	Punjab, Haryana, Chandigarh, Delhi, U.P., Uttarakhand	fri.icfre.gov.in
Himalayan Forest Research Institute (HFRI)	HFRI	1977	Shimla	Himachal Pradesh, Jammu and Kashmir	hfri.icfre.gov.in
Institute of Forest Biodiversity (IFB)	IFB	2012	Hyderabad	Telangana, Maharashtra	frc.icfre.gov.in
Institute of Forest Genetics and Tree Breeding (IFGTB)	IFGTB	1988	Coimbatore	T.N., Kerala, A & Nicobar, Lakshadweep, Pondicherry	ifgtb.icfre.gov.in#/
Institute of Forest Productivity (IFP)	IFP	1993	Ranchi	Bihar, Jharkhand, Sikkim, West Bengal	ifpranchi.co.in
Institute of Wood Science and Technology (IWST)	IWST	1938	Bengaluru	Karnataka, Telangana, Andhra Pradesh, Goa	iwst.icfre.gov.in#/
Rain Forest Research Institute (RFRI)	RFRI	1988	Jorhat	North-east India	rfri.icfre.gov.in
Tropical Forest Research Institute (TFRI)	TFRI	1988	Jabalpur	M.P., Chhattisgarh, Maharashtra, Odisha	tfri.icfre.gov.in

Advanced Research Centres

Institute and their locations, sorted alphabetically					
Name	**Acronym**	**Established**	**City**	**Jurisdiction**	**Website**
Advanced Research Centre for Bamboo and Rattan (a unit of RFRI)	ARCBR	2004	Aizawl	Northeast India	www.icfre.org
Centre for Forestry Research and Human Resource Development (satellite centre of TFRI)	CFRHRD	1995	Chhindwara	M.P., Chhattisgarh, Maharashtra, Odisha	www.icfre.org
Centre for Social Forestry and Eco-Rehabilitation (a centre of ICFRE)	CSFER	1992	Allahabad	Eastern U.P., North Bihar, Vindhya Range	www.icfre.org
Centre for Forest Based Livelihood and Extension[2][14]	CFLE	2013	Agartala	Tripura	tripurainfo
Centre for Urban Forestry Research (a centre of AFRI)	CUFR	(Planned)	Gandhinagar	Gujarat	

Institutes under the Indian Council of Forestry Research and Education

- Advanced Research Centre for Bamboo and Rattan, Aizawl
- Arid Forest Research Institute, Jodhpur
- Centre for Forest-based Livelihoods and Extension (CFLE), Agartala
- Centre for Forestry Research and Human Resource Development, Chhindwara
- Centre for Social Forestry and Eco-Rehabilitation, Allahabad
- Forest Research Institute (India), Dehradun
- Himalayan Forest Research Institute, Shimla
- Institute of Forest Biodiversity, Hyderabad
- Institute of Forest Genetics and Tree Breeding, Coimbatore
- Institute of Forest Productivity, Ranchi
- Institute of Wood Science and Technology, Bangalore
- Rain Forest Research Institute, Jorhat
- Tropical Forest Research Institute, Jabalpur
- Van Vigyan Kendra (Forest Science Centres)

Other National Institutes

Other research institutes under the Ministry of Environment and Forestry

Subordinate offices

- Forest Survey of India, Dehradun
- Botanical Survey of India, Kolkata
- Directorate of Forest Education, Dehradun
- Indira Gandhi National Forest Academy, Dehradun
- National Institute of Animal Welfare, Faridabad
- National Zoological Park, New Delhi
- National Museum of Natural History, New Delhi
- Zoological Survey of India, Kolkata
- Wildlife Crime Control Bureau (WCCB)

Authorities

- Central Zoo Authority of India, New Delhi
- National Biodiversity Authority, Chennai
- National Ganga River Basin Authority, New Delhi
- National Tiger Conservation Authority, New Delhi

Centres of excellence

- Centre for Environment Education, Ahmedabad
- C.P.R. Environmental Education Center, Chennai
- Centre for Animals and Environment, Bengaluru
- Center of Excellence in Environmental Economics, Chennai
- Foundation for Revitalisation of Local Health Traditions, Bengaluru
- Center for Ecological Sciences, Bengaluru
- Center for Environmental Management of Degraded Ecosystem, Delhi
- Center for Mining Environment, Dhanbad
- Salim Ali Center for Omithology and Natural History (SACON), Coimbatore
- Tropical Botanic Garden and Research Institute, Thiruvananthapuram

Under State Governments

- Kerala Forest Research Institute, Peechi, Thrissur
- Forest College and Research Institute, Tamil Nadu Agricultural University, Mettupalayam
- Forest Research Institute, Kanpur, Uttar Pradesh Forest Department
- Gujarat Forest Research Centre, Rajpipla, Gujarat
- State Forest Department, Jammu
- State Forest Research and Training Institute, Raipur, Chhattisgarh
- State Forest Research Institute, Jabalpur, Madhya Pradesh
- State Forest Research Institute, Chennai, Tamil Nadu
- State Forest Research Institute, Itanagar, Arunachal Pradesh

Appendix - II

List of Universities and Colleges of India Working in the Field of Forestry

- Forest Research Institute, Dehradun
- PDKV University, Akola
- Arid Forest Research Institute Jodhpur
- Aspee College of Forestry and Horticulture, Navsari Agricultural University, Navsari, Gujarat
- College of Forestry and Hill Agriculture, Ranichauri, G. B. Pant University of Agriculture and Technology, Pantnagar
- College of Forestry, Dr. Balasaheb Sawant Konkan Krishi Vidyapeeth University (BSKKV), Dapoli, Maharashtra
- College of Forestry, Kerala Agricultural University
- College of Forestry, Ponnampet, UAHS, Shimoga
- College of Forestry, Sirsi, University of Agricultural Sciences Dharwad
- College of Horticulture and Forestry, Maharana Pratap University, Jhalawar, Rajasthan
- Department of Forest Sciences, Desh Bhagat University (DBU), Mandi Gobindgarh, Punjab
- Department of Applied Science, North Eastern Regional Institute of Science and Technology (NERIST), Nirjuli, Arunachal Pradesh
- Department of Ecology and Environmental Science, Assam University, Silchar, Assam
- Department of Forestry, Dr. Panjabrao Deshmukh Krishi Vidyapeeth University (PDKV), Akola, Maharashtra
- Department of Forestry, Hemwati Nandan Bahuguna Garhwal University
- Department of Forestry, Jawaharlal Nehru Agricultural University, Jabalpur, Madhya Pradesh
- Department of Forestry, Wildlife and Environment Science, Guru Ghasidas University, Bilaspur
- Dr. Yashwant Singh Parmar University of Horticulture and Forestry, Nauni, Solan, Himachal Pradesh

- Forest College and Research Institute, Tamil Nadu Agricultural University, Mettupalayam, Tamil Nadu
- Forest Department, Forest Rangers College, Angul, Odisha
- Forest Research Institute University, Dehradun
- Indian Institute of Forest Management, Bhopal
- Gujarat Forest Research Institute, Gujarat Forest Rangers College, Rajpipla, Gujarat
- Faculty of Forestry, Sher-e-Kashmir University of Agricultural Sciences and Technology of Kashmir, Ganderbal Jammu and Kashmir.

Ranks in Union Ministry and State Government

Grade	Union Ministry Designation
Apex Scale	Director General of Forests (वन महानिदेशक)
HAG + Scale	Additional Director General of Forests (अपर वन महानिदेशक)
Higher Administrative Grade	Inspector General of Forests (वन महानिरीक्षक)
PB-4	Additional Inspector General of Forests (अपर वन महानिरीक्षक)
PB-4	Deputy Inspector General of Forests (उप वन महानिरीक्षक)
PB-4	Director (निदेशक)
PB-3	Assistant Inspector Gerneral o Forests (सहायक वन महानिरीक्षक)
Grade	**State Government Designation**
Apex Scale	Principal Chief Conservation of Forests (प्रधान मुख्य वन संरक्षक)
Higher Administrative Grade	Additional Principal Chief Conservation of Forests (अपर प्रधान मुख्य वन संरक्षक)
PB-4	Chief Conservation of Forests (मुख्य वन संरक्षक) Regional Chief Conservation of Forests (क्षेत्रीय मुख्य वन संरक्षक)
PB-4	Conservation of Forests (वन संरक्षक)
PB-3	Deputy Conservation of Forests (उप वन संरक्षक) Divisional Forest Officer (तन प्रमंडल पदाधिकारी)
PB-3	Probationary Officer (प्रशिक्षु पदाधिकारी)

Appendix - III

Karnataka Forest Department

The Forest Department State Head Quarters is situated at Aranya Bhavan, 18th Cross, Malleswaram, Bengaluru-560003.

The Administrative head of the Department is the **Principal Chief Conservator of Forests (Head of Forest Force)**, who is a technical and professional adviser of the Government on forest matters. The Principal Chief Conservator of Forests (Wild life) is Chief Wildlife Warden of the state. He is responsible for the management of National Parks and Sanctuaries and all the wildlife matters of the state. For Territorial Administrative purpose of the Department, the State is divided into thirteen Territorial Circles, besides Functional Circles namely Forest Research and Utilization, Field Director (Project Tiger), Working Plan, Training & Forest Mobile Squad.

Territorial

- The Principal Chief Conservator of Forests (HOFF) controls the activities of the Territorial Units.
- Administratively, the State is divided into 13 Forest Territorial Circles under which there are 40 Territorial Divisions.
- Chief Conservator of Forests oversees the working and control of Territorial Forest Divisions, Social Forestry divisions (Technical Control) and Wildlife divisions coming under their circle jurisdiction.
- Deputy Conservator of Forests is the administrative head of a Forest Division. He is assisted by Assistant Conservators of Forests in the sub-divisions and Range Forest Officers in the Ranges. The Territorial Ranges are divided into Sections headed by Section Foresters and Beats headed by Forest Beat Guards.
- The jurisdictional boundaries of the Forest Divisions are independent of Revenue Department jurisdictions and are based on forest area and density. The Districts of Uttara Kannada, Shivamogga, Kodagu, Dakshina Kannada and Mysuru have more than one forest division each. However, in Eastern Plain areas the Forest Divisions are co-terminus with the districts.

Forest Circles and Divisions of Karnataka Forest Department

S.No.	Circle Name	Division Name
1.	APCCF (Research)	ACF Utilisation Bangalore
2.	APCCF (Research)	CCF Bangalore (Research)
3.	APCCF (Research)	CF Research Bellary
4.	APCCF (Research)	CF Research Dharwad
5.	APCCF (Research)	CF Research Madikeri
6.	APCCF (Research)	DCF SF Research Bangalore
7.	APCCF(EWPT)	CCF (WP) Bangalore
8.	APCCF(EWPT)	CCF Training
9.	APCCF(EWPT)	Test
10.	APCCF(PT), Mysore	Bandipur Project Tiger
11.	APCCF(PT), Mysore	BRT Tiger Reserve Chamarajanagar
12.	APCCF(PT), Mysore	Nagarahole Tiger Reserve
13.	Bangalore	Bangalore Rural
14.	Bangalore	Bangalore Urban
15.	Bangalore	Bannerghatta National Park
16.	Bangalore	Chikkaballapura
17.	Bangalore	Kolar
18.	Bangalore	Ramanagara
19.	Belgaum	Bagalkot
20.	Belgaum	Belgaum
21.	Belgaum	Bijapur
22.	Belgaum	Gokak
23.	Bellary	Bellary
24.	Bellary	Chitradurga
25.	Bellary	Daroji Bear Sanctuary
26.	Bellary	Davanagere
27.	Bellary	Koppal
28.	Chamarajanagara	BRT Tiger Reserve, Chamarajanagara
29.	Chamarajanagara	Cauvery WL, Kollegal
30.	Chamarajanagara	Male Mahadeshwara WL, Kollegala
31.	Chikkamagalur	Bhadra Wildlife
32.	Chikkamagalur	Chikkamagalur
33.	Chikkamagalur	Koppa
34.	Dharwad	Dharwad
35.	Dharwad	Gadag
36	Dharwad	Haveri
37	Dharwad	Ranebennur WL Sub-Division
38	Gulbarga	Bidar
39	Gulbarga	Gulbarga
40	Gulbarga	Raichur
41	Gulbarga	Yadagiri
42	Hassan	Hassan
43	Hassan	Tumkur
44	Kanara	Dandeli Wildlife
45	Kanara	Haliyal
46	Kanara	Honavar
47	Kanara	Karwar
48	Kanara	Sirsi
49	Kanara	Yellapura
50	Kodagu	Madikeri
51	Kodagu	Madikeri SF
52	Kodagu	Madikeri WL Division
53	Kodagu	Virajapet
54	Mangalore	Karkala Wildlife
55	Mangalore	Kudremukh
56	Mangalore	Kundapur
57	Mangalore	Mangalore
58	Mysore	Hunasur
59	Mysore	Mandya
60	Mysore	Mysore
61	Mysore	Mysore Wildlife
62	PCCF (HOFF)	APCCF HQ
63	PCCF (HOFF)	PCCF
64	Shimoga	Bhadravathi
65	Shimoga	Sagar
66	Shimoga	Shimoga
67	Shimoga	Shimoga Wildlife

Forest Ranges in Canara Circle of Karnataka Forest Department

Sr.No	Circle Name	Division Name	Range Name
1	Kanara	Dandeli Wildlife	Anshi
2	Kanara	Dandeli Wildlife	Gund
3	Kanara	Dandeli Wildlife	Kulgi
4	Kanara	Dandeli Wildlife	Kumbarwada
5	Kanara	Dandeli Wildlife	Phansoli
6	Kanara	Haliyal	Barchi
7	Kanara	Haliyal	Bhagwati
8	Kanara	Haliyal	Dandeli
9	Kanara	Haliyal	Haliyal
10	Kanara	Haliyal	Jagalbet
11	Kanara	Haliyal	Sambrani
12	Kanara	Haliyal	Tinaighat
13	Kanara	Haliyal	Virnoli
14	Kanara	Honavar	Bhatkal
15	Kanara	Honavar	Gersoppa
16	Kanara	Honavar	Hiregutti
17	Kanara	Honavar	Honavar
18	Kanara	Honavar	Katgal
19	Kanara	Honavar	Kumta
20	Kanara	Honavar	Manki
21	Kanara	Karwar	Ankola
22	Kanara	Karwar	Gopshitta
23	Kanara	Karwar	Joida
24	Kanara	Karwar	Kadra
25	Kanara	Karwar	Karwar
26	Kanara	Karwar	Mastikatta
27	Kanara	Karwar	Ramanguli
28	Kanara	Sirsi	Banavasi
29	Kanara	Sirsi	Hulekal
30	Kanara	Sirsi	Janmane
31	Kanara	Sirsi	Kyadgi
32	Kanara	Sirsi	Siddapur
33	Kanara	Sirsi	Sirsi
34	Kanara	Yellapura	Idagundi
35	Kanara	Yellapura	Katur
36	Kanara	Yellapura	Kirwatti
37	Kanara	Yellapura	Manchikeri
38	Kanara	Yellapura	Mundagod
39	Kanara	Yellapura	Yellapur

Appendix - IV

List of Agricultural Universities in India

State Agricultural Universities/Central University

1. Acharya NG Ranga Agricultural Univ., Rajendranagar, Hyderabad-500030, A.P
2. Anand Agricultural University, Anand-388110, Gujarat
3. Assam Agricultural University, Jorhat-785013, Assam
4. Bidhan Chandra Krishi Viswavidyalaya, P.O Krishi Viswavidyalaya, Mohanpur, Nadia-741252, West Bengal
5. Birsa Agricultural University, Kanke, Ranchi- 834006, Jharkhand
6. Central Agricultural University, Imphal -795004, Manipur
7. Chandra Shekar Azad Univ. of Agriculture & Technology, Kanpur- 208002, U.P
8. Chaudhary Charan Singh Haryana Agricultural University, Hissar-125004,Haryana
9. Chaudhary Sarwan Kumar Himachal Pradesh Krishi Vishwavidyalaya, Palampur, Kangra- 176062, Himachal Pradesh
10. Dr Balasaheb Sawant Konkan Krishi Vidyapeeth, Dapoli, Ratnagiri-415712, Maharashtra
11. Dr Panjabrao Deshmukh Krishi Vidyapeeth, Krishi Nagar, Akola-444104, Maharashtra
12. Dr Yashwant Singh Parmar Univ. of Horticulture & Forestry, Solan, Nauni - 173230, Himachal Pradesh
13. Govind Ballabh Pant University of Agriculture & Technology, Pantnagar, Udhamsingh Nagar-263145, Uttarakhand
14. Guru Angad Dev University of Veterinary and Animal Sciences, Ludhiana-141004, Punjab
15. Indira Gandhi Krishi Vishwavidyalaya, Krishak Nagar, Raipur-492006, Chhattisgarh
16. Jawaharlal Nehru Krishi Vishwavidyalaya, Krishi Nagar, Jabalpur- 482004, M.P.
17. Junagadh Agriculture University, Moti Baug, Agril. Campus, Junagadh-362001, Gujarat

18. Karnataka Veterinary Animal and Fisheries Science University, P.B. No. 6, Nandinagar, Bidar-585401, Karnataka
19. Kerala Agricultural University, P.O Vellanikkara, Thrissur-680656, Kerala
20. Maharana Pratap Univ. of Agriculture & Technology, Udaipur-313001, Rajasthan
21. Maharashtra Animal Science & Fishery University, Nagpur, Maharashtra
22. Mahatma Phule Krishi Vidyapeeth, Rahuri-413722, Maharashtra
23. Marathwada Agricultural University, Parbhani -431402, Maharashtra
24. Narendra Deva University of Agriculture & Technology, Kumarganj, Faizabad- 224229, Uttar Pradesh
25. Navsari Agricultural University, Vijalpore, Navsari-396450, Gujarat
26. Orissa Univ. of Agriculture & Technology, Siripur, Bhubaneswar-751003, Odisha
27. Punjab Agricultural University, Ludhiana -141004, Punjab
28. Rajasthan AgriculturalUniversity, Bikaner -334006, Rajasthan
29. Rajendra Agricultural University, Pusa, Samastipur-848125, Bihar
30. Sardar Vallabh Bhai Patel Univ. of Agriculture & Technology, Modipuram, Meerut-250110, Uttar Pradesh
31. Sardarkrushinagar-Dantiwada Agricultural University, Sardarkrushinagar, Dantiwada, Banaskantha-385506, Gujarat
32. Sher-E-Kashmir Univ. of Agricultural Sciences & Technology, Railway Road, Jammu- 180012 (J&K)
33. Sher-E-Kashmir Univ. of Agricultural Sciences & Technology, Shalimar, Srinagar- 191121, (J&K)
34. Sri Venkateswara Veterinary University, Tirupati, Chittoor-517502, A.P.
35. Tamil Nadu Agricultural University, Coimbatore-641003, Tamil Nadu
36. Tamil Nadu Veterinary & Animal Sciences University, Madhavaram Milk Colony, Chennai- 600051, Tamil Nadu

37. University of Agricultural Sciences, Dharwad, Karnataka
38. University of Agricultural Sciences, Bangalore- 560065, Karnataka
39. UP Pandit Deen Dayal Upadhaya Pashu Chikitsa Vigyan Vishwa Vidhyalaya Evam Go Anusandhan Sansthan, Mathura- 281001, Uttar Pradesh
40. Uttar Banga Krishi Vishwavidyalaya, P.O. Pundibari, Distt. Cooch Behar-736165, West Bengal
41. West Bengal University of Animal & Fishery Sciences, 68 KB Sarani, Kolkata700037, West Bengal
42. University of Horticultural Sciences, Venkataramnagudem, West Godavari, A.P.
43. Rajmata VRS Agricultural University, Gwalior-474002, Madhya Pradesh
44. University of Horticultural Sciences, Navanagar, Bagalkot-587101, Karnataka
45. University of Agricultural Sciences, Raichur-584102, Karnataka

Deemed-to-be Universities

1. Indian Agricultural Research Institute, Pusa-110012, New Delhi
2. Indian Veterinary Research Institute, Izatnagar, Bareilly-243122, Uttar Pradesh
3. National Dairy Research Institute, Karnal-132001, Haryana
4. Central Institute of Fisheries Education, Mumbai-400061, Maharashtra
5. Allahabad Agricultural Institute, Allahabad-211007, Uttar Pradesh

Central Universities with Agriculture Faculty

1. Benaras Hindu University, Varanasi, U.P.
2. Aligarh Muslim University, Aligarh, U.P.
3. Vishwa Bharti, Shantiniketan, West Bengal
4. Nagaland University, Medizipherma, Nagaland

Appendix - V

Karnataka Forest Department

Forms and Records

1. Warrant to Search Suspected Place of Deposit
2. Search List
3. First Information Report" (F.I.R.)
4. Seizure of Property
5. Bail Bond
6. Bond for the Release of Property Seized
7. Summons to Witness
8. Charge Sheet

Karnataka Forest Department
(Karnataka Forest Manual)
Form No15 (Rule 64 (B)h)
"Warrant to search suspected place of Deposit"

To

____

____

(Name and designation of a forest Officer above the rank of a forest Guard) Where information has been laid before me and on the inquiry there upon had. I have been led believe that is used as a place for the deposit (or sale) of property.

This is to authorize and require you to enter the said house (or other place) with such assistance as shall be required and to use if necessary, reasonable force for that purpose and to search every part of the said house (or other place or if the search is to be confined to a part, specify the part clearly) and to seize and take possession of any property (or document, or stamps or seals as the case may be) (add when the case requires it) and also of any instruments and materials which you may reasonably believe to be kept for the manufacture of forgot documents, or counterfeit stamps, or false scales (as the case may be) and forthwith to bring before this Officer such of the said things as may be taken possession of, returning this warrant , with an endorsement certifying what you have done under it immediately upon its execution.

Dated this ....day of ....year
Seal of the office

Karnataka Forest Department

(Karnataka Forest Manual)

Farm No16 (Rule 64 (5BL))

(Section 62 and 99 © of the Karnataka Forest Act, 1963)

"Search List"

Forest ______________________Division ______

1. Forest Offence Case Number ______________________
2. Name and address of the accused ______________________
3. Nature of offence and section of ______________________

   Forest Act or other Law applicable. ______________________
4. Search warrant number and date by who issued and to whom.

   ____
5. Name and rank of the forest officer who conducted the search.

   ____
6. House premises and the village where search is made.

   ____
7. Name of the owner of the house of premises searched.

   ____
8. Date and hour of search ______________________
9. Names of search witnesses ______________________
10. Did the house owner attend the search? ______________

    If not did any, do so on his behalf? ______________________
11. Description, quantity and value of the property seized during the search. ______________________________________
12. Mark of identification put on the seized property.

    ____
13. Name and address of the person or official to whom the property seized is entrusted for safe custody.

    ____
14. Whether the property seized has been released to the owner on the execution of a bond by the owner under section 63 of the Act? If so, date release.

____

15. Name of persons arrested, if any during the search. If so, how disposed off _______________________________________

16. Date of dispatch of the seizure report to the Magistrate.

____

Signature of witnesses.

1. ....

2. ....

3. ....

4. ....

Place .... Signature of the Forest Officer

Date .... Conducting the search

To be printed in quadruplicate

1. Original to be retained by the forest officer conducting the search.
2. Duplicate to be sent to the magistrate.
3. Triplicate to be sent to the forest officer authorizing the search.

4. Quadruplicate copy to be delivered to the occupant at his.

Karnataka Forest Department

(Karnataka Forest Manual)

Form No. 17 (Rule 65(1))

"First Information Report" (F.I.R.)

Number________________Date____________________

1. Name of Beat, Section , Range and Division

____

2. Place where the offence took place or discovered

____

3. Nature of the offence

____

4. Description and quantity of the property Seized where when and what arrangements made for its safe custody.

____

5. Names of witnesses

____

Station .... Signature and Designation of the Forest Officer reporting

Date ....

To be printed in quadruplicate.

1. Original to be submitted to the Magistrate having jurisdiction.
2. Duplicate to be sent to the concerned Range Forest Officer.
3. Triplicate to be sent to the Divisional Forest Range Forest Officer.

4. Quadruplicate to be retained at the reporting office.

Karnataka Forest Department

(Karnataka Forest Manual)

Form No 20 (Rule 67 (3)

Sub: Report of "**seizure of property**" concerned in a forest offence u/s____________ ____________________ of KFA, 1963, R/W Rule__________ of KFA, 1969.

To

The Hon' ble judicial magistrate.

First class ___________________.

I have to report that, I have seized the following property on .... In connection with a forest offence committed by the persons named below in the ....

Particular of property seized	Name/ Names of accused persons

reserve forest land. A full report on the case will be furnished in due course by the Range Forest officer.

Date:

Signature

No:

Designation

Karnataka Forest Department
(Karnataka Forest Manual)
Form No 19 (Rule 66 (16))
"Bail Bond"
(Section 75 of the Karnataka forest Act, 1963)

I, ... of .... being charged with offence .... of .... do hereby I bind myself to appear before .... on .... at .... and continue to so appear when required until otherwise directed by the said officer or any other competent court.

And in case of my making default herein I bind myself to forfeit to the Government of Karnataka, the sum of Rs..............................

Dated this .... Day of .... year

Witnesses

....

....

Signature

Before me

Place.................................... Signature and Designation

Date.................................... of the forest officer

I declare myself (we jointly and severally declare ourselves and each of us) surety (sureties) for the above named .... that be shall appear before .... on .... at .... and continue to so appear when required until otherwise directly by the said officer , or any other competent court.

And in case of his making default there in I bind myself (we bind ourselves and each of us) to forfeit to the Government of Karnataka, the sum of Rs... ....

Dated this .... day of ....year

Witnesses

....

....

Sureties

....

....

Before me

Place.................................... Signature and Designation

Date.................................... of the forest officer

Karnataka Forest Department

(Karnataka Forest Manual)

Form No 21 (Rule 67 (4))

"Bond For The Release of Property Seized"

(Section 63 of the Karnataka forest Act, 1963)

I..of......................... being charged with offence of .... in case No .... do hereby bind myself to produce before the Magistrate .... if and when required the following property seized in the above named offence and released to me under, section 63 of the Karnataka forest Act, 1963 and in case of my making default there in I bind myself to forfeit to the Government the sum of Rs. .... in addition to any other punishment according to law.

Dated this ....day of ....Year

Particulars of property

Witness: ....

Signature..............................

'Before me'

Place........... Signature and Designation of the forest officer

Date................

Karnataka Forest Department

(Karnataka Forest Manual)

Form No22 (Rule 69 (6) H)

"Summons to Witness"

To

....

....

....

Where complaint has been made before me that (name of the accused) of (address) has (or is suspected to have) committed the offence of (state the offence concisely with time and place and it appears to me that you are likely o give material evidence or to produce any document or other thing for the prosecution)

You are hereby summoned to appear before this office on the .... Day of .... next at ten 'O' clock in the forenoon, , to produces such document or thing or testify what you know concerning the matter of the said complaint, and you are here by warned that , if you shall without just excuse neglect or refuse to appear on the said date a warrant will be issued to compel your attendance.

Dated this ....day of .... year

Seal of the office

Karnataka Forest Department

(Karnataka Forest Manual)

Form No.26 (Rule 75(1))

"Charge Sheet"

No___________________ Date ____________

1. Name of range __________________________________
2. Offence case number __________________________________
3. Number and date of first information report

   ____
4. Enquiry report number and date _______________________
5. Orders of the Divisional forest officer in form No.

   ____
6. Name and official designation of the complaint

   ____
7. Names and addresses of accused personsa. a) Forwarded in custody b) On bail, sent up for trail c) Not sent for trail

   ____
8. Charge: Nature of offence and circumstance connected with it in brief and section of forest Act or other law applicable

   ____
9. Description quantity and value of the property seized where, when and by whom seized and how disposed of and the number and date of submitting the seizure report in form No.

   ____
10. Names and address of witnesses and what point each is called on to prove. __________________________________

Signature and Designation of the RFO

□□□